DAN MCCARTHY

DAN
MCCARTHY

First Edition 2008

Published by Anton Kern Gallery and the journal Books
Art Direction by Sean Carmody
Production by Michael Nevin
Printing by Magnum Offset, Hong Kong
Retouching by Dodge + Burn
Mechanics by Poppie van Herwerden

Anton Kern Gallery

532 West 20th Street / New York, NY 10011
Phone 212.367.9663 / Fax 212.367.8135
E-mail info@antonkerngallery.com
www.antonkerngallery.com

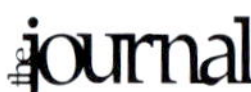

168 North 1st Street / Brooklyn, NY 11211
Phone 718.218.7148 / Fax 646.390.3395
E-mail info@thejournalinc.com
www.thejournalinc.com

ISBN 13: 978-0-615-15858-7
Printed in Hong Kong

For exhibition information, contact Christoph Gerozissis at Anton Kern Gallery.

Dan McCarthy's work speaks to me of mastery, not only of paint and
a surface, but of the moments of joy and sorrow that are woven into
the life of a creative person. I admire his ability to make a life in the
world that is comfortable enough to let his imagination luxuriate. I've
enjoyed his work and his friendship since we both emerged in the New
York art world over 15 years ago. His opinion is always one I seek. His
knowledge and acceptance of most things is vast, which makes his
input worthy and sincere.

This little piece of writing should be a picture. I photographed Dan early
in our friendship in a studio I had on 42nd Street. My itinerancy since
then has made locating said pictures improbable. He was making things
with figures and pickle jars at the time, I was still working out what I
was doing.

Anyway, if I could lay my hands on one of those frames it would be great,
He hasn't changed much in the years I've known him. His clean living
and the love of a good woman have kept him from decay. He may be
descended from one of the Eskimos that were "imported" to live in the
Eskimo village at Coney Island during the turn of the century, because
to me he looks Hawaiian or Eskimo (he is neither). Maybe that's a result
of me picturing him in the beach-y or mountainous terrains he paints
so often. I guess because he likes snowboarding in the winter and
deep-sea fishing in the summer.

I'm sure I'm among many who think of him as a brother. So sweet is
it to be able to count upon his countenance.

Jack Pierson
Provincetown, 2007

DAN MCCARTHY: LAND WITH NO SIGN
Nick Stillman

FIGURE .1
Deckhand, 2003
Oil on Canvas
68 x 62 inches

FIGURE .2
Sunrise, 2005
Oil on Canvas
45 x 59 inches

FIGURE .3
Through the Night, 2006
Oil on Canvas
52 x 46 inches

FIGURE .4
Surfers in Huntington
Beach, mid-1960s

FIGURE .5
Six Banger, 2006
Oil on canvas
57 x 84 inches

FIGURE .6
Burnt, 2006
Oil on canvas
36 x 30 inches

A contortionist deckhand glides through a spotlit cabaret, his hands and smile the burning red of the carelessly guilty. Man and woman share a turquoise stage of beach at daybreak. He poses *contrapposto* with a surfboard. She lofts a Japanese umbrella, balances on tiptoe, and rides the sand beneath her flipflops. A woman frozen in a field of nothing waits silently on hands and knees. A puddle of red, white, and blue camouflage for skin, her stoned eyes lock on something behind you, beyond you. Soaring rainbows bleed pastel yolks. Bodies coil in crouches. Surfers hold waves. People hoist fish. Characters pose like limpid statues within landscapes, extreme weather systems, and frenzied patterns mostly lacking objects. These forms, situations, and characters are a few of many appearing again and again in Dan McCarthy's paintings. Stubborn repetition can beget stale dogma, but it'd be a reach to cite any specific credo that dictates McCarthy's imagery. This, as another painter has already noted, is a "land with no sign."[1]

Vladimir Nabokov, advocate of "pure" imagination as the only respectable inspiration for artmaking, wrote,

"It is strange, the morbid inclination we have to derive satisfaction from the fact (generally false and always irrelevant) that a work of art is traceable to a 'true story.' Is it because we begin to respect ourselves more when we learn that the writer, just like ourselves, was not clever enough to make up a story himself? Or is it something added to the poor strength of our imagination when we know that a tangible fact is at the base of the 'fiction' we mysteriously despise?"[2]

So much current art bombards with signs skimmed from a world we know and see and live, an overexposure ostensibly mirroring our surfeit of consumer, media, and entertainment possibilities. The arc of McCarthy's work since he began exhibiting in the early 1990s has been an exercise in scaling back, of purging his imagery of all manifestations of material surplus and eschewing the digital era's inexhaustible catalogue of imagery. His deviant "copies" from models distort their proportions and smear their faces with clownish-whorish smudges. His landscapes, whether sublime or apocalyptic, are defiantly otherworldly. Where are the objects the consumer products so endemic to an American lifestyle? In McCarthy's paintings, the only "things" not of the natural world to appear with any regularity are makeup, flip-flops, surfboards, skateboards, snowboards, and the accompanying gear appropriate for each extreme sport.

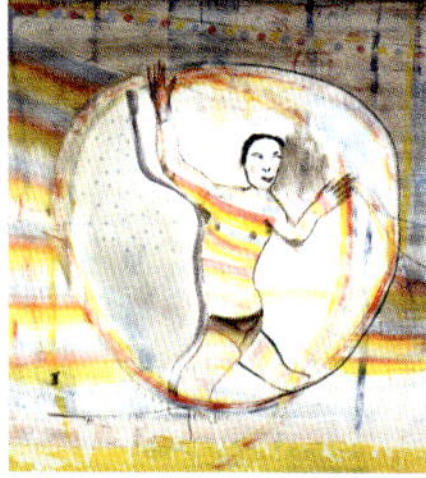

FIGURE .1

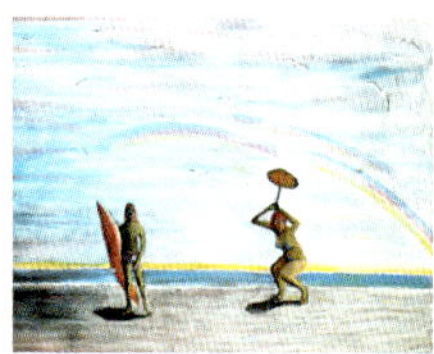

FIGURE .2

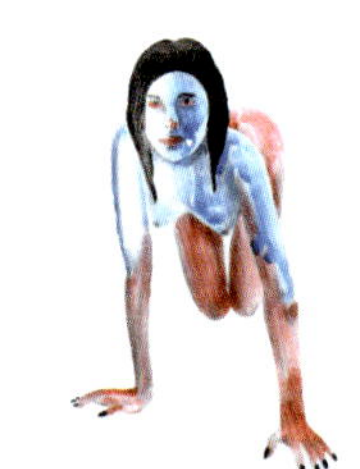

FIGURE .3

1. Philip Taaffe's haiku for McCarthy's 1993 painting *South China Sea:*
    Letters on walrus, South China Sea
    yellow pink dusk
    and with no sign
    In McCarthy, Dan. Dan McCarthy: *Paintings, Drawings 1992-1994* (Anton Kern Gallery, 2003) (Not paginated).
2. Nabokov, Vladimir. *Nikolai Gogol* (New Directions, 1961), pg. 40.
3. There are also several alpine scenes, a few of which show Swiss flags or include the word "Switzerland" in the title.
4. Author interview with the artist, June 2007.

The environs McCarthy's paintings distortedly mirror are mostly southern Californian,**3** sometimes Huntington Beach—McCarthy's hometown and the place that has officially trademarked itself Surf City USA. "I grew up in southern California in the 1960s to the 1980s," McCarthy says. "From the Beach Boys to the Germs. The beach was it… still is."**4** California's honeyed mystique bloomed in the 1960s and on into the 1970s while the cultural capital of the east, New York City, sank into economic depression and social chaos. Legends of the Golden State's sun, sand, and bodies made it the mythical endpoint for road-tripping Americans. This was a national image America could export. And history shows that it sold. Peter Dixon's vaguely technical and always totally stoked *The Complete Book of Surfing* describes how by 1965 surfing had become a new hallmark of Americana, joining the requisite cowboys, mountains, and sunsets as an advertising gimmick to evoke the good life.**5** It was cool, a little sexual, and whispered promises of transcendence. Inevitably, the culture spawned a specific form of reverb-drenched surf music. Jan & Dean and the Beach Boys ruled this scene on the popular level, their breezy glorifications of California beach ethos the aural equivalent of the Luminists, whose oversized paintings propagandized America's resplendent 19th-century landscapes. California had hip slang, better pot, and was a haven for ambassadors from two marginalized groups of romanticized American dissidents: hippies and surfers.

The frenzy of uncritical idealization can seriously fuck up a good thing. Artist Mike Kelley, writing on Paul Thek's 1967 installation *Death of a Hippie,* a wax hippie corpse rotting inside his dank, claustrophobic environment: "[It] *is* Manson, *is* the Altamont Hell's Angel; the degraded end of hippie utopianism and the beginning of the notion of hippie as criminal burnout."**6** Hippies, Kelly continues, became a "cartoon of American otherness" when popular context divorced them from their ideology of negating and disrespecting bourgeois values. What was left was the waste product of hippie style, an easy target for their reduction to, as Kelley correctly calls it, caricatures. Nabokov, in his biography of Nikolai Gogol, invokes the author's play with *poshlost,* Russian for something close to, but not exactly kitsch: "A kind of satellite shadow world in the actual existence of which neither sellers nor buyers really believe."**7** *Poshlost:* this is the territory occupied by the modern hippie, the post-hippie-era hippie, whose ethos can be pegged as historically frozen in a moment some 40 years

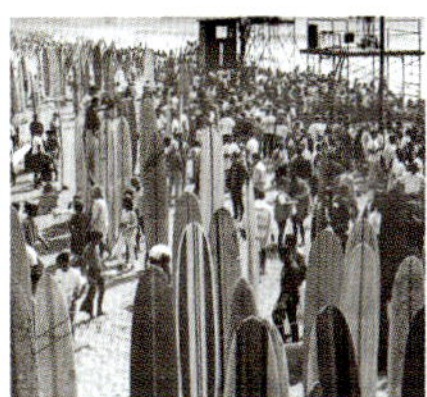

FIGURE .4

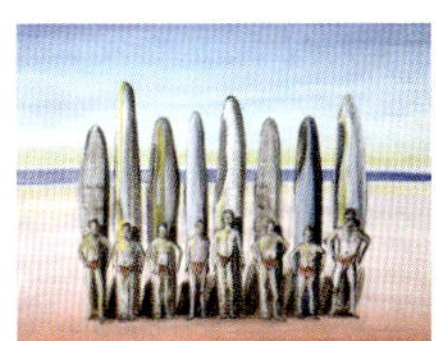

FIGURE .5

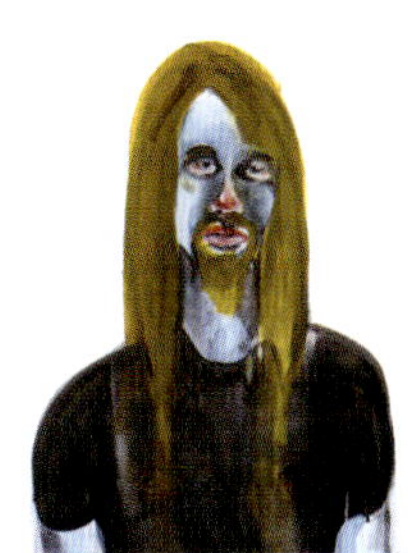

FIGURE .6

5. Dixon, Peter. *The Complete Book of Surfing* (Ballantine, 1965), pg.20
    Dixon's surfer prose is worth quoting here: "The image of surfing is used to sell every thing from autos to soft drinks to instant-dry-non-fat-low-cal-good-for-mothers-and-surfers powdered milk." Cowboys, mountains, and sunsets happen to be the titles of the three sections forming artist Richard Prince's 1983 novel *Why I Go to the Movies Alone.* Prince, like McCarthy, mines the mythic America of popular imagination, and while this essay isn't the space to do it, there are affinities between Prince and McCarthy's work would reward further investigation.

6. Kelley, Mike. *Foul Perfection: Essays and Criticism,* "Death and Transfiguration" (MIT Press, 2003), pg. 144.

distant. But its endurance is proof of the timeless temptation of freedom from modern life's vulgarity. The hippie remains a potent archetype (albeit an almost exclusively white and/or middle class one) encompassing those who renounce normative work and voting habits, style, and opinions on "family values." *Poshlost* dwells in this conflicted space between revered and ridiculous, tired but timeless tropes. Like sun, sand, and girls in bikinis.

"Are these for real"? The question hangs in an invisible thought bubble over McCarthy's paintings. Put another way, McCarthy's attitude toward his own imagery isn't discernibly positive or negative, sincere or ironic. His people are too statuesque, too completely iconic, to be quite human. They constantly revert to a repeated repertoire of poses. Many tote surfboards or balance as if negotiating invisible waves. Rainbows stream through skies, some crystalline and serene, others filthy and toxic. A vague notion of transcendence, of "the ultimate," is everywhere in these paintings—the rainbows, the silent snowy mountains, the bathing suit-clad beauties. But the idyllic is compromised, not quite as good as its rumored promises. Faces are rife with imperfections. Makeup is slapped on vulgarly. Metallic silver washes of paint pollute an epic landscape. Characters' skin is freaked with acid stains. In McCarthy's paintings there is *poshlost,* and there is also its infection.

Willem de Kooning's paintings famously laced epic with vulgar, but McCarthy's primary models extend further back than AbEx, specifically to Edvard Munch, Henri Rousseau, and Pablo Picasso. Especially in his early paintings, McCarthy's color treatments evoke Munch's; his 1993 painting *Harvest* even seems to reference the same tortured seascape of *The Scream.* But the primary thing McCarthy gleaned from Munch is texture—or rather, its lack. McCarthy cites the radical flatness of Munch's canvases as revelatory. "Munch's paintings are so flat that when viewed from the side there is little or no texture whatsoever… [Texture] was something to be avoided as it detracted from the immediacy of the subject, an unnecessary barrier that made the experience of both painting and viewing illegitimate."[8] By layering coat after coat of gesso onto his canvases, McCarthy crafts a perfectly smooth surface to accommodate the effects he executes with almost no paint at all. Sometimes paint is applied quickly and allowed to bleed over the smooth surface; sometimes it's left to congeal in little pools; sometimes it's blotted with newspaper. Descending hazes of washy color slide down the face of canvases in ribbons of Technicolor pollution. Recently, McCarthy has taken effects previously used for atmosphere or landscape and transposed them onto the skin of characters painted against blank white backgrounds, whose traumatized blotches of rotting, phosphorescent skin mimic weather's chance operations.

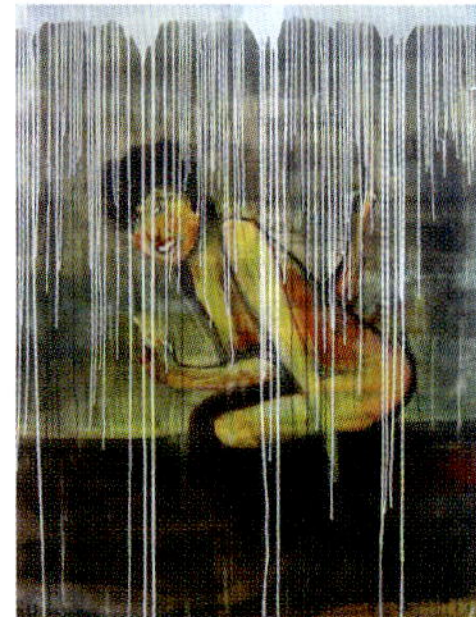

FIGURE .7

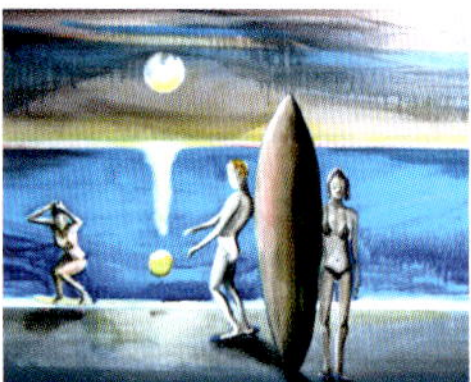

FIGURE .8

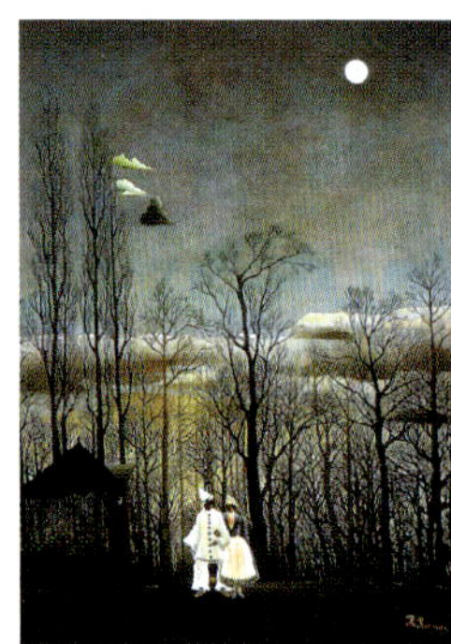

FIGURE .9

7. Nabokov, Vladimir. *Nikolai Gogol* (New Directions, 1961), pg. 67.
8. Gingeras, Alison. "Dan McCarthy: The Silver Surfer." Included with press materials for McCarthy's 2005 exhibition at Anton Kern Gallery, New York.

McCarthy has described himself as a "psychological painter." Some of this is accomplished through the chromatic drama and washy effects that come with using thin paint, but just as much stems from his distortions of scale and perception, his invasion of Picasso and Rousseau's territory. McCarthy's "dreamy, goofy, and naughty" iconography led one reviewer to pan his paintings as "professionally contrived," the implication being that their weirdness was a put-on, that they weren't *believably* weird.[9] Rousseau was almost universally disparaged by critics for the opposite reason: his paintings' blundering amateurishness. In truth, any "outsider" qualities read into Rousseau's paintings are undermined by his writings, in which he clearly explains that his late, fantasist style was a slowly acquired process; he even coyly mentions "maintaining his naiveté."[10] One so conscious of his naiveté isn't naïve in the least. Rousseau, in his most interesting work, was inventing image-constructions. His jungle and overseas military scenes belong to a world he never experienced. Leo Steinberg's argument that "Most [art] is dedicated precisely to the imitations of nature, the likeness-catching to the portrayal of objects and situations—in short, to representation," is still true, but Rousseau's steroidal flora and impossible treatments of natural light are a perverse interpretation of "representation."[11]

T.J. Clark, discussing a photo Picasso snapped of a group of his own 1912 paintings, wrote that Picasso was perched on a frontier, "…and not just painting, by the looks of it, but picturing in general; and not just picturing but maybe perceiving; and not just perceiving but maybe being-in-the-world."[12] This is the language of Modernism, of art as a conduit to a higher plane of consciousness and awareness. Clark's point is that Picasso's interpretations of vision and structure kicked open a door of possibility, one that Rousseau (whose work Picasso loved and owned) had cracked. Whereas his peers and predecessors bent reality, Picasso's project was to reinvent it while unmasking it as constructed and subjective. Then, just after sufficiently fracturing all perceptual logic with Analytical Cubism, Picasso abruptly returned to figurative painting. McCarthy's quietly misproportioned figures (often with very short legs or heads much too large or small for the body) echo the proportional play evident during Picasso's Neoclassical period, which occupied him from the mid-1920s through the early 1930s. The enduring impression given by Picasso's Neoclassical work is the heaviness of the figures; they're more statues than people.

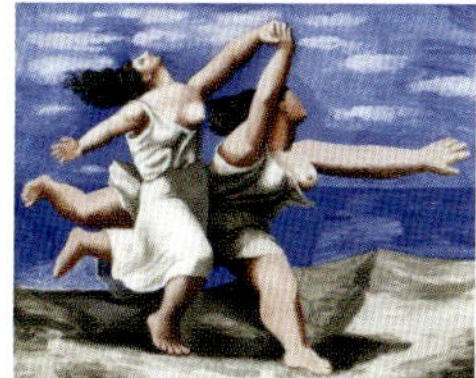

FIGURE .10

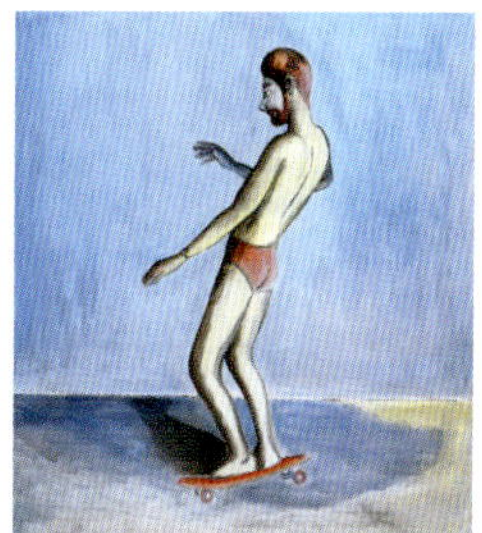

FIGURE .11

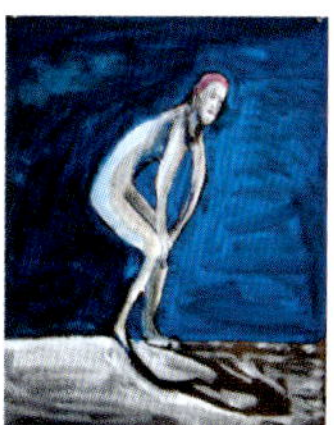

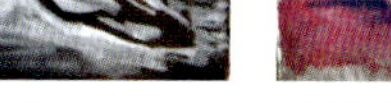

FIGURE .12   FIGURE .13

9.   Johnson, Ken. *New York Times,* June 20, 2003. Arts and Leisure section, Weblink: http://query.nytimes.com/gst/fullpage.html?res=9B00E3DD1F38F933A15755C0A9659C8B63

10. Lanchner, Carolyn and William Rubin. "Henri Rousseau and Modernism," in *Henri Rousseau* (Museum of Modern Art, 1984), pg. 35.

11. Steinberg, Leo. "The Eye Is a Part of the Mind," in *Other Criteria* (Oxford University Press, 1972), pg. 291.

12. Clark, T.J. "Cubism and Collectivity," in *Farewell to an Idea: Episodes from a History of Modernism* (Yale University Press, 1999), pg. 174.

From the work included in his 2003 show at Anton Kern Gallery until now, McCarthy's figures have become discernibly more statuesque. Knees bent, the torso hunched over with its weight on the hands, as they grip the knees. Hands held over head, both knees bent. Holding a large fish aloft. McCarthy's people constantly repeat physical situations; they're models, eternally holding repetitive poses, and this repetition is what makes them convincing statues. There's nothing spontaneous about these postures, so many of which seem derived from stances assumed on surfboards and skateboards. These are people conscious of our scrutiny, conscious of their status as performers. Statues are idealizations, and so are the characters in McCarthy's paintings, especially the women, who easily outnumber men. Since 2005, McCarthy's women are almost invariably nude or dressed only in bathing suits.[13] They casually kill time, avoid eye contact, and confidently expose their bodies. McCarthy says they are based on an accepted Western cultural ideal of feminine physicality: the 25-year-old. "Women should never age beyond 25," Michel Subor's character Bruno Forestier opines in Jean-Luc Godard's 1963 film Le Petit Soldat. According to conventional wisdom it's all downhill after 25, but that doesn't stop advertisers from incessant summertime prattle urging women to chisel themselves into their "bathing suit body." Bodies and the poses they strike are a form of non-verbal communication, part of the human mating ritual. As if channeling one of McCarthy's female figures, a J. Crew bikini model photographed in this summer's catalogue flaunts a top nearly identical in shape to those McCarthy's women wear. She's not just selling a bikini, she's selling a lifestyle fueled by an imagined communion with nature: of course, she sits on a surfboard.

The observation of nature is a constant in McCarthy's paintings. Mountains, underwater views, and ubiquitous beach scenes describe the majority of his work since the early 1990s. In 2006 McCarthy made a series of winter scenes seeming to take place at the crest of a mountain, the summit of a hike. The colors of the snowy landscapes—scarlet, cerulean blue, pink—are some of McCarthy's most surreal, and yet the characters' activities are his most banal. They pose frontally, ostensibly acknowledging the presence of the unseen painter or cameraperson. They jab triumphant fingers skyward. They affect stylized postures with the tools of their hobby. They grimace heroically under silver moons. Having reached a plateau, McCarthy's hikers do exactly what is expected of them. Conscious of being watched, they obediently perform the least creative action conceivable. McCarthy had previously used streaks and jabs of paint to communicate an ambiguous but palpably looming negativity. In the winter paintings he communicates the same through the characters' adherence to the generic. Shortly after completing this series, McCarthy deleted the landscapes and backgrounds entirely; the resultant "white paintings" are even more freezing, arguably his bleakest work yet.

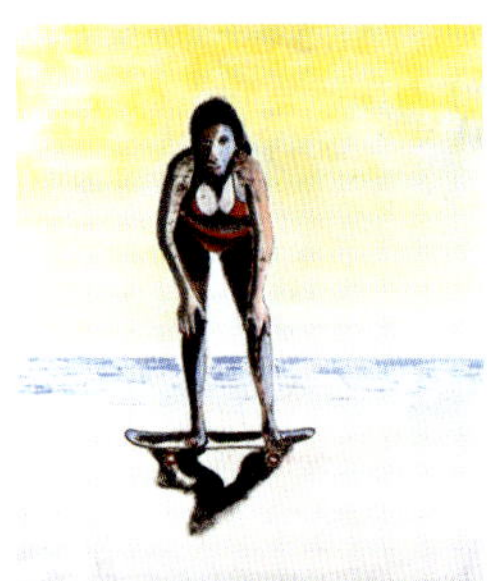

FIGURE .14

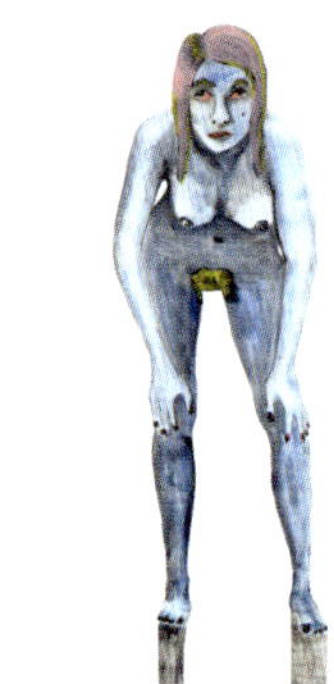

FIGURE .15

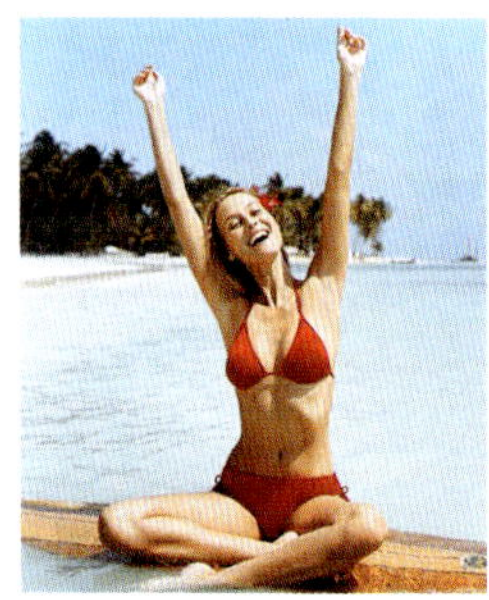

FIGURE .16

13. A few women wear burkas or nuns' habits.
14. Author interview with the artist, June 2007.
15. Author interview with the artist, June 2007.

No nature and much less frequent communion between people. Two of McCarthy's trademarks are reduced or diminished in the white paintings. The protagonists are almost exclusively women alone in an empty netherworld. When joined by men, both characters appear so statuesque as to be monuments to the once-human. The same cerulean blue McCarthy used for his winter landscapes frosts the bodies of these inaccessible cyborgs and their superior and stoned gazes. Dropped into a glaring spotlight, they become billboards with exposed, color-coded skin, not quite human. Ana Karinas from *Alphaville.* It would be a stretch to argue that a concrete politics is espoused in McCarthy's work, but the white paintings come closest to a sustained political gesture. Most obvious is the characters' skin color: America's national colors are bluntly evoked. The removal of landscape contains specifically American political implications. *Kyoto Protocol,* an earlier painting and McCarthy's most specifically political image preceding the white pieces, is a nighttime scene of a woman on the water in a small fishing boat. Against a snowcapped backdrop of mountains flying Japanese and Swiss flags, she gestures to the sky, apparently pleading. America's non-ratification of the international Kyoto Protocol and the Bush administration's brazen refusal to admit the facts of global warming seem the likely referents. There's impending danger in images like *Kyoto Protocol* and two dramatic paintings of icebergs emerging from an oceanic horizon, the latter of which could be read as references to the rapid melting of icecaps and the corresponding rise in sea levels. In the wake of paintings like these, the wholesale removal of natural landscape makes the white paintings the stage of disaster's aftermath. The washy paint effects used for a sky's reflective nimbus or an ocean's silver glare have been transported to the body as repulsively damaged skin. Whatever sexuality is initially communicated by these figures' nudity unravels and is revealed as a decoy. These alien, almost grotesque women are alone and vulnerable under a hot spotlight. "Front and center. Red, white, and blue."**14**

"I thought the white would make things really clear… and undeniable," McCarthy said of his decision to eliminate landscape.**15** Objects of mass production have always been nearly nonexistent in McCarthy's paintings. The white paintings initiate a new level of removal: viewers are denied a context with which to judge the situation. The world as we know it, see it, and are trained to deconstruct it is junked and isn't replaced. In making

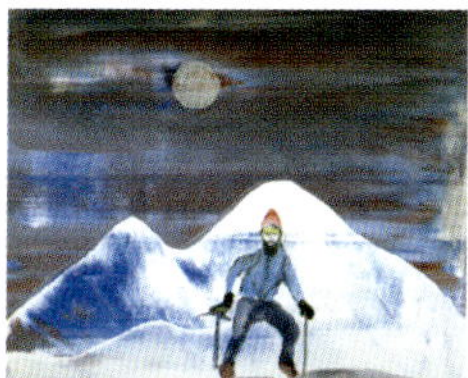

FIGURE .17

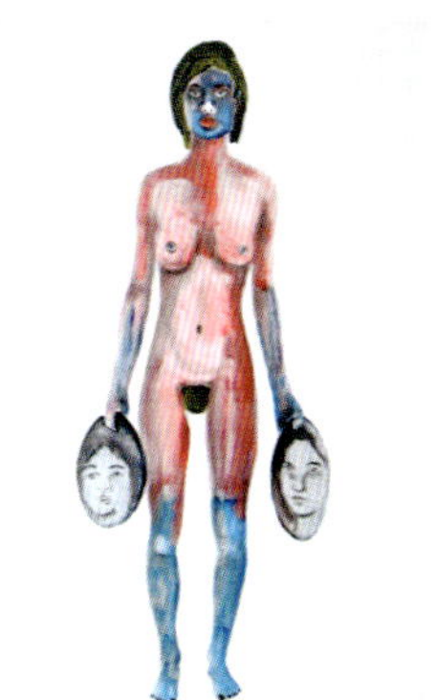

FIGURE .18

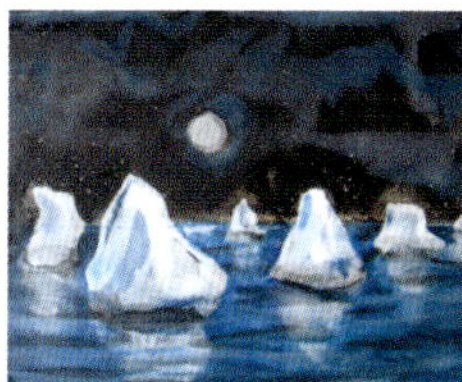

FIGURE .19

this new work, McCarthy first sketches a model with pencil onto a gessoed canvas before filling in the drawing with thin washes of very wet paint. The process is a self-imposed restraining order; the white paintings are a study of economy and wastelessness, a distinctly un-American technique.

It's important to keep in mind Taaffe's "land with no sign" phrase and it's relationship to McCarthy's paintings. His work resists instant gratification. There is no clear "message." No discernible advocacy. Except this: Keep looking. Continue decoding what you see on a daily basis, because reality is the construction of those inclined to invent it themselves. A painter rendering rainbows, placid beach landscapes, portraits, and practitioners of extreme sports might initially seem to be wallowing in *poshlost*. But who determines what's considered hackneyed? If in 2007, extreme sports are considered passé, isn't this the product of their commodification and elevation by corporations? If the ecstasy of surfing has become a trope, isn't this because advertising agencies appropriate what's "extreme" or "alternative" and present it in a palatable, saleable package, draining it of all oppositional significance? In describing *poshlost*, I used the example of the modern hippie in part because McCarthy has painted post-hippie burnouts and also to show how the reduction of anything to a stereotype is contextually determined. I believe this is what McCarthy means when he says, "Through confronting the standard gaze we get past the banal and toward a clearer perception."[16] This involves the extrication of the self from an identity determined by brands. Assuming that the beautiful 25-year-olds who populate McCarthy's paintings are an evocation of society's sexualized "standard gaze," he confronts this most articulately with the individual women in his white paintings who hold up mirrors with disembodied faces reflected in them. Are the reflections (often homely, not necessarily young, sometimes deformed) the actual visages of these women? Some women hold the mirrors over their faces; others hold bags over their heads, masking themselves. Appearance is artifice. What we see—what is sold—is the mask, the show. Nabokov describes the idea with perfect accuracy: "All reality is a mask."[17]

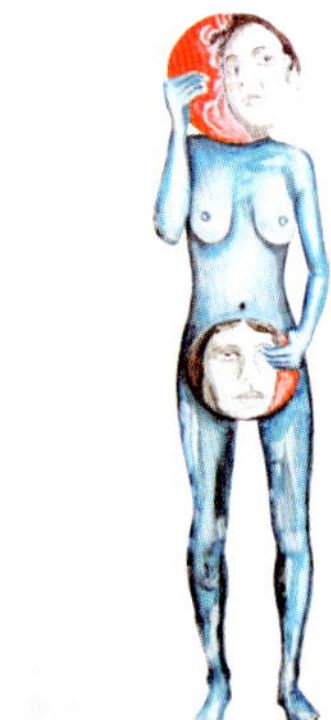

FIGURE .20

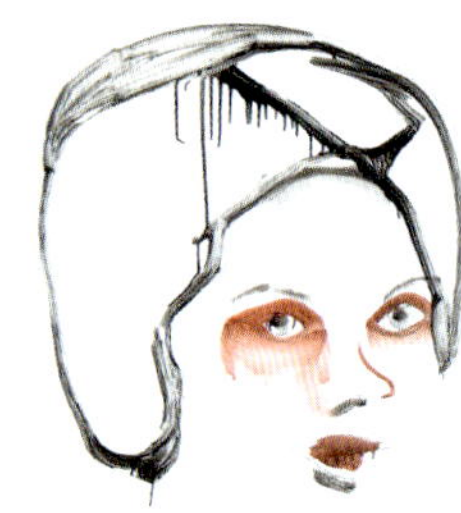

FIGURE .21

16. Author interview with the artist, June 2007.
17. Nabokov, Vladimir. Nikolai Gogol (New Directions, 1961), pg. 148.

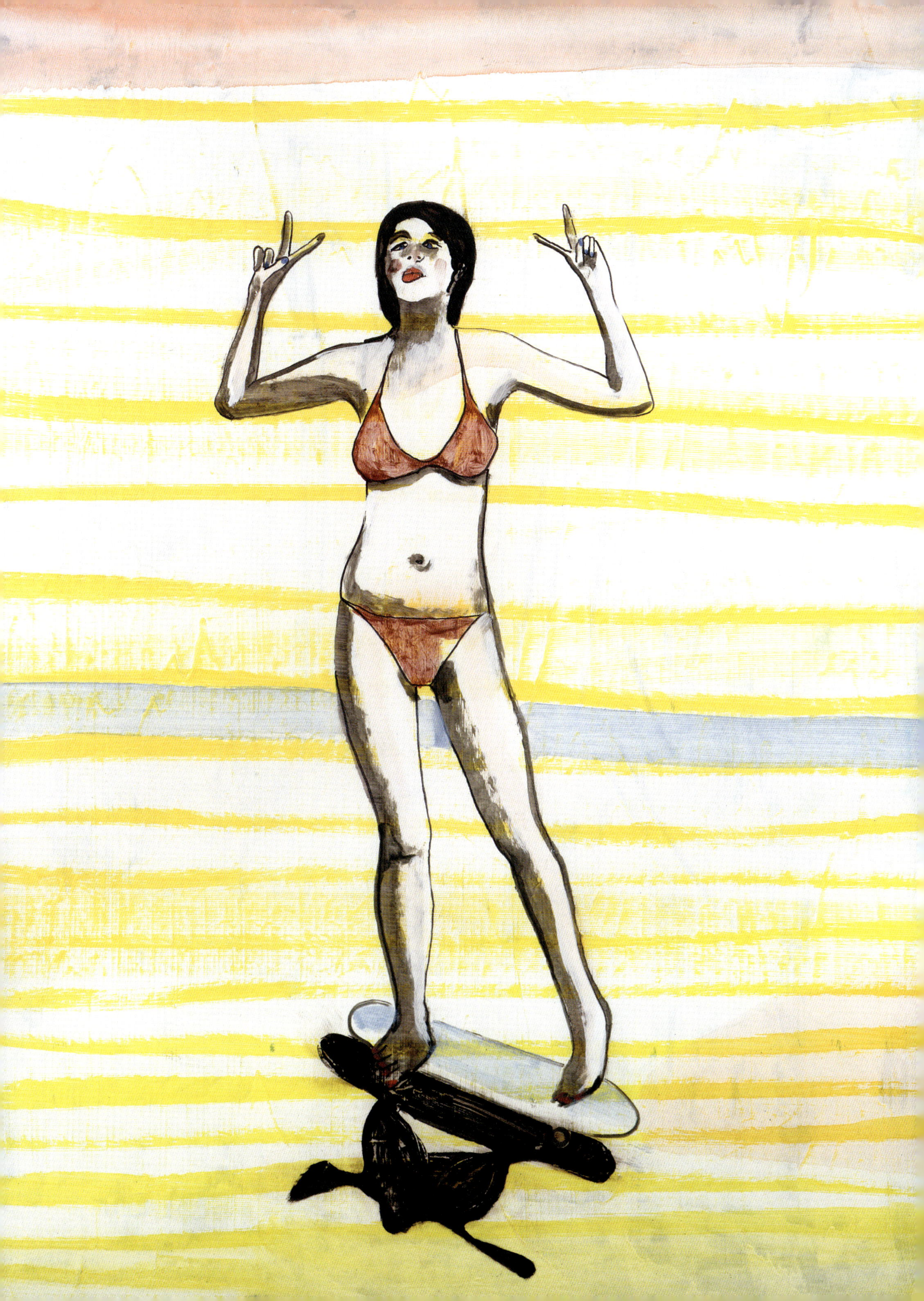

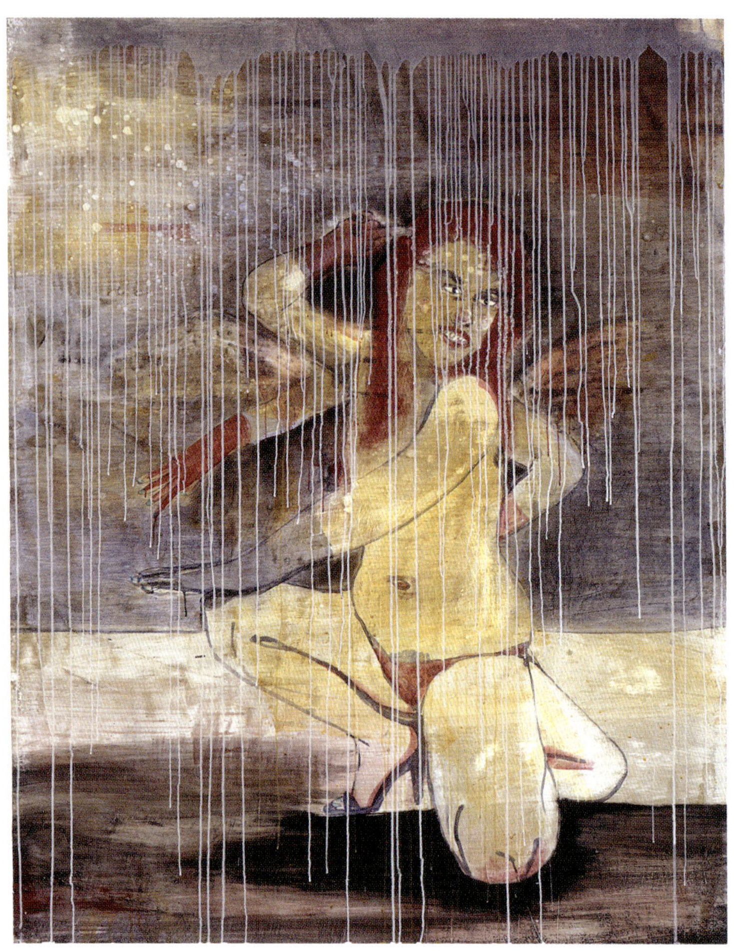

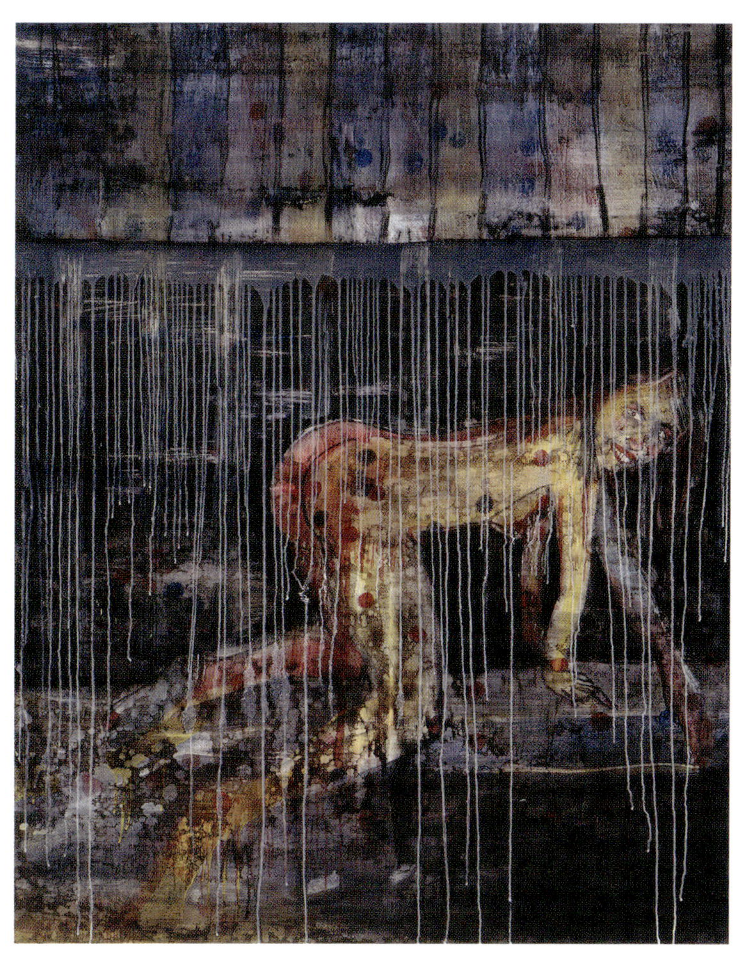

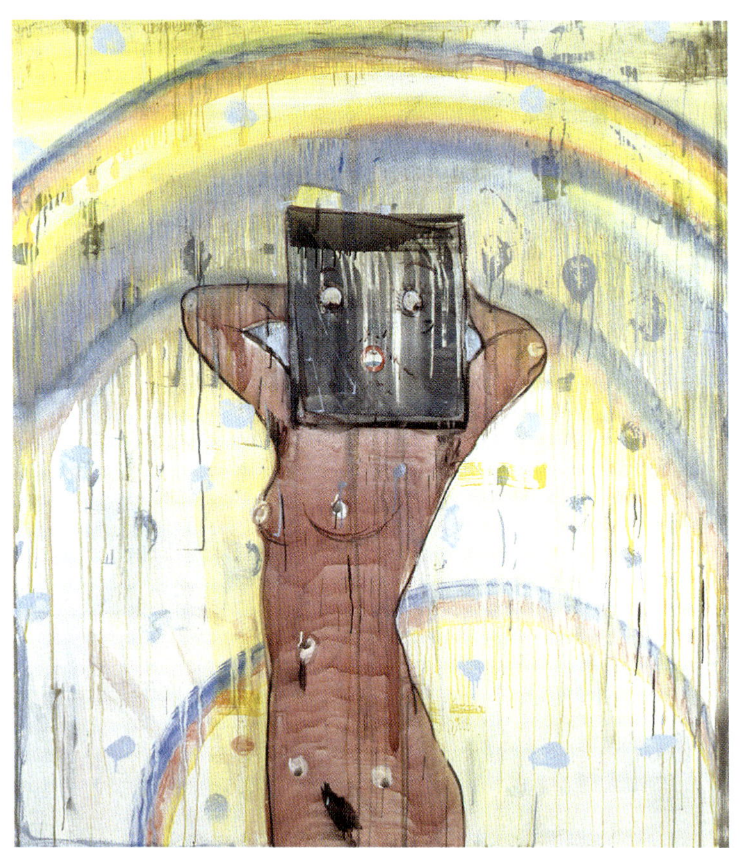

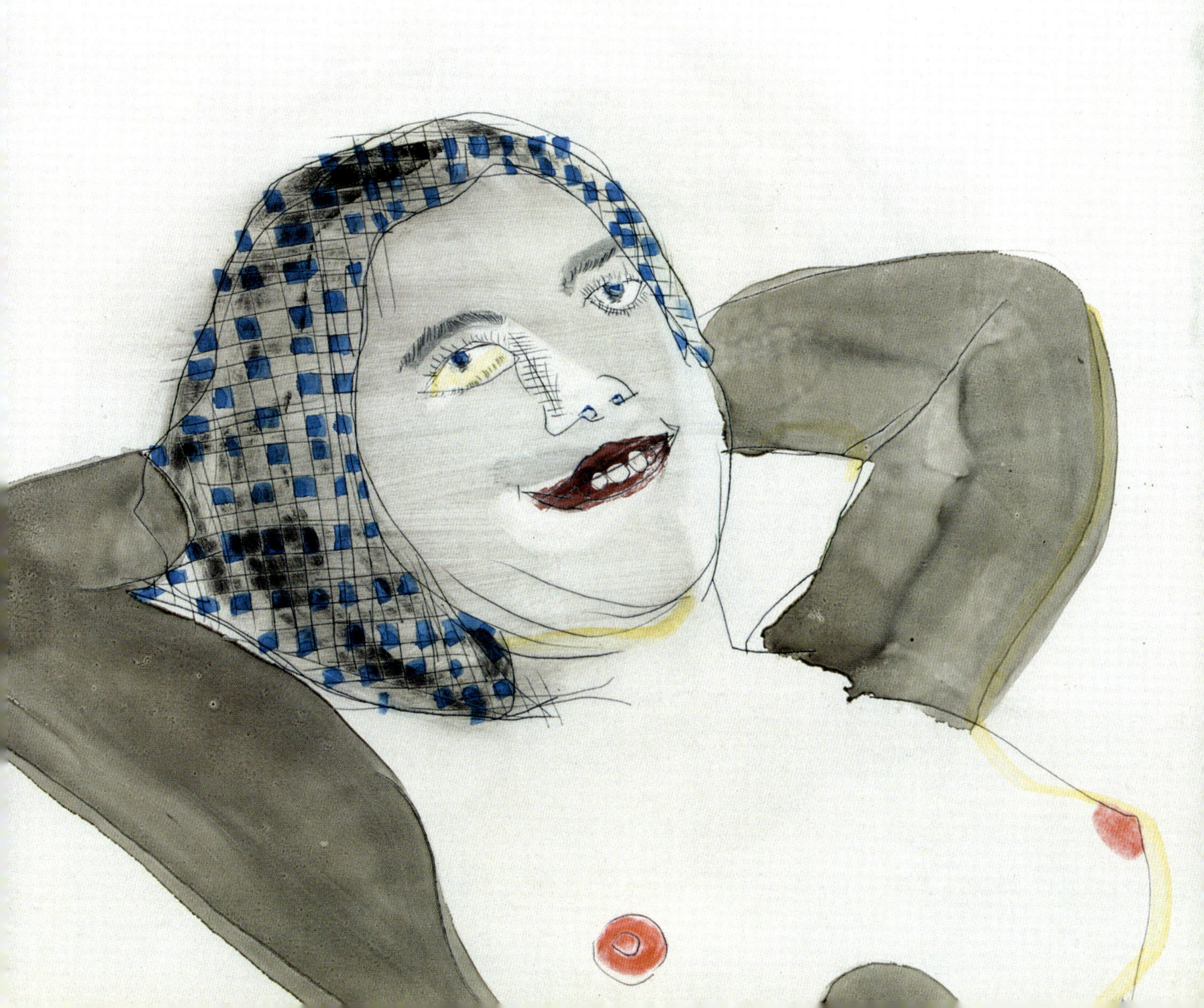

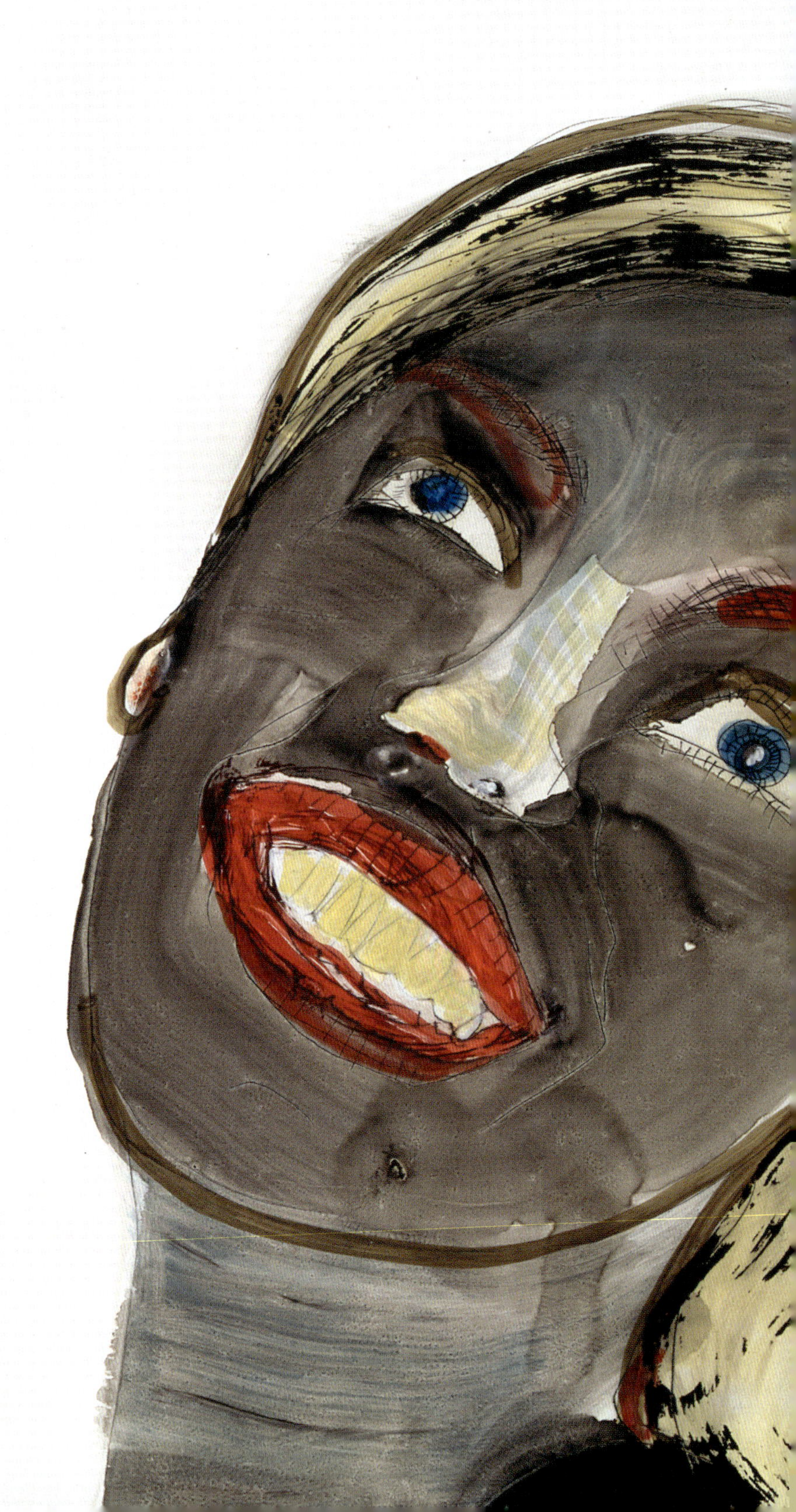

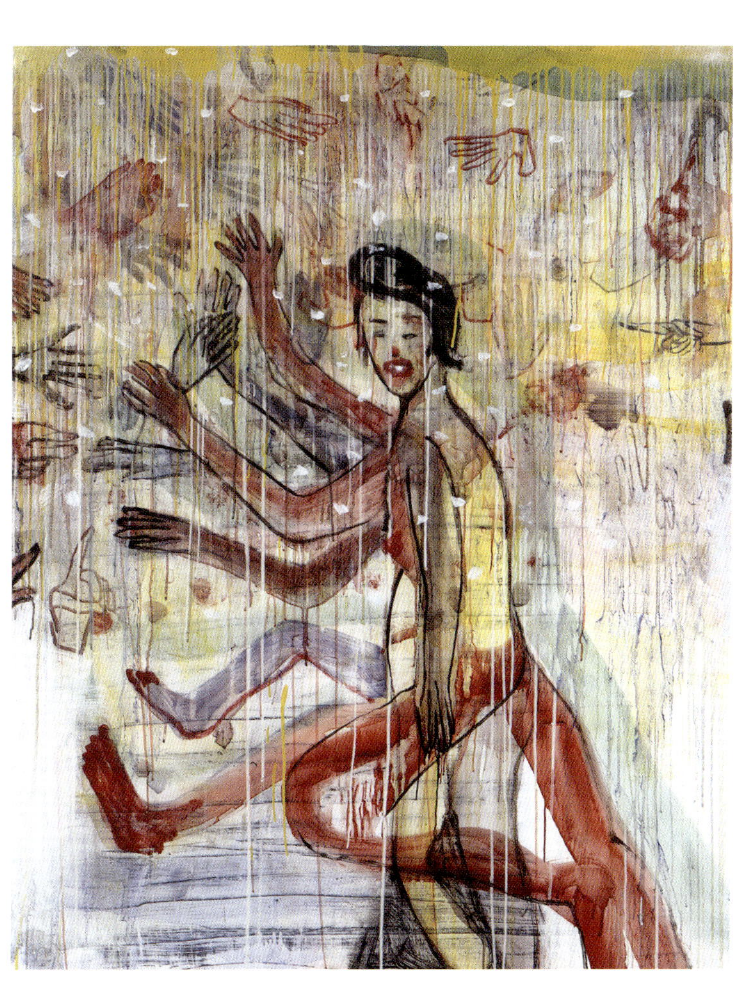

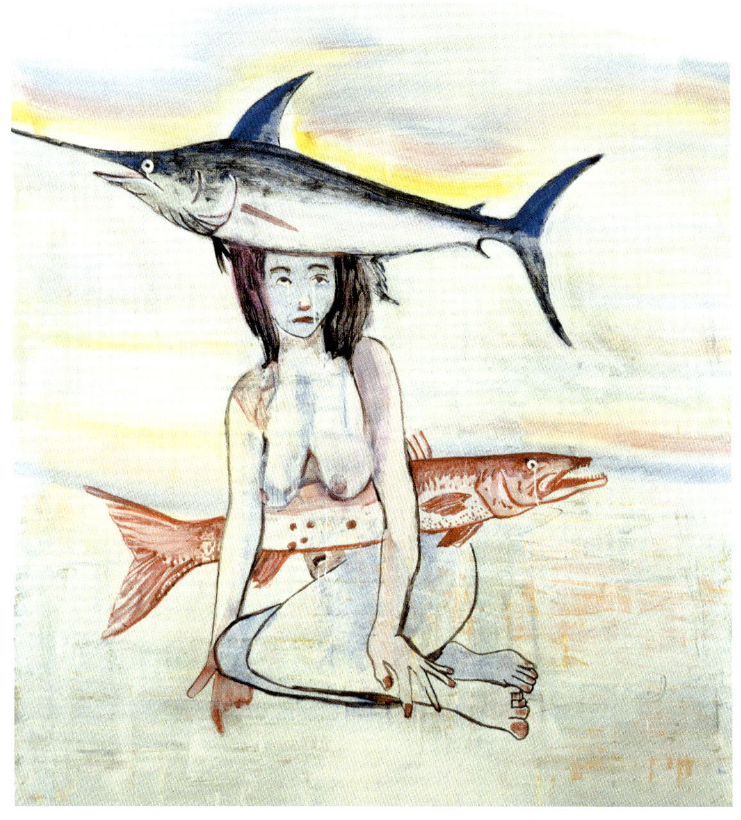

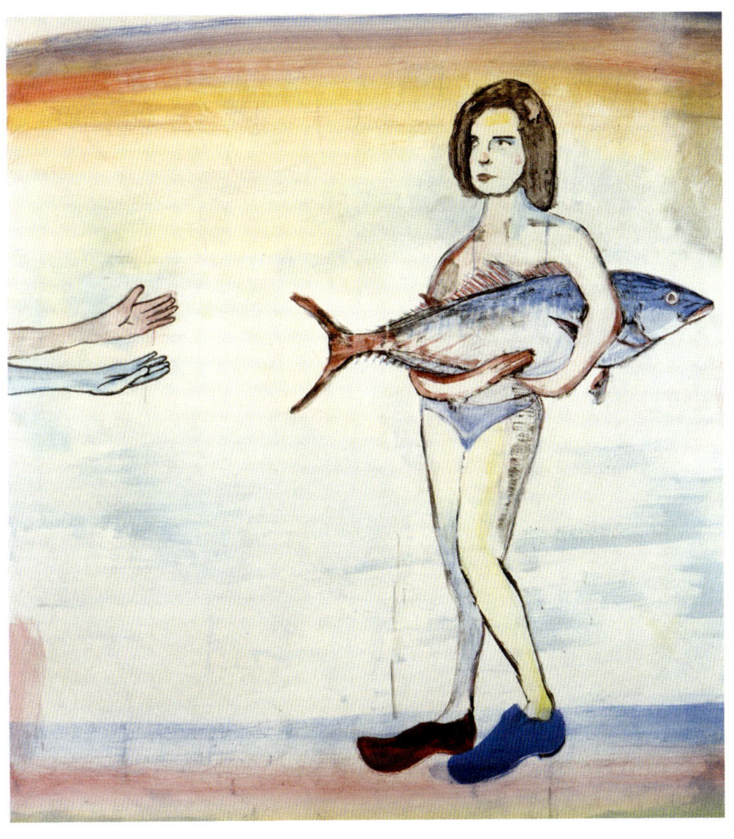

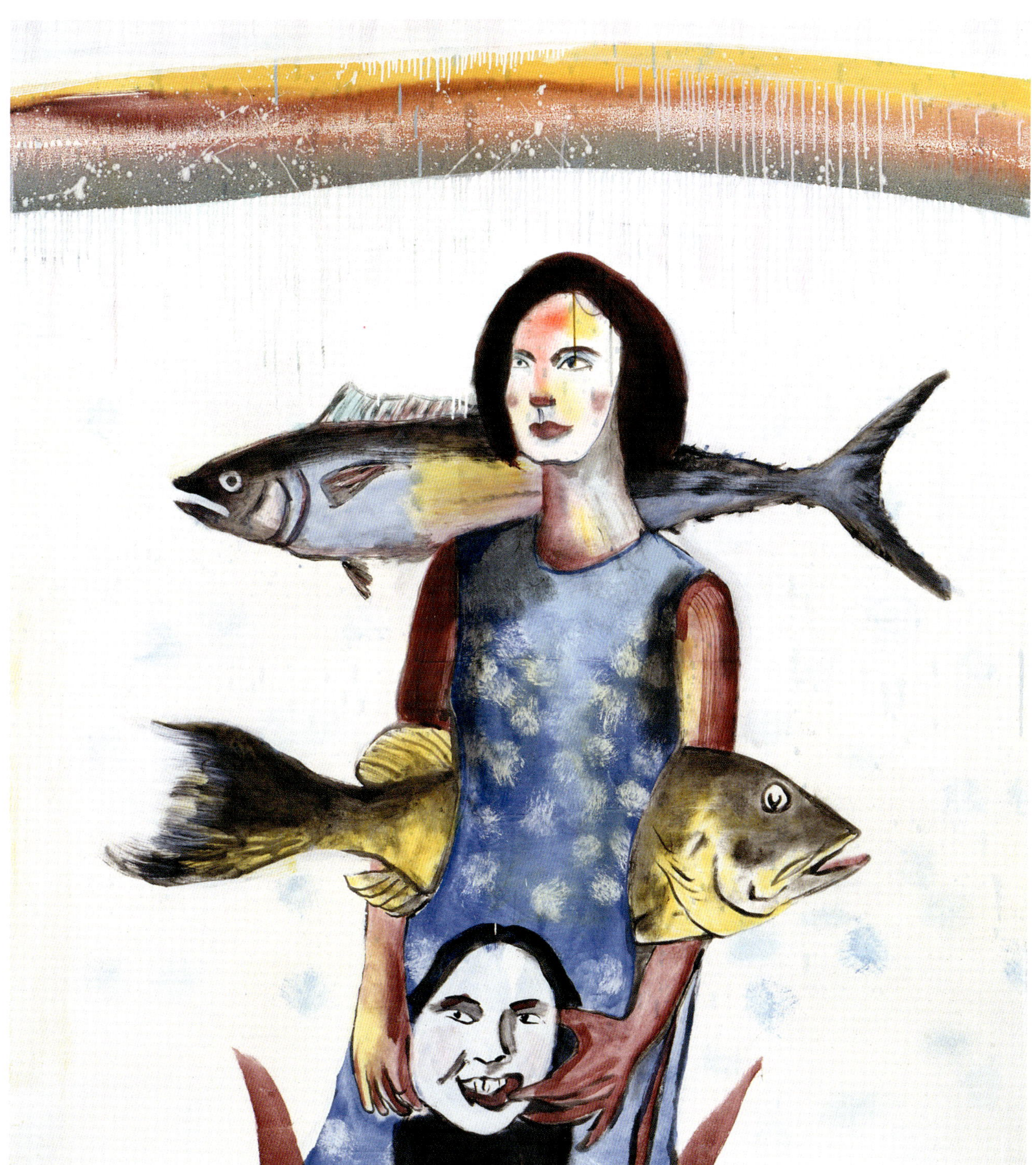

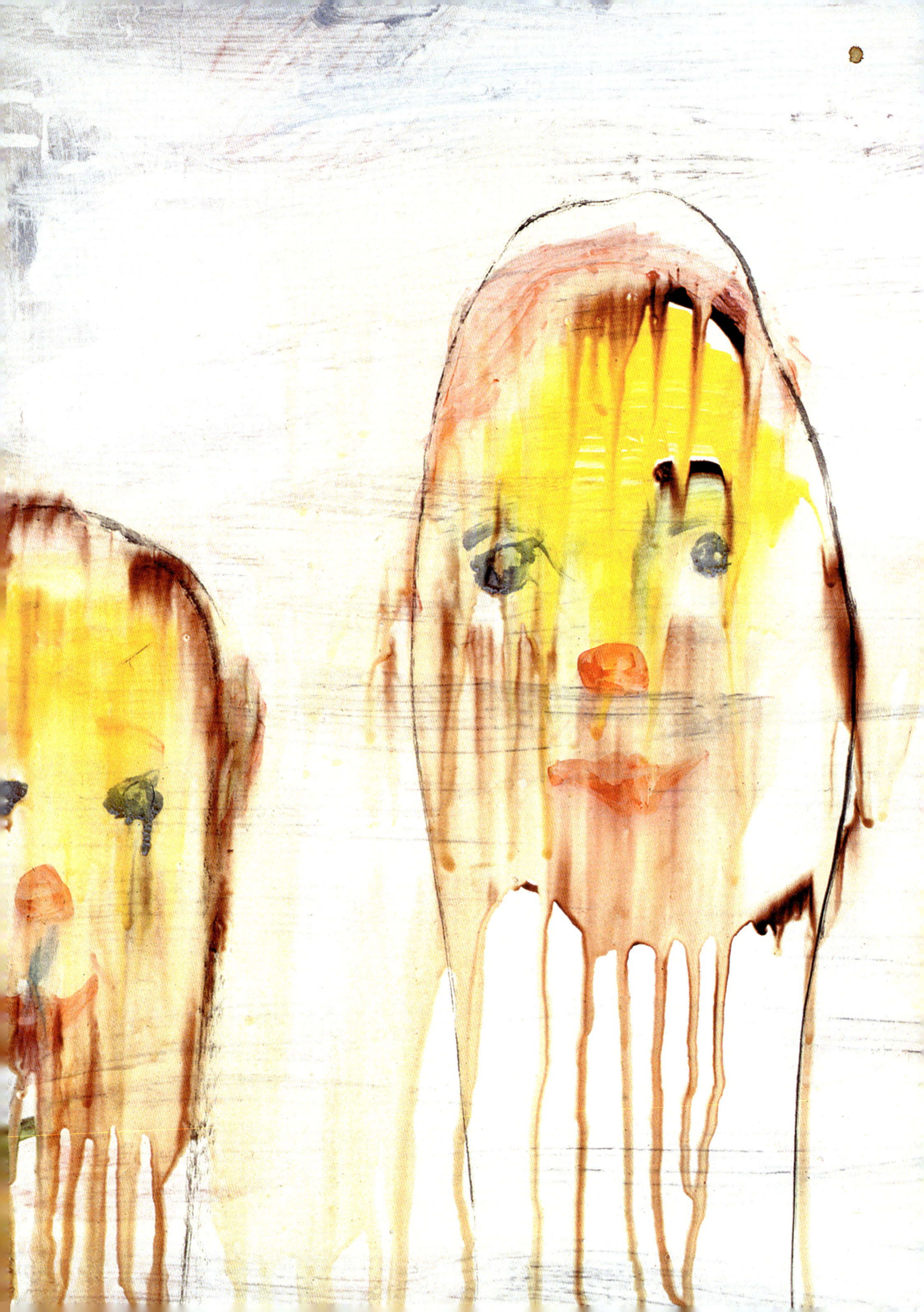

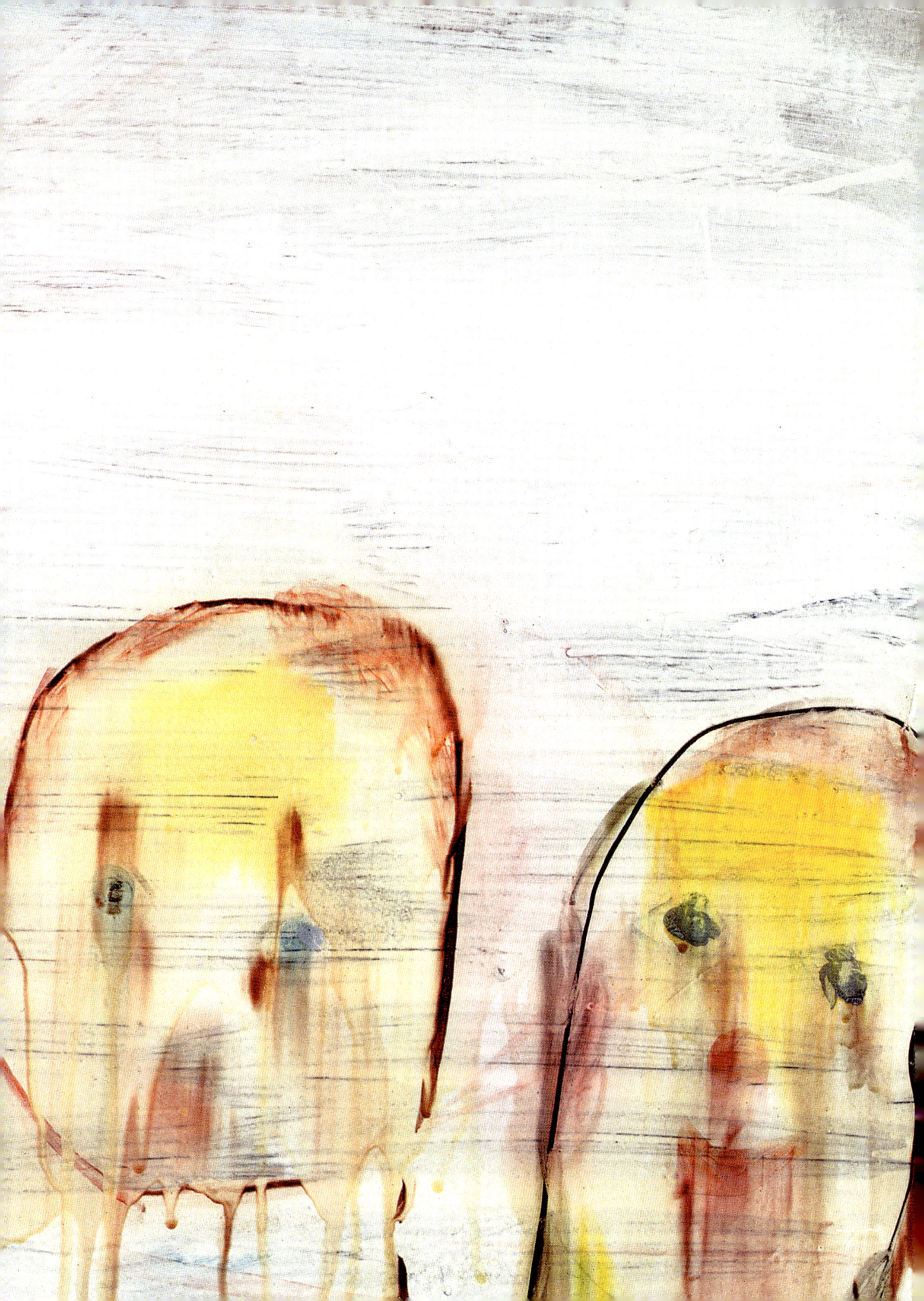

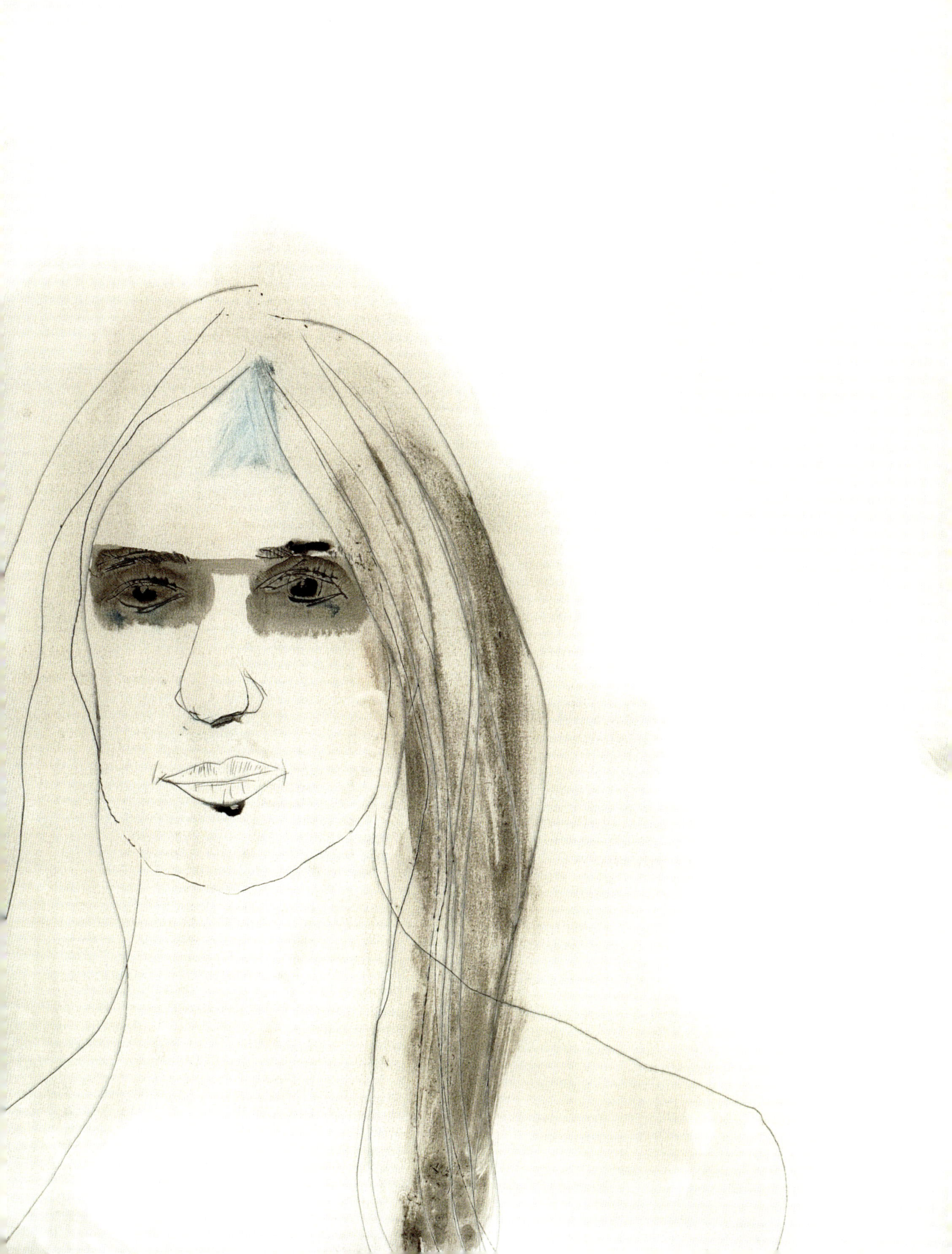

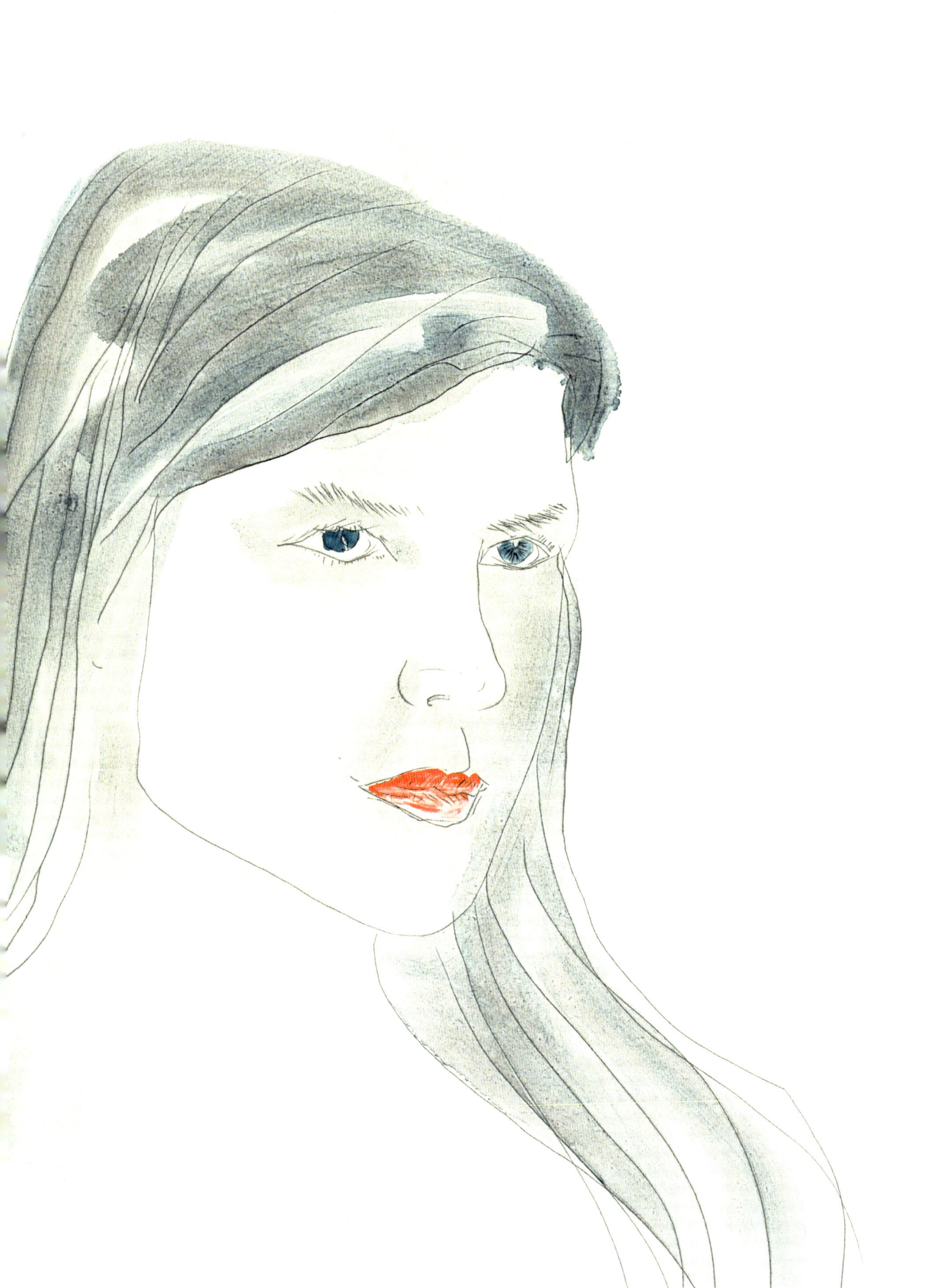

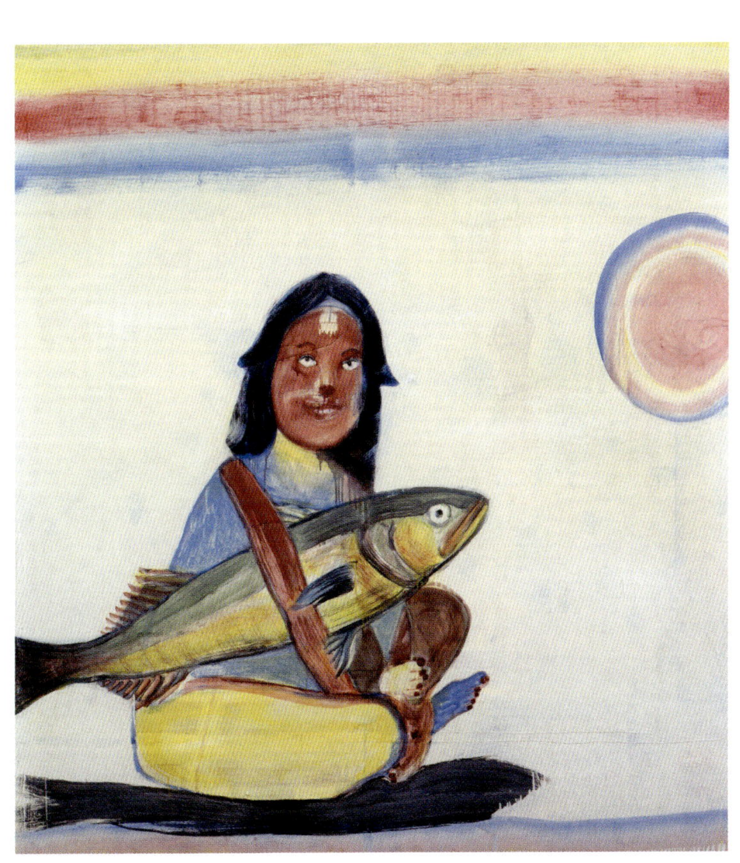

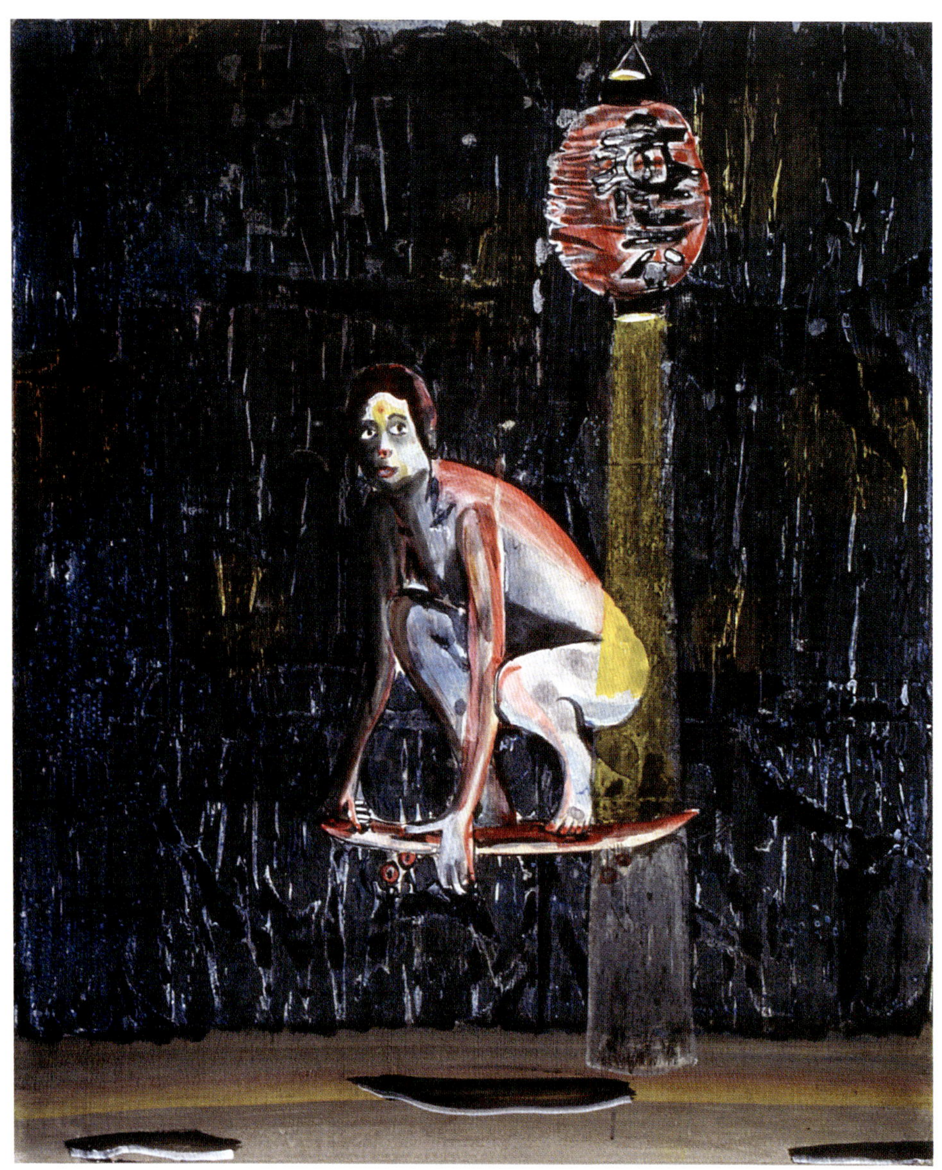

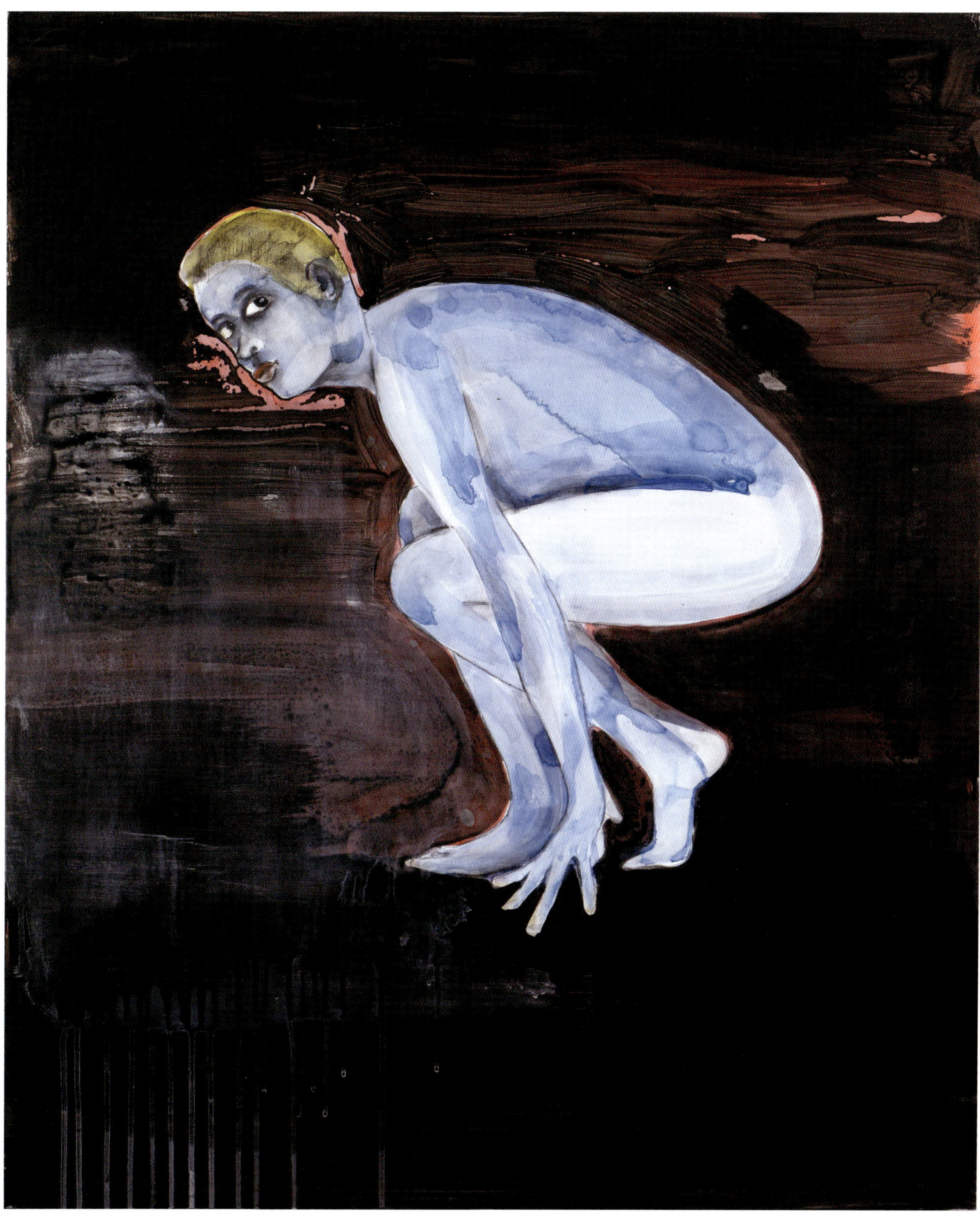

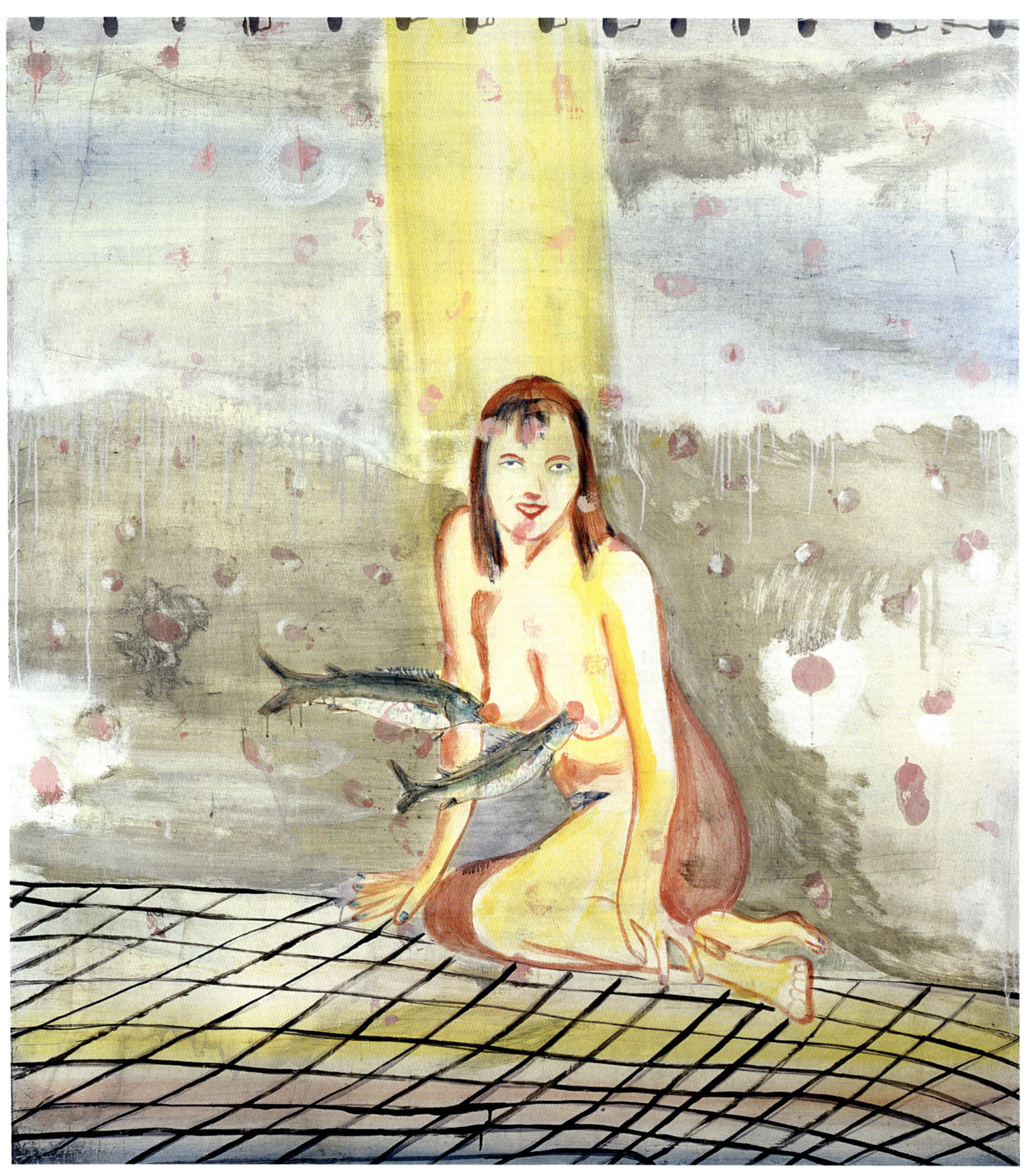

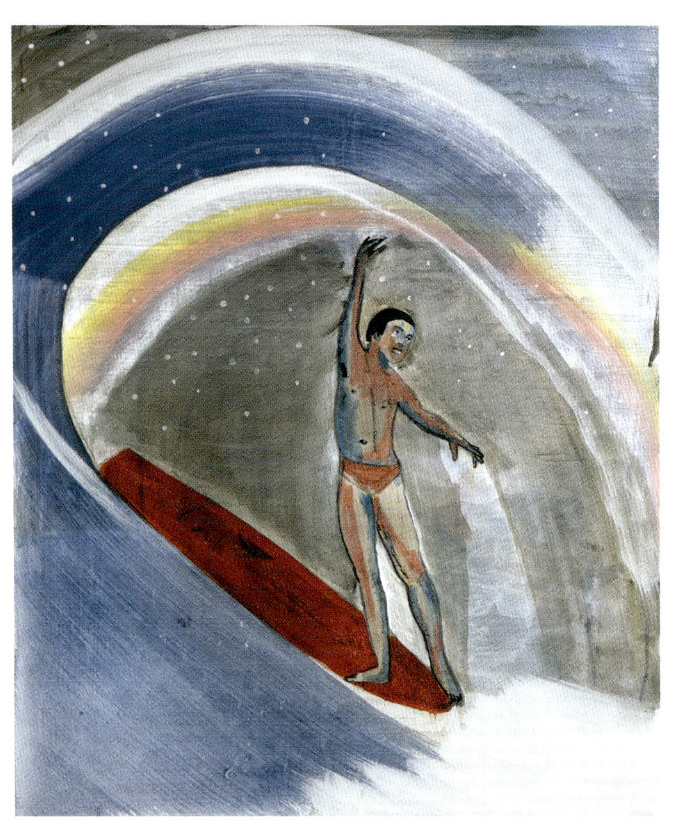

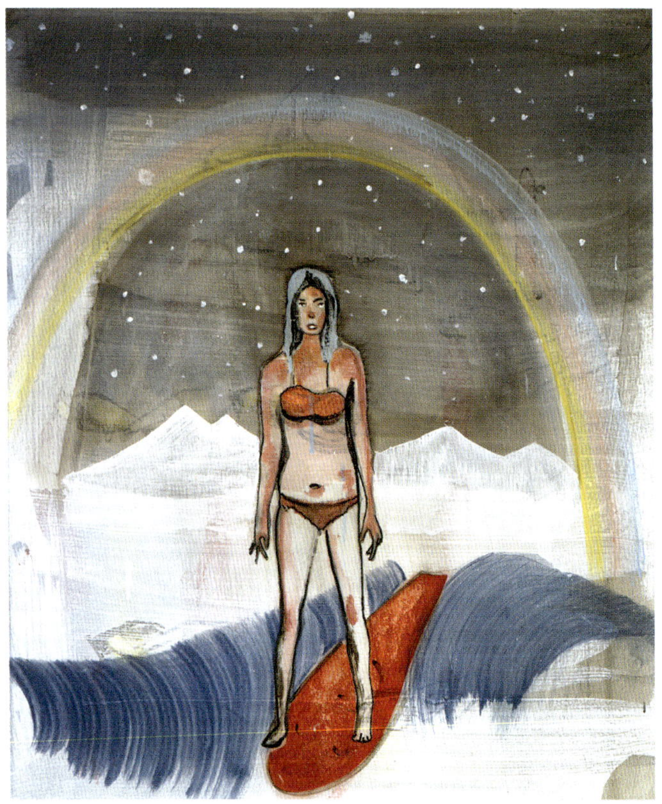

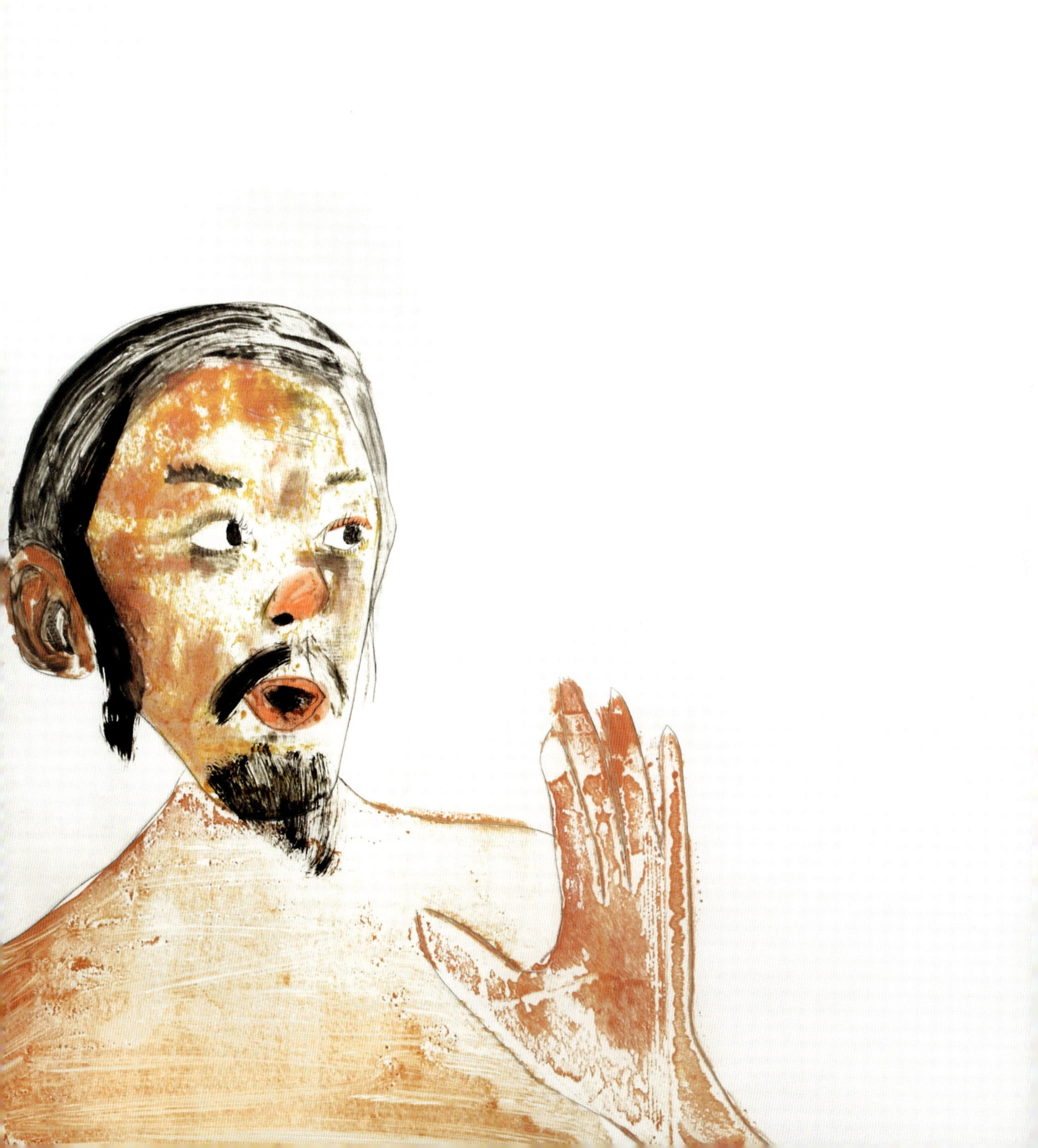

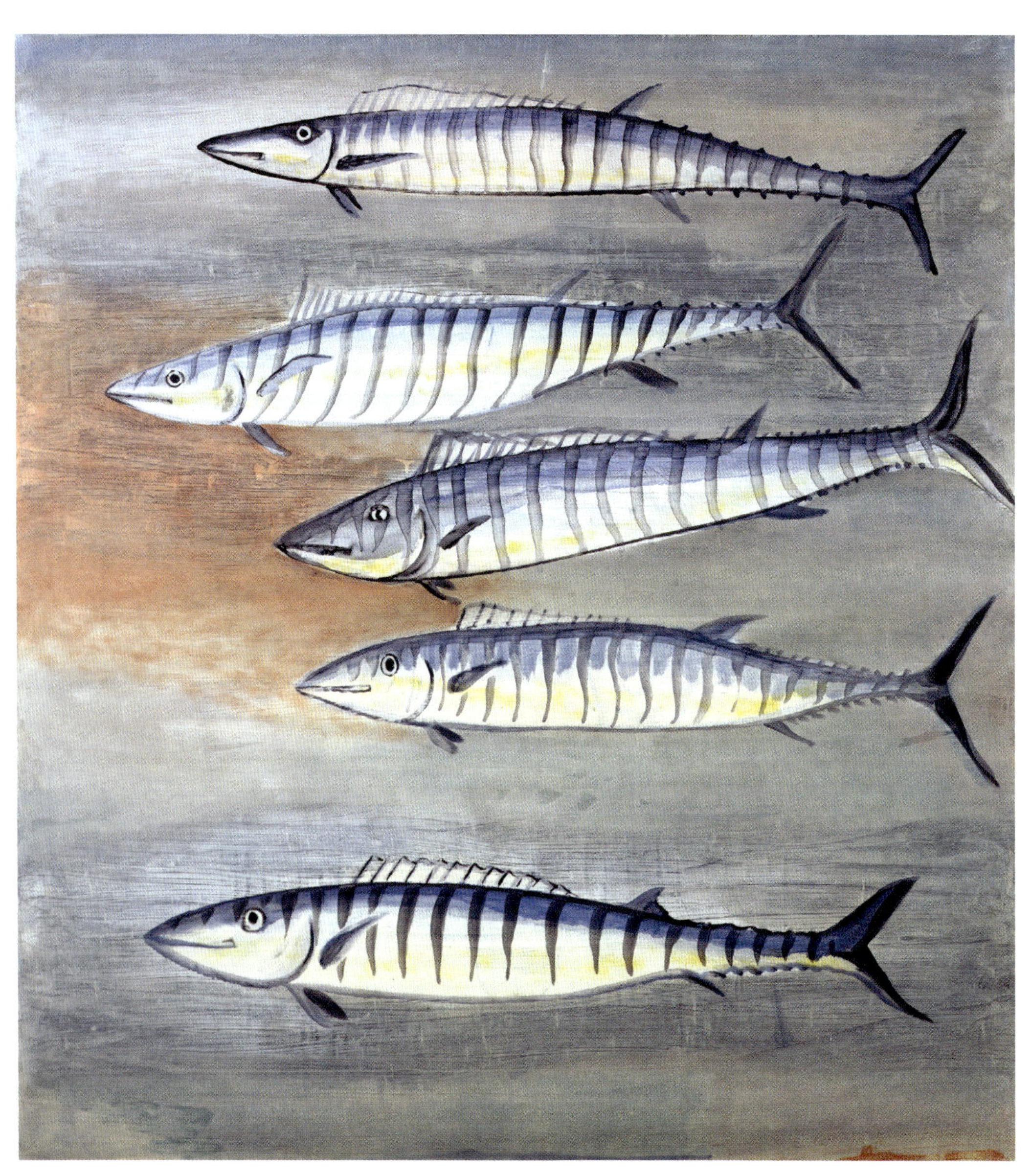

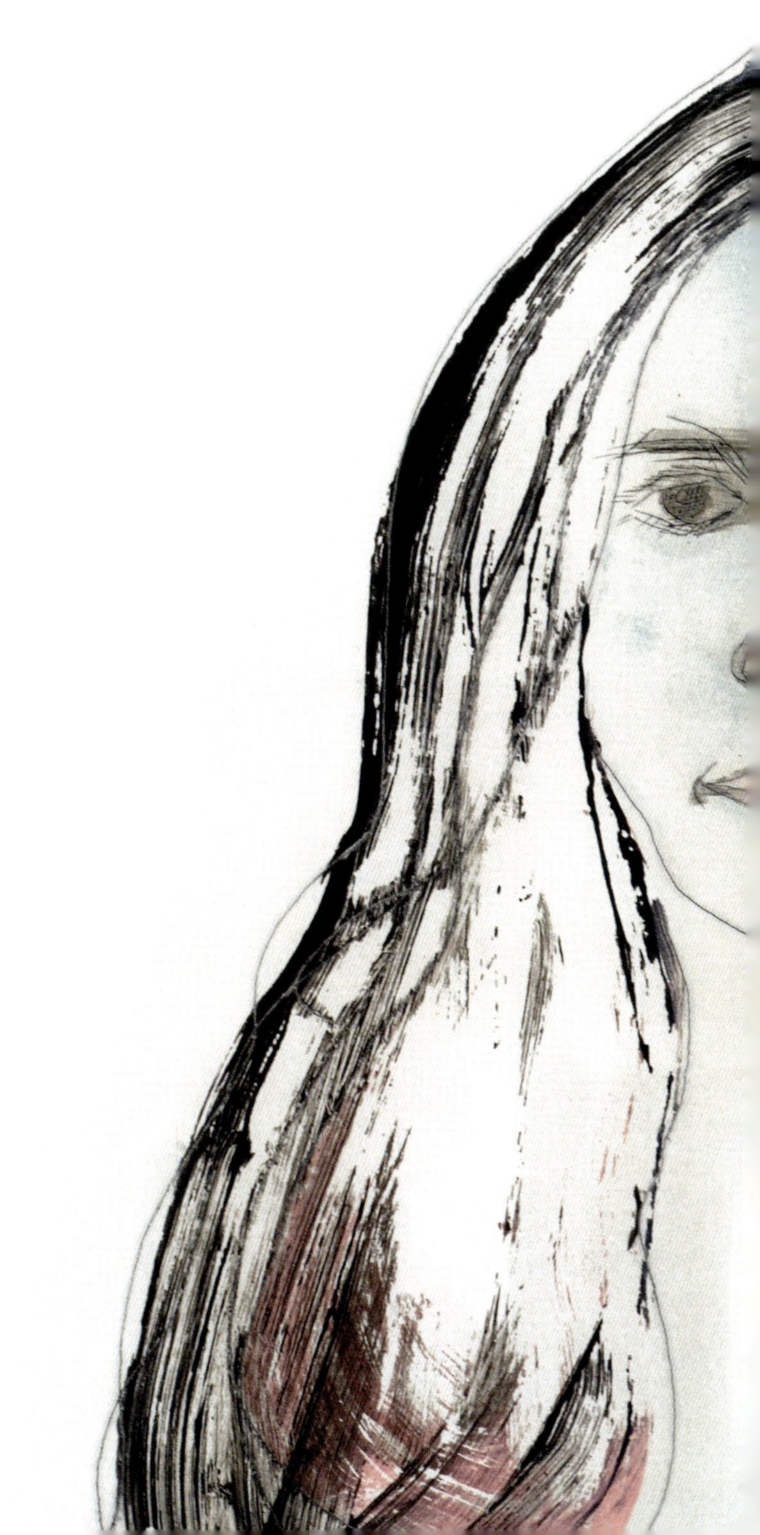

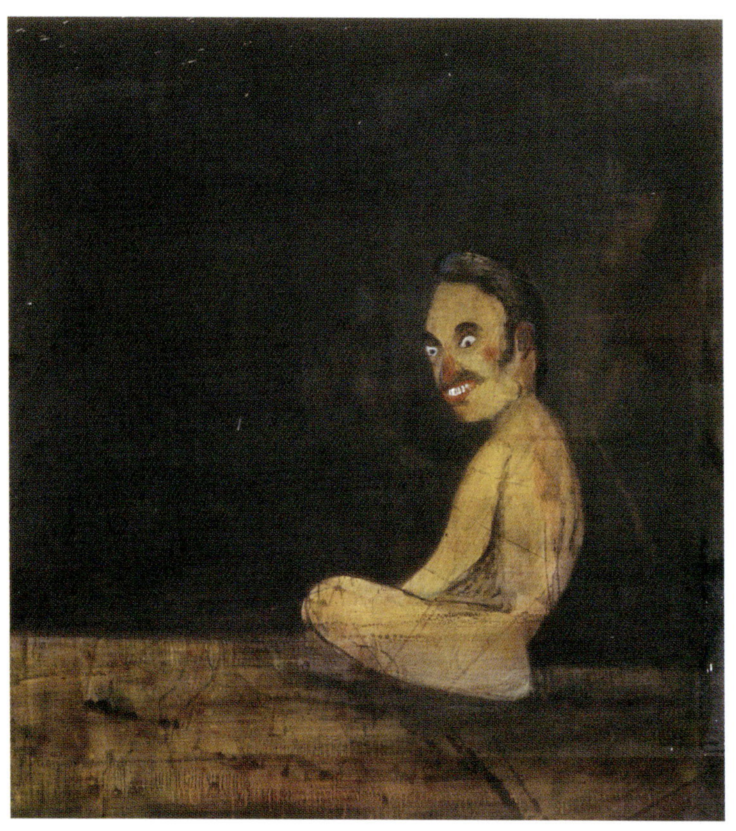

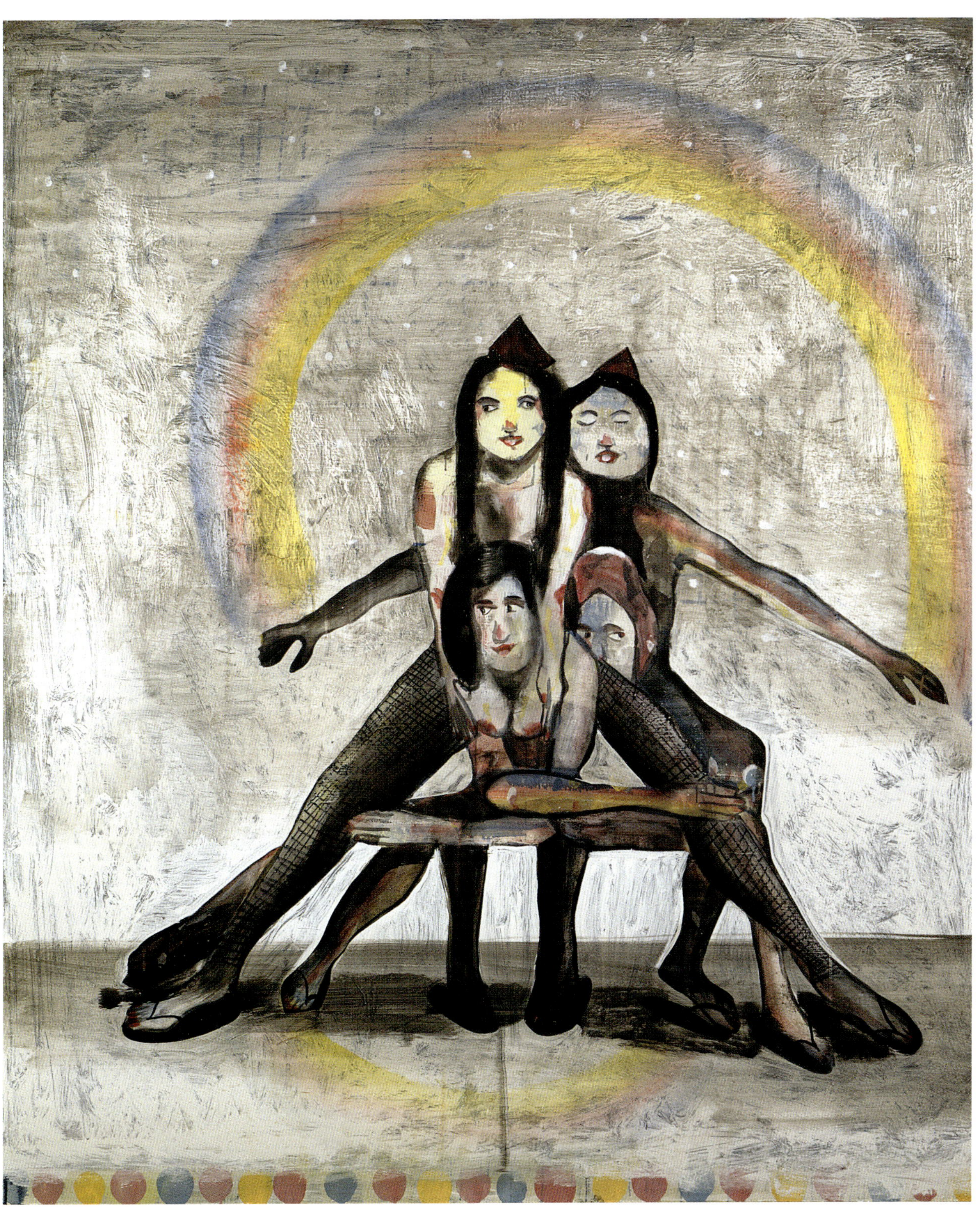

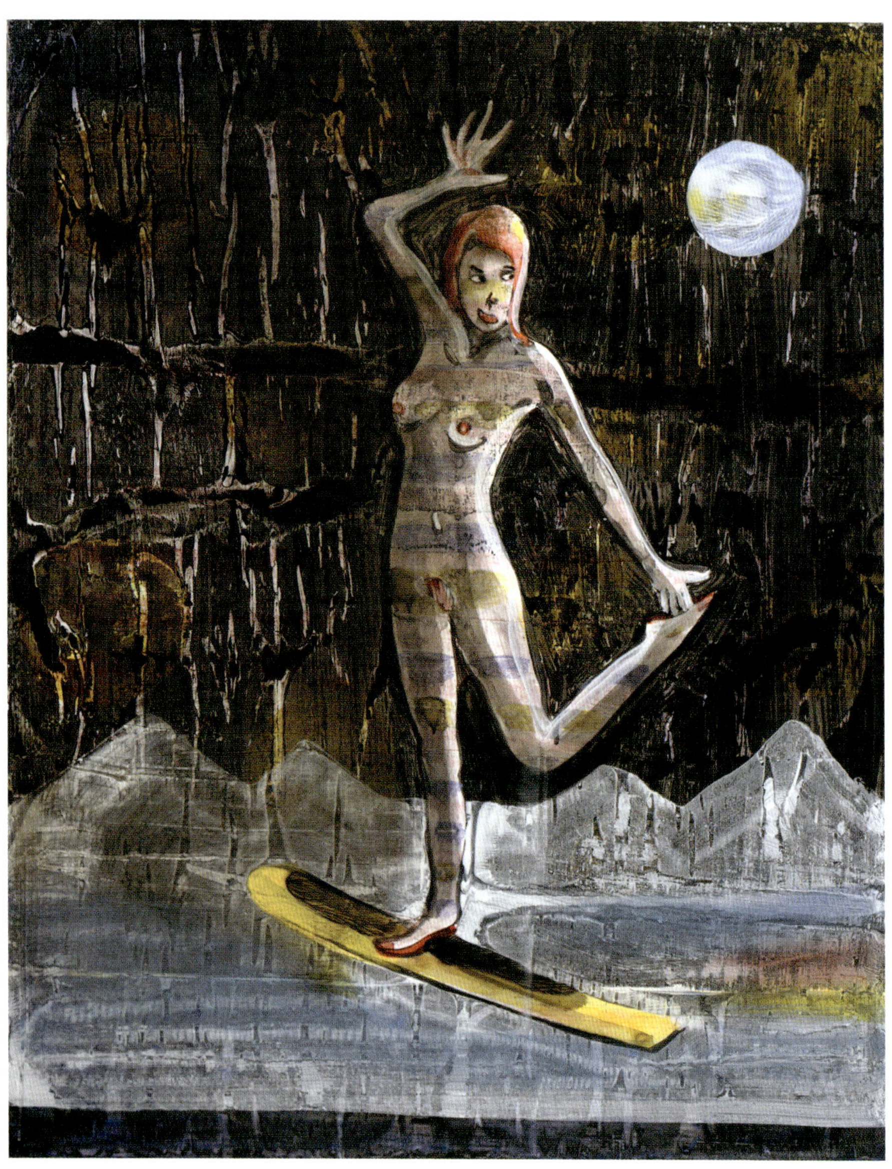

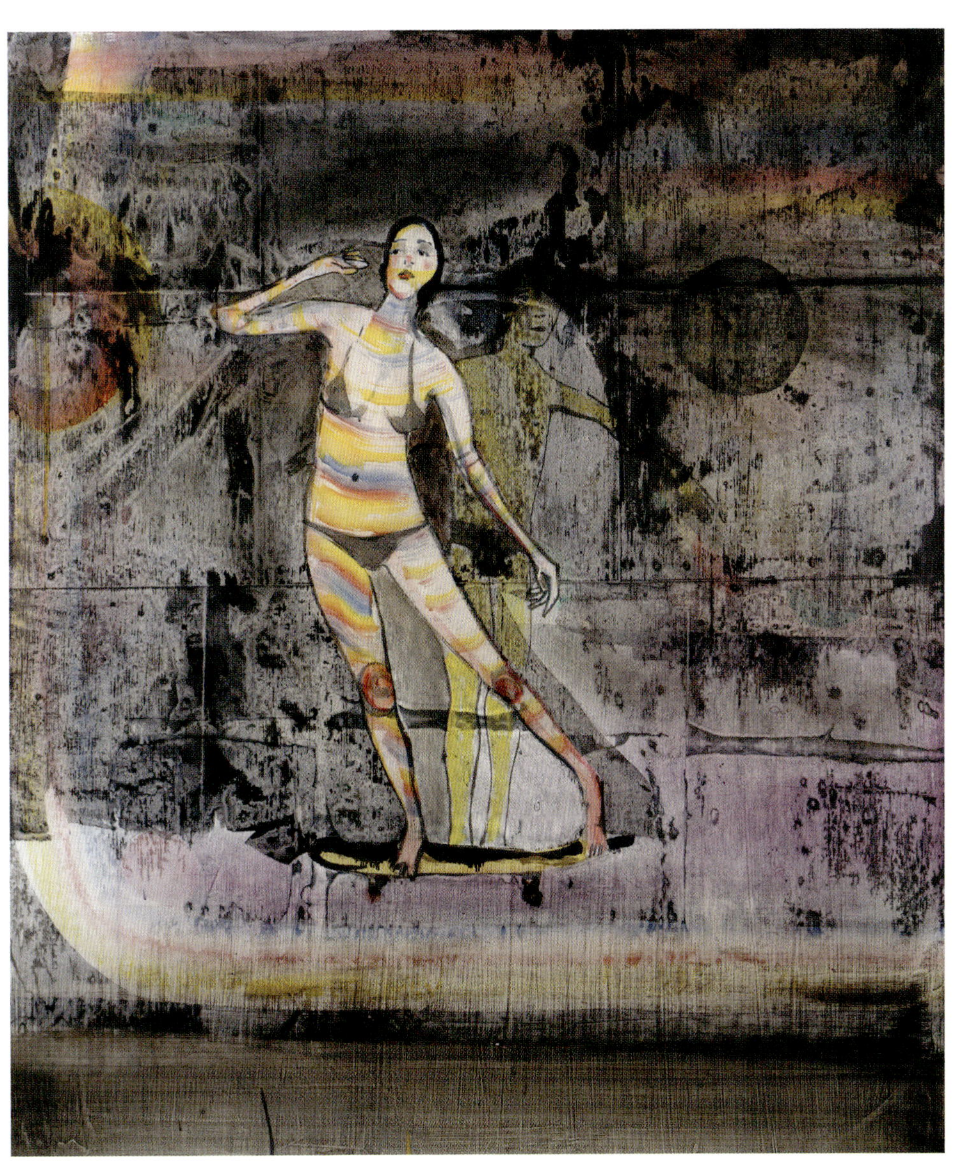

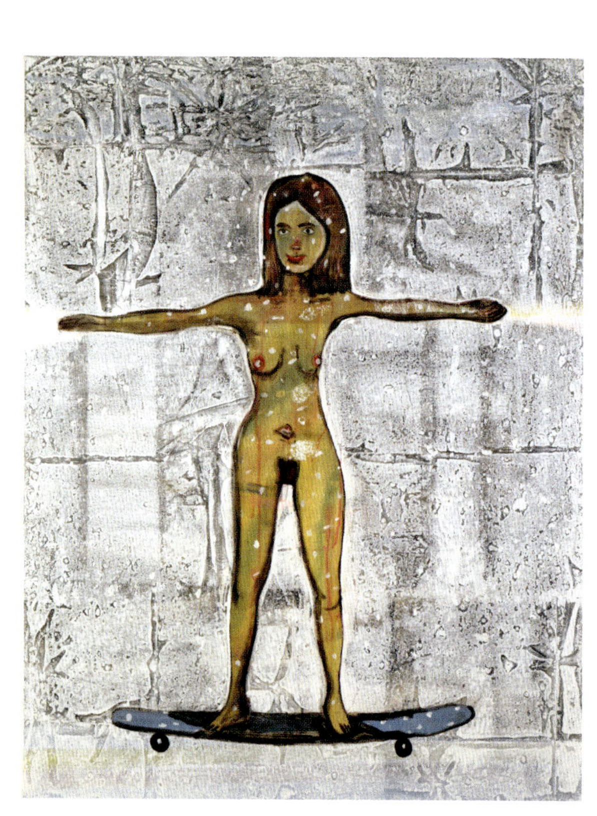

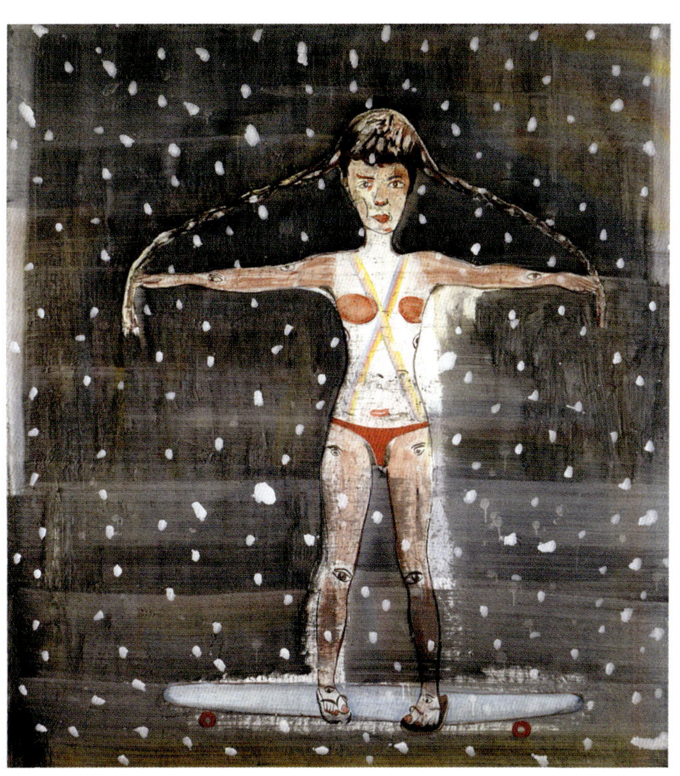

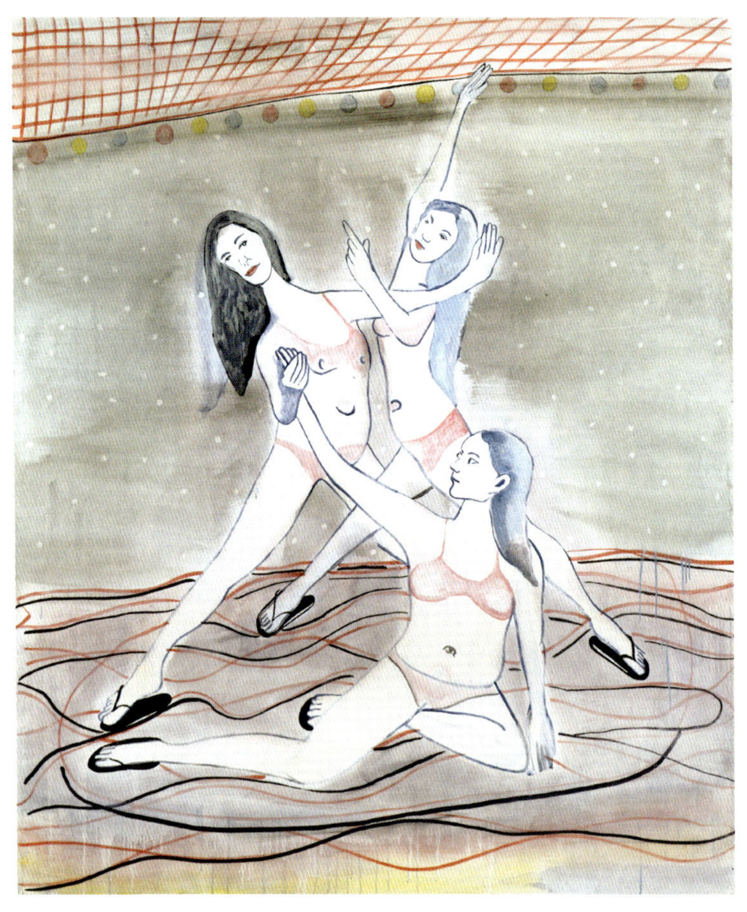

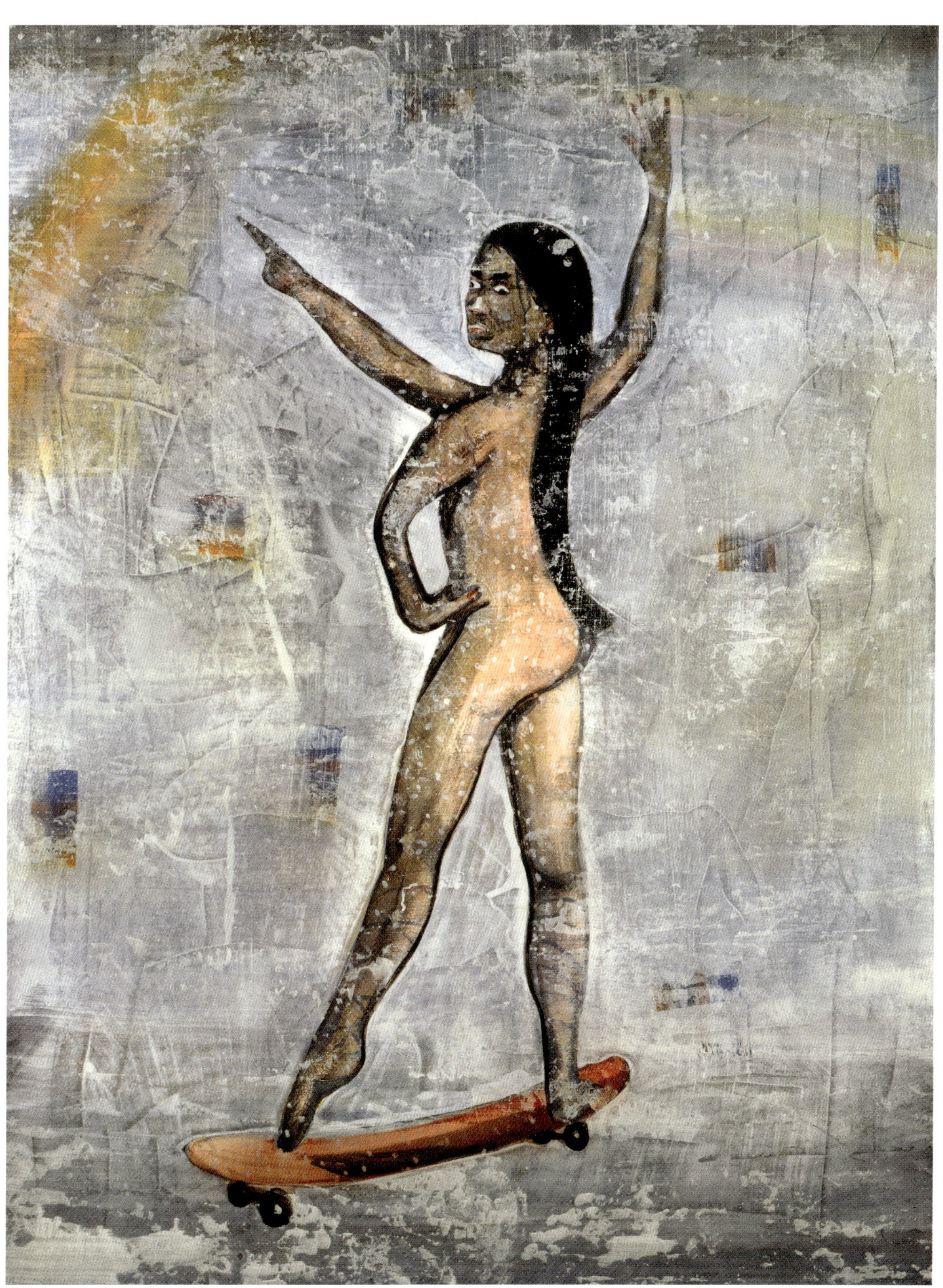

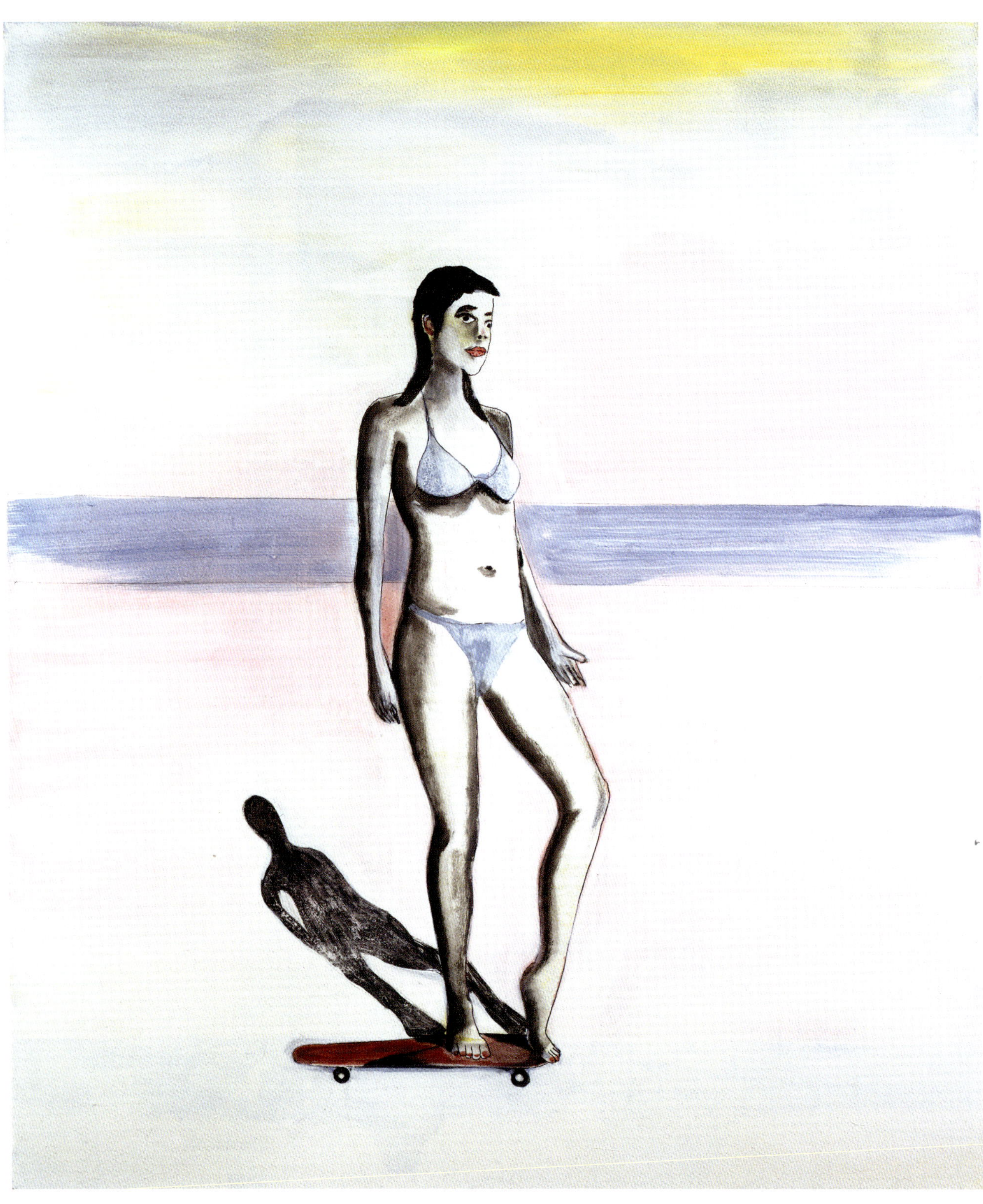

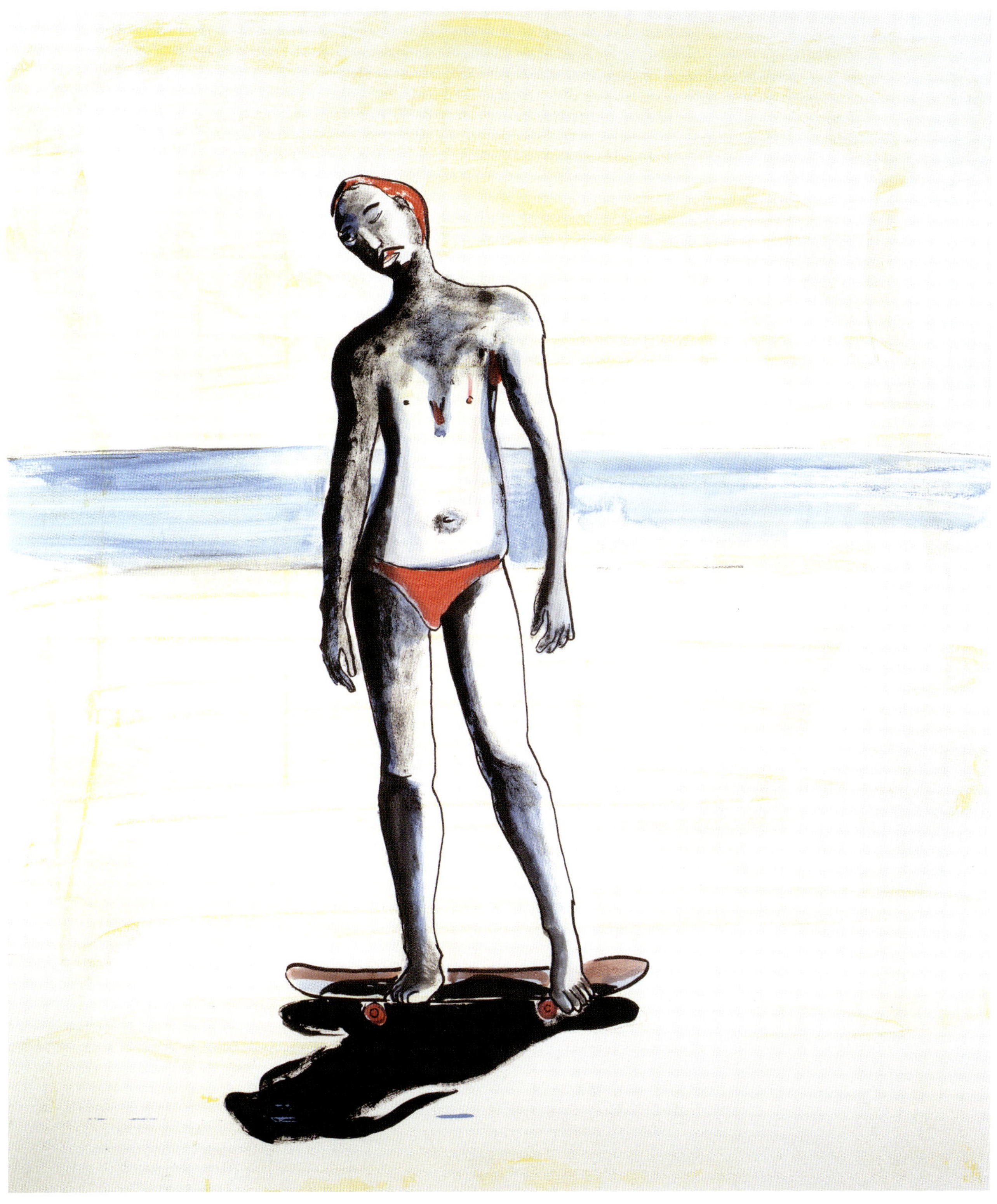

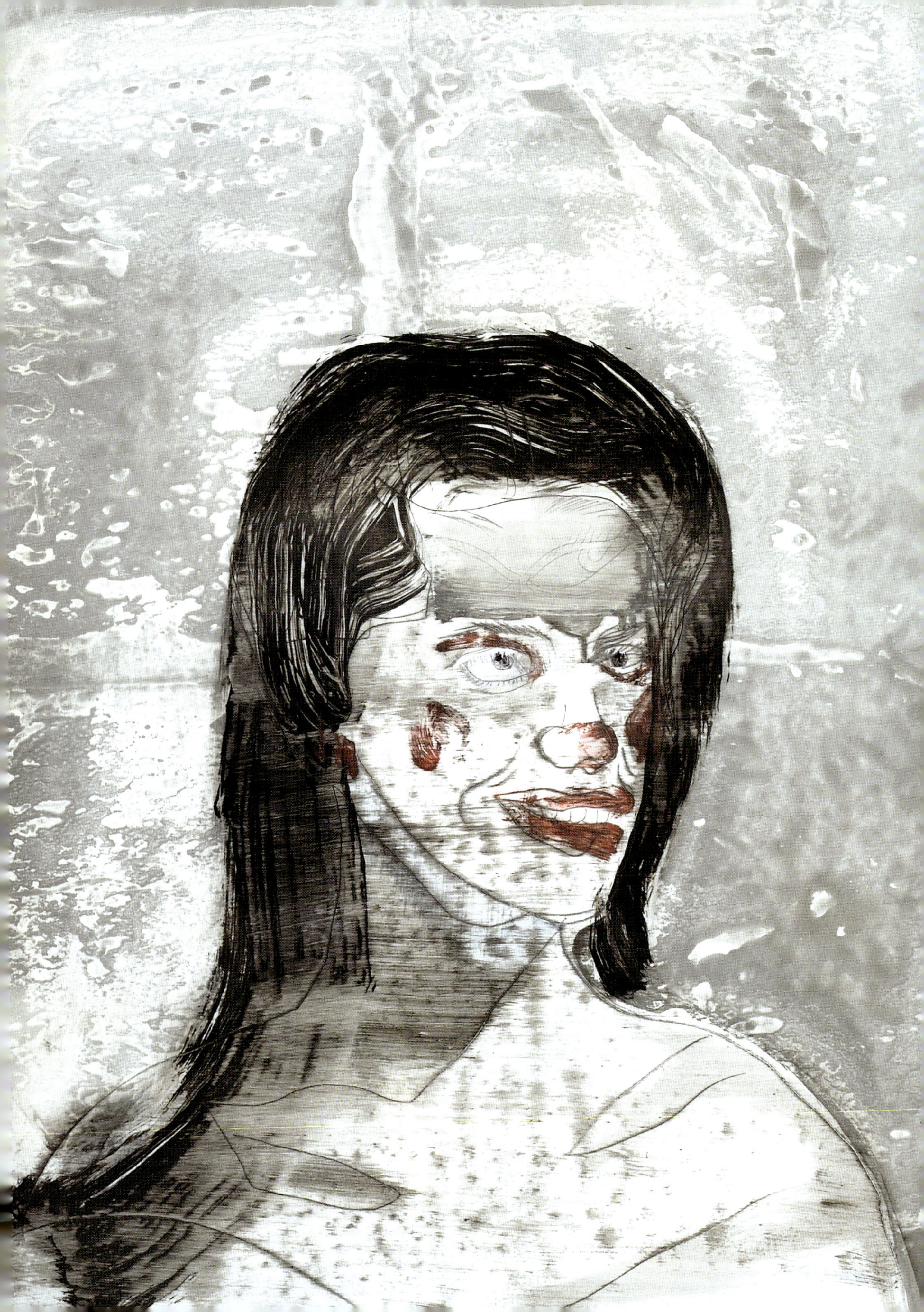

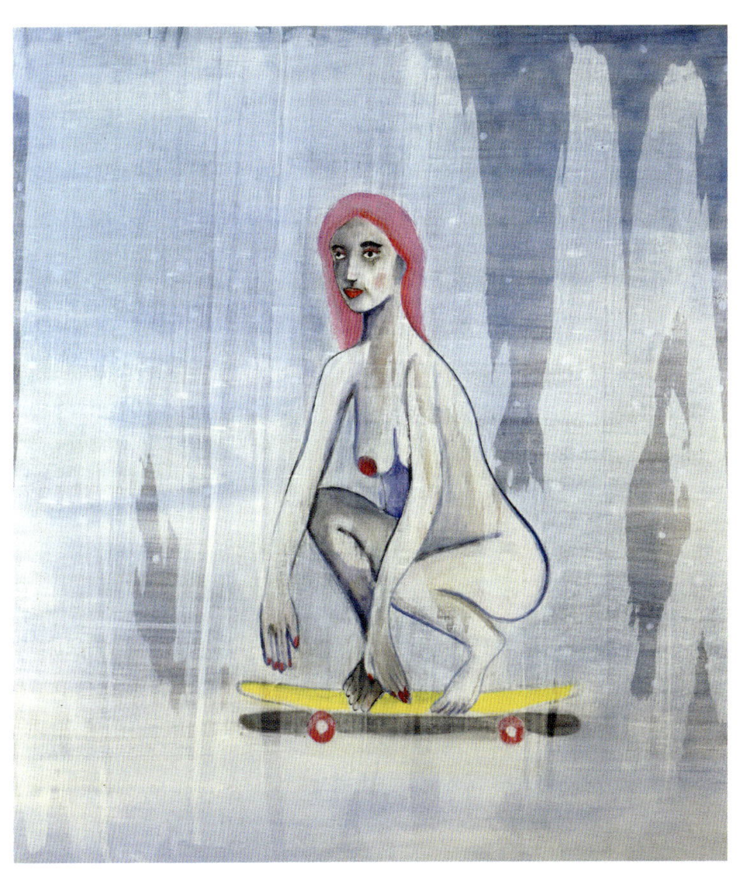

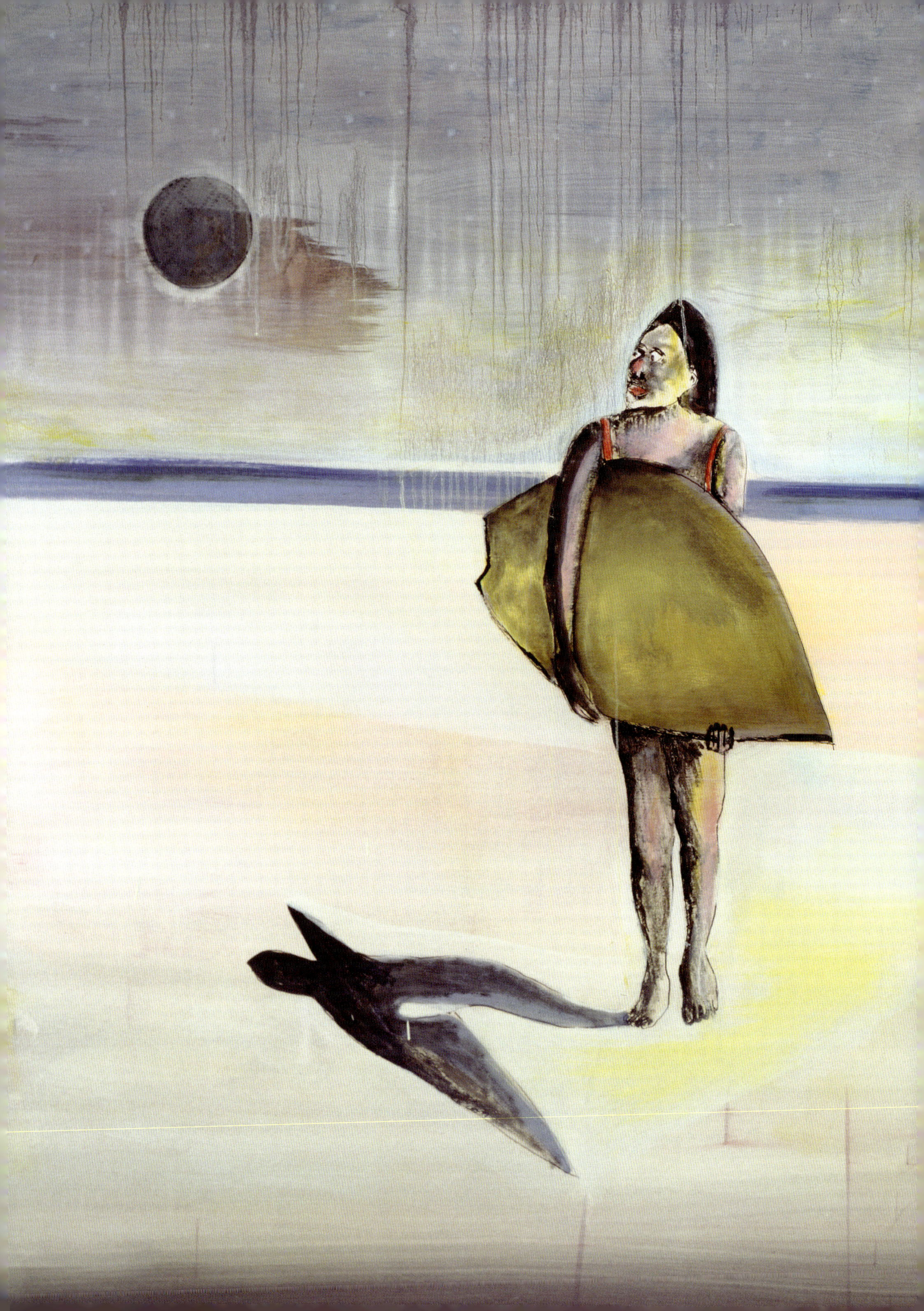

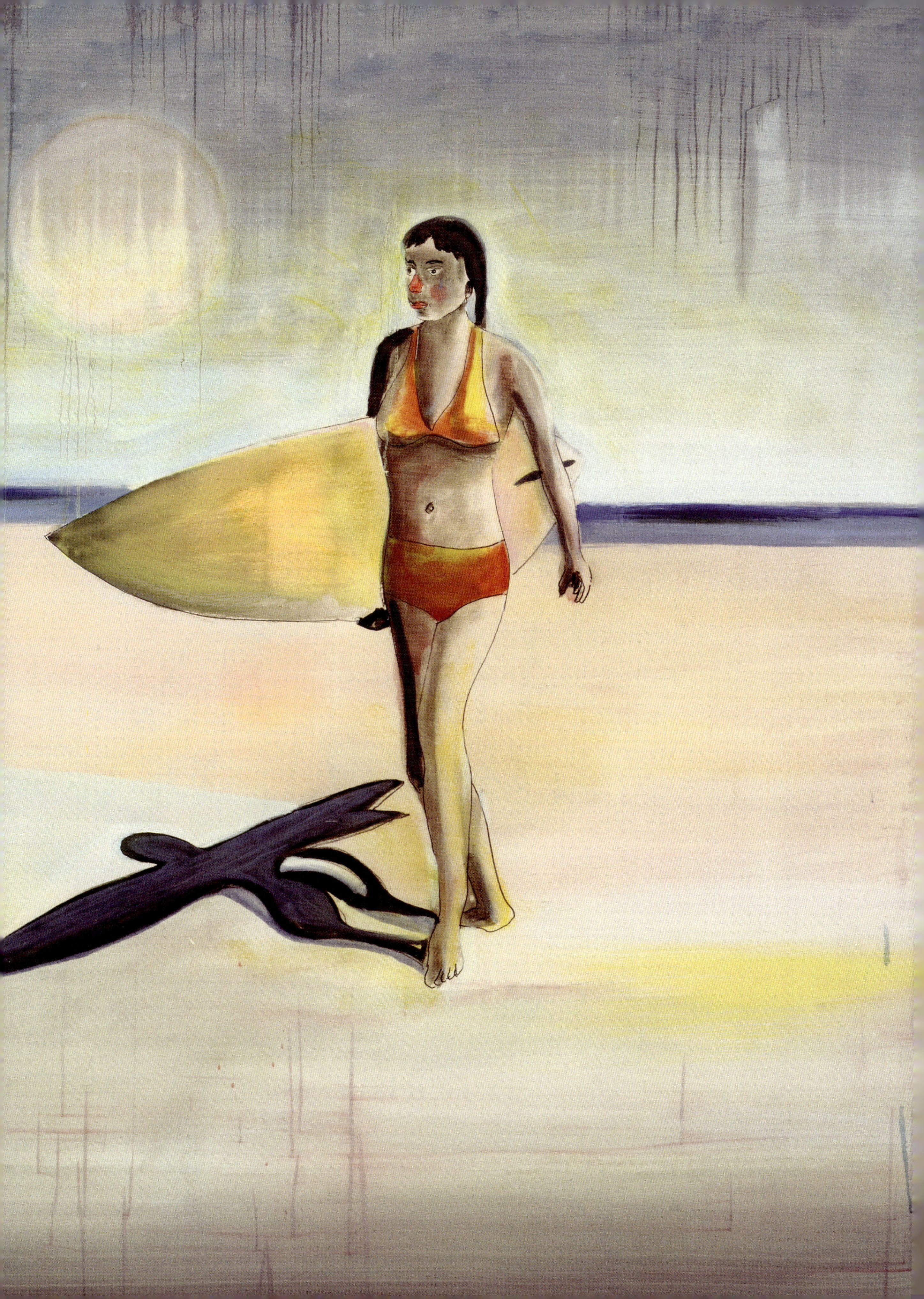

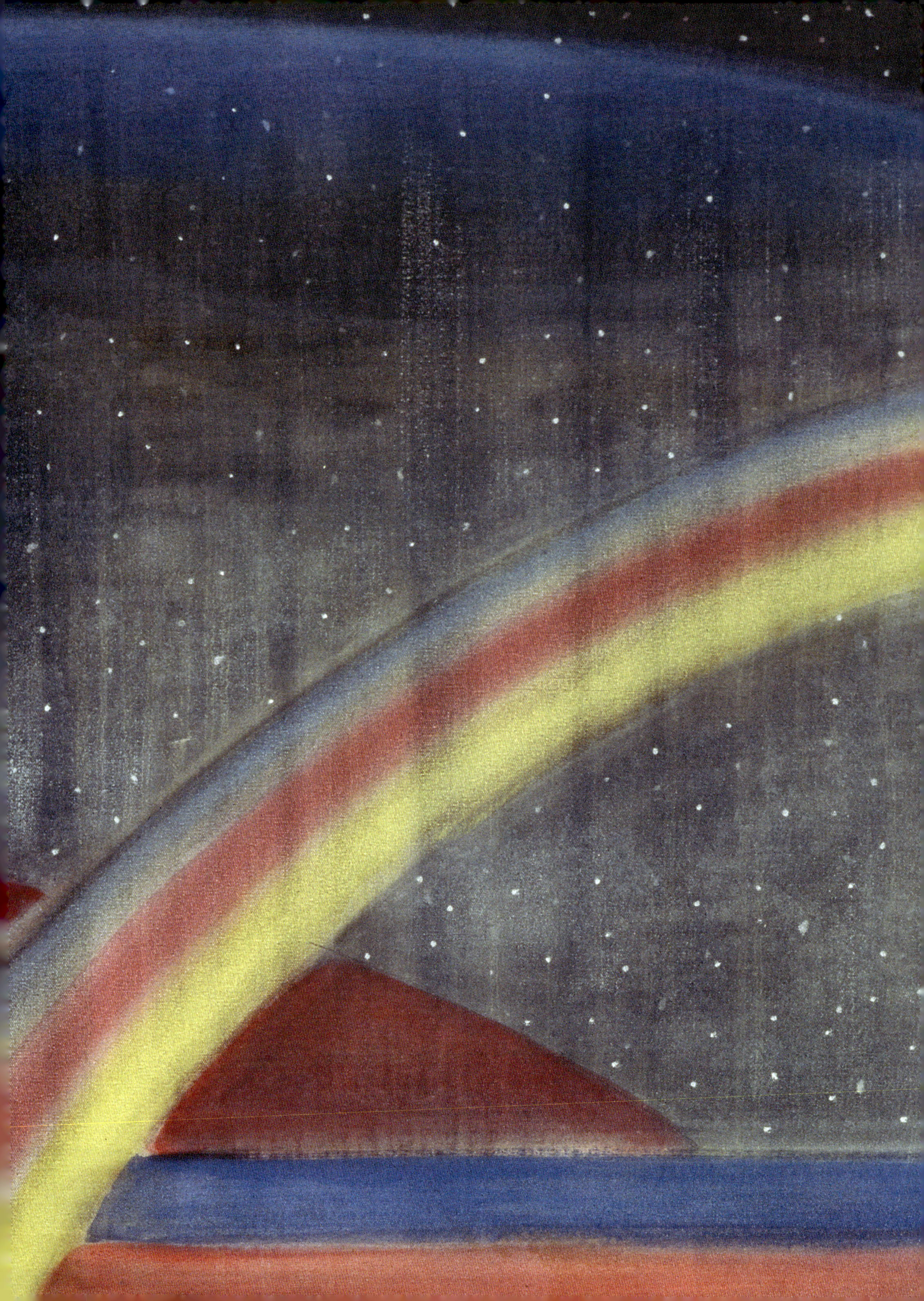

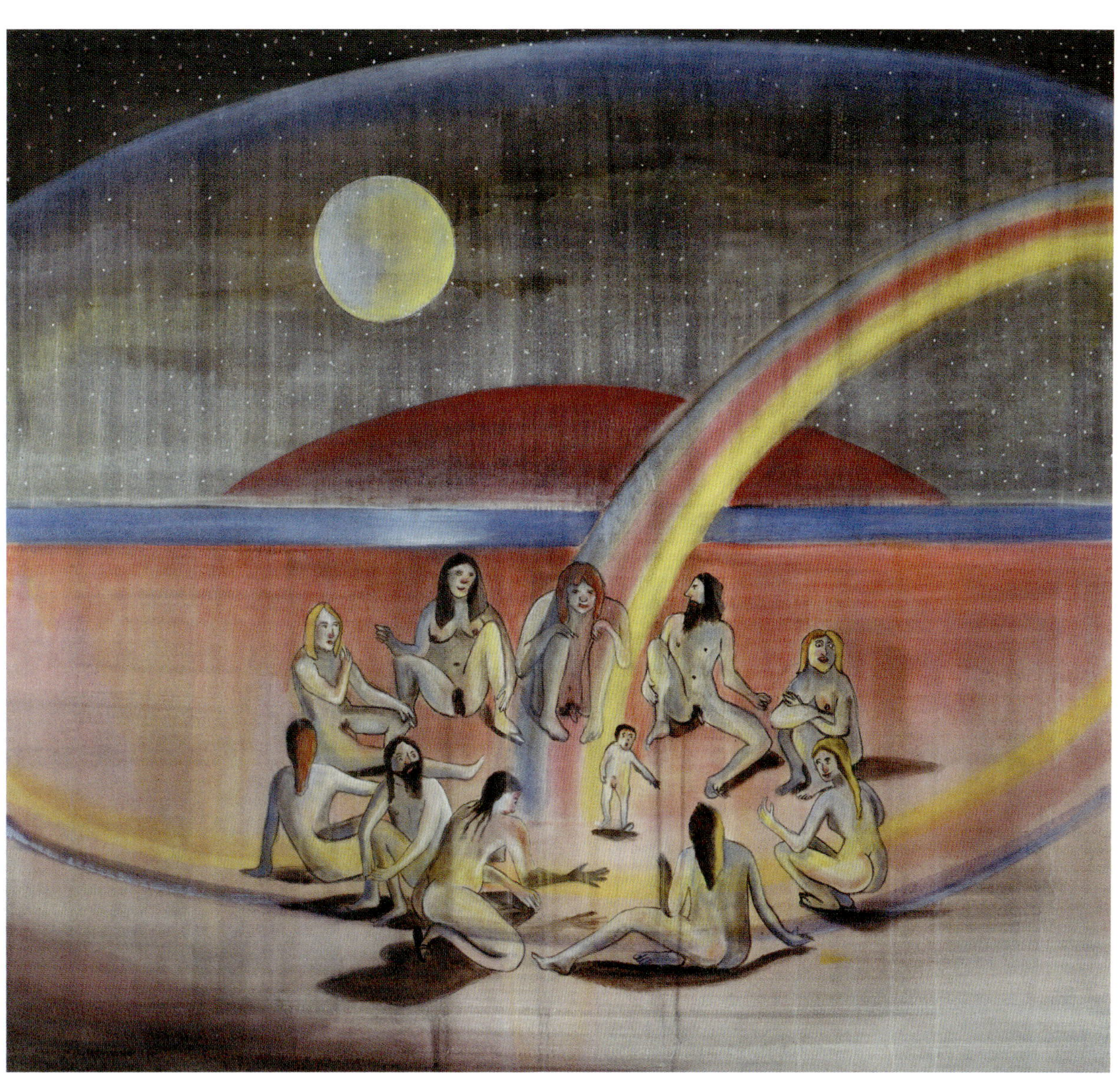

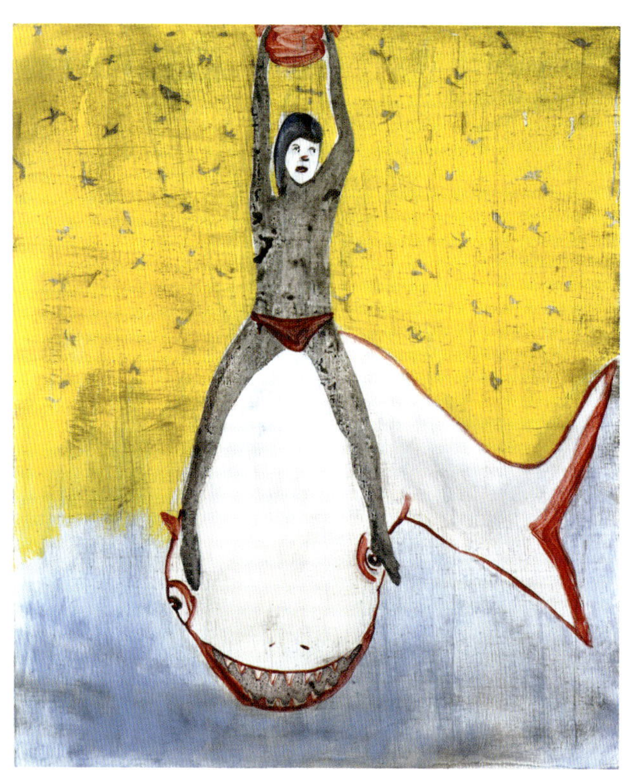

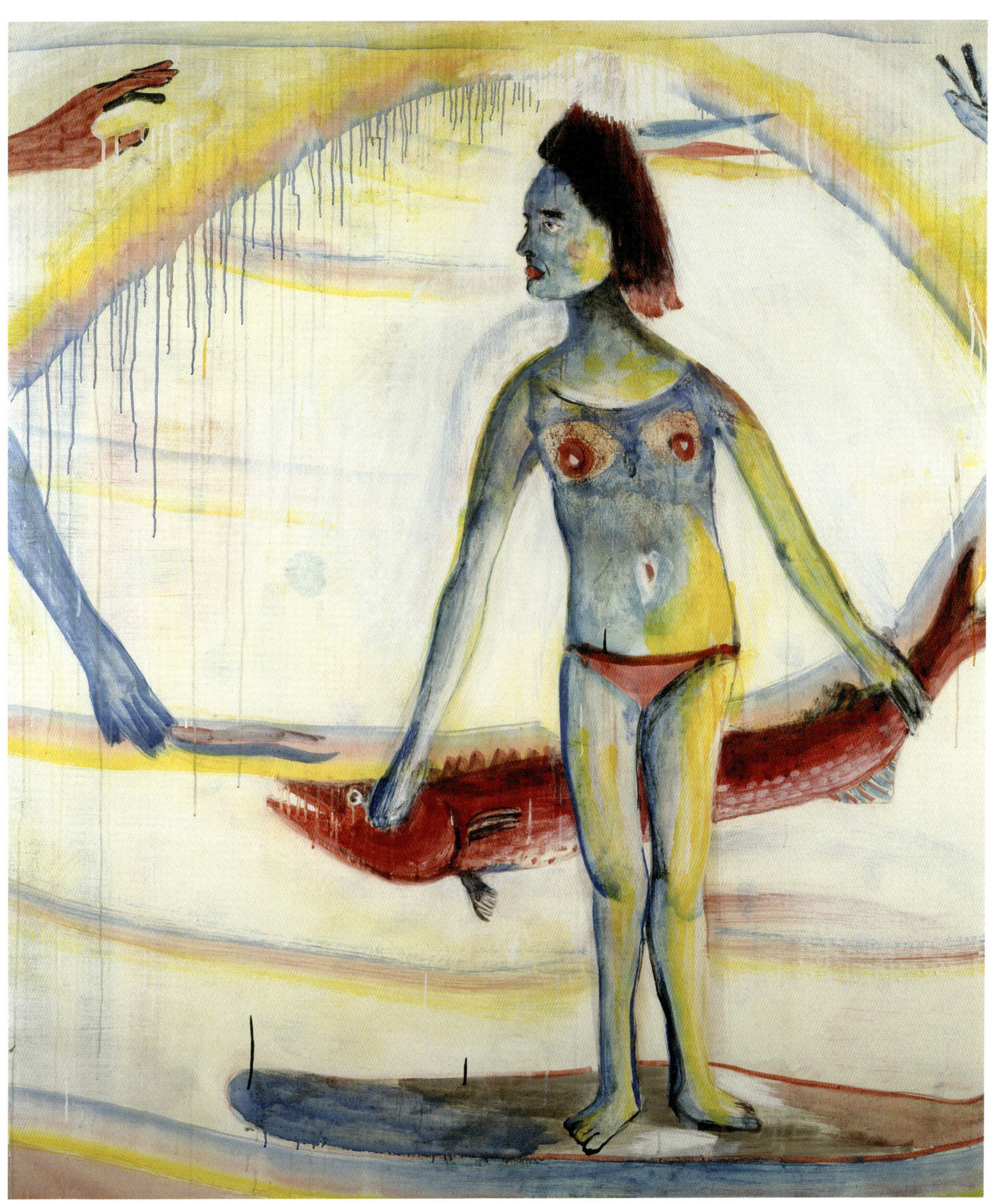

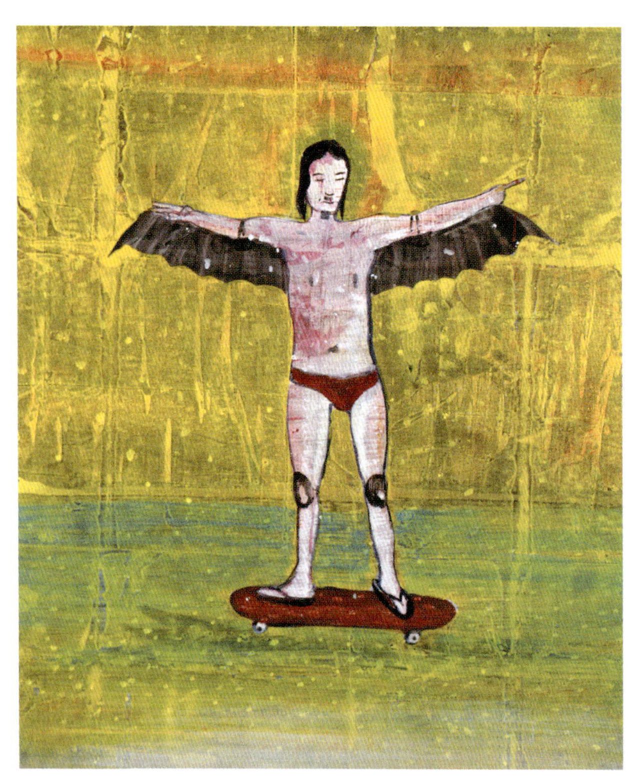

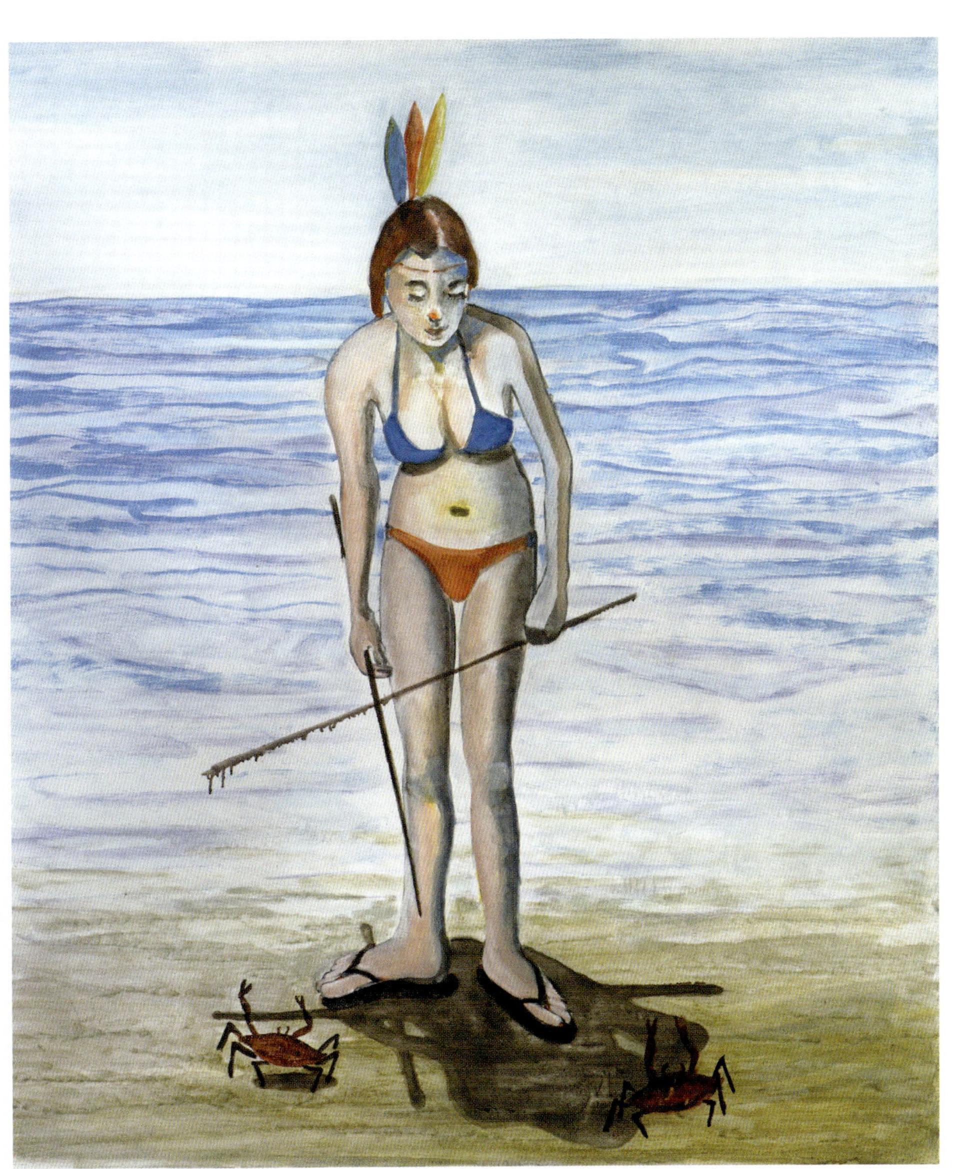

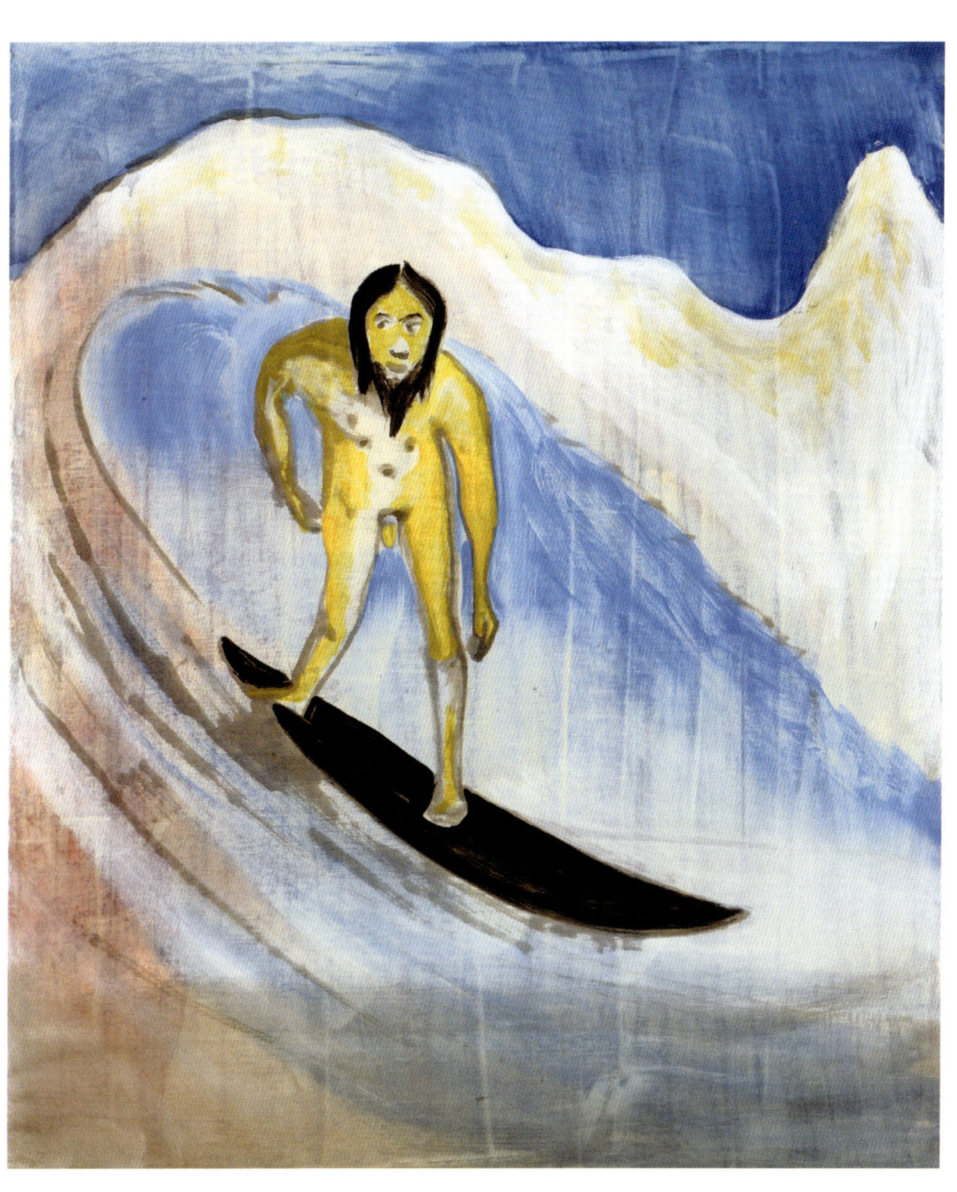

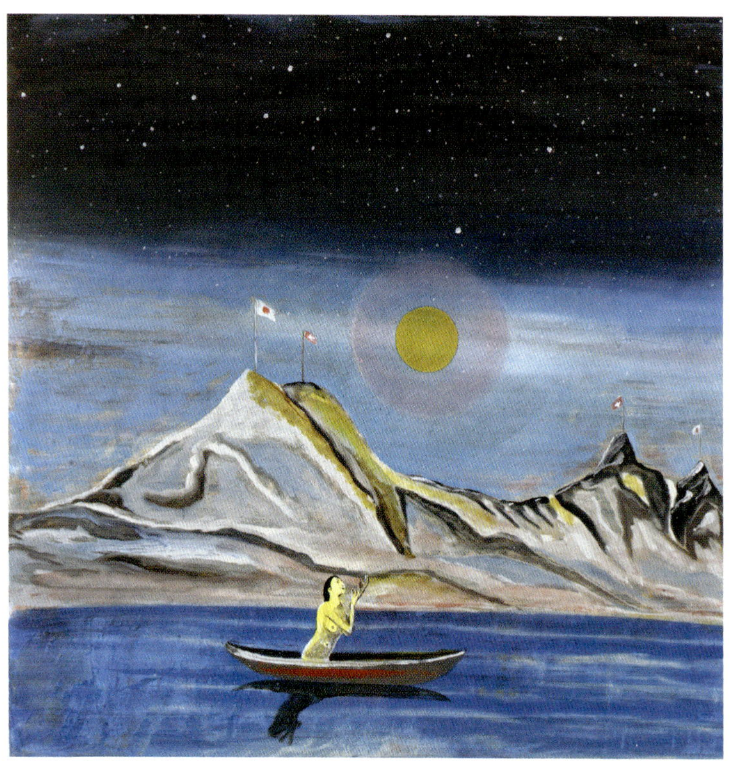

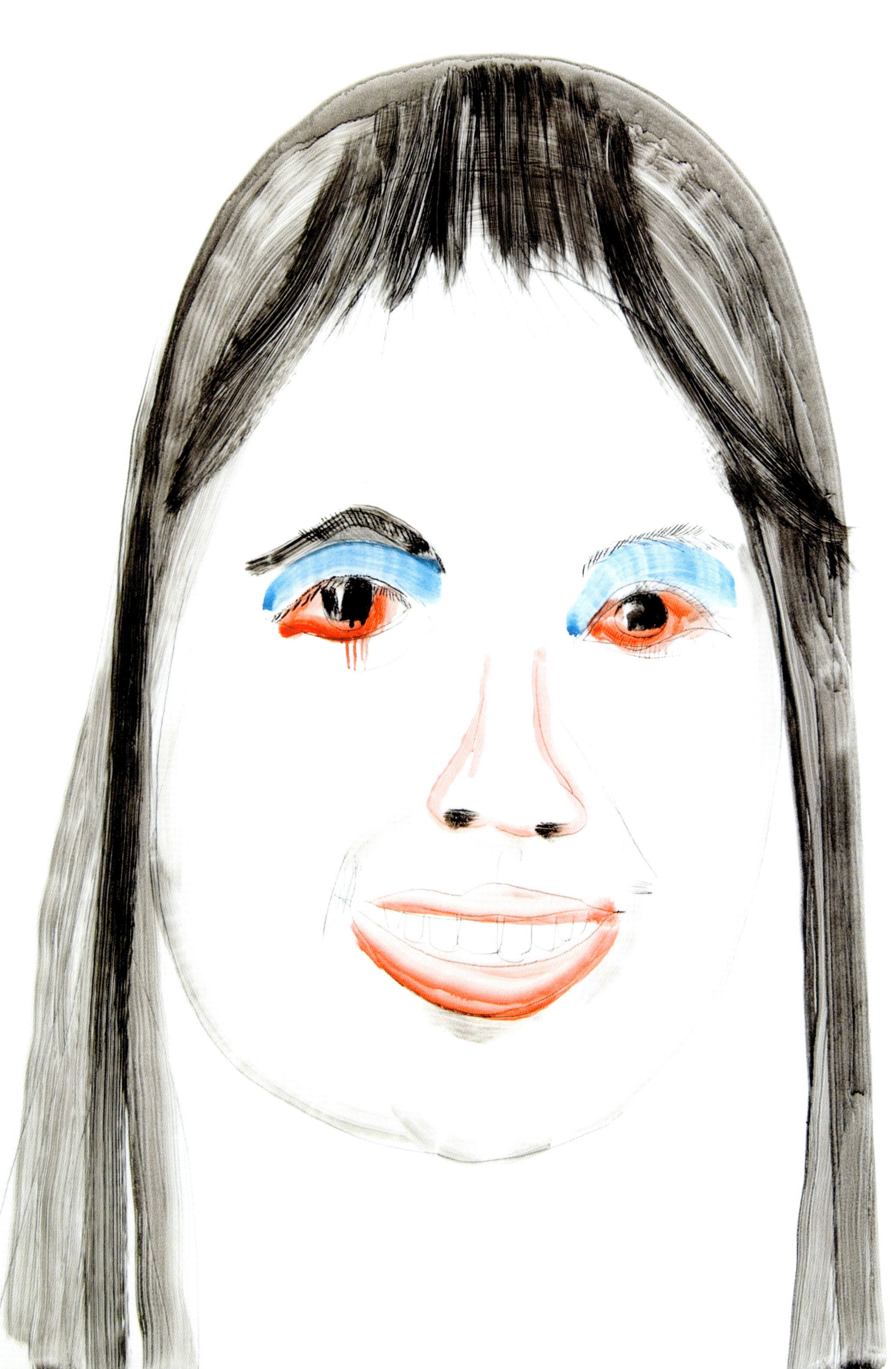

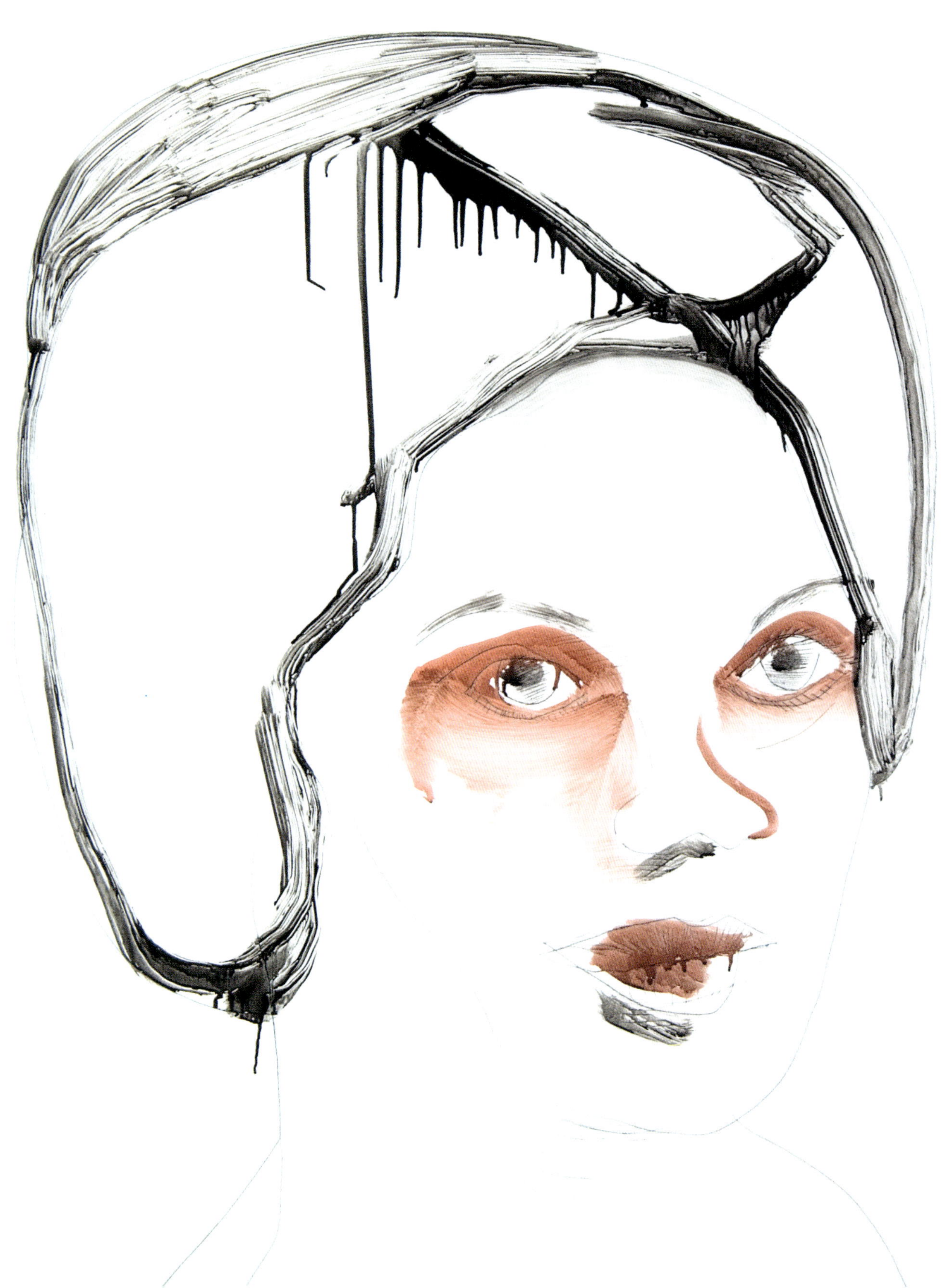

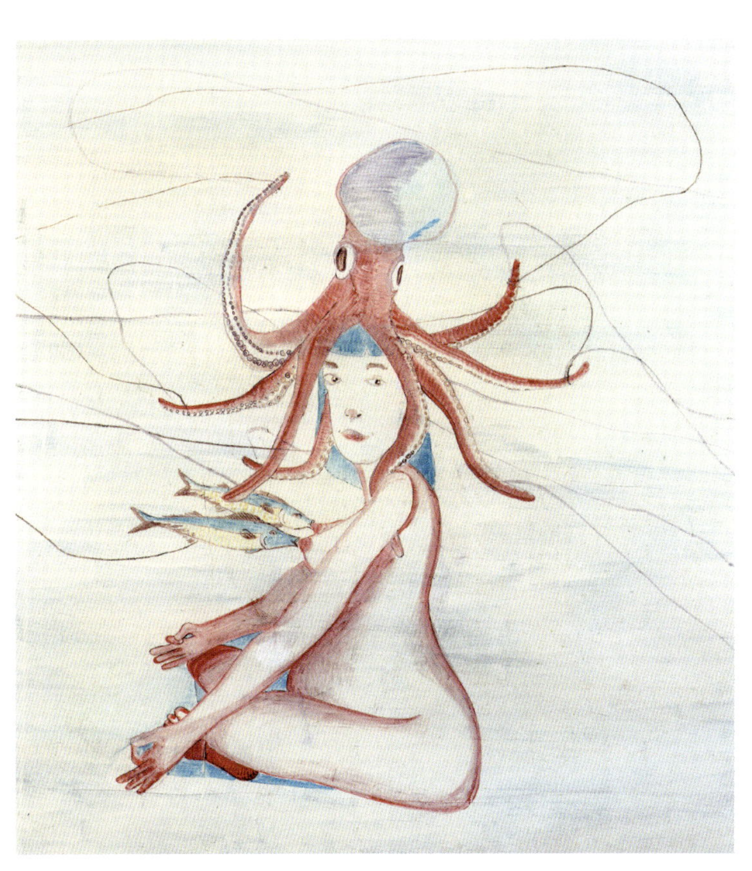

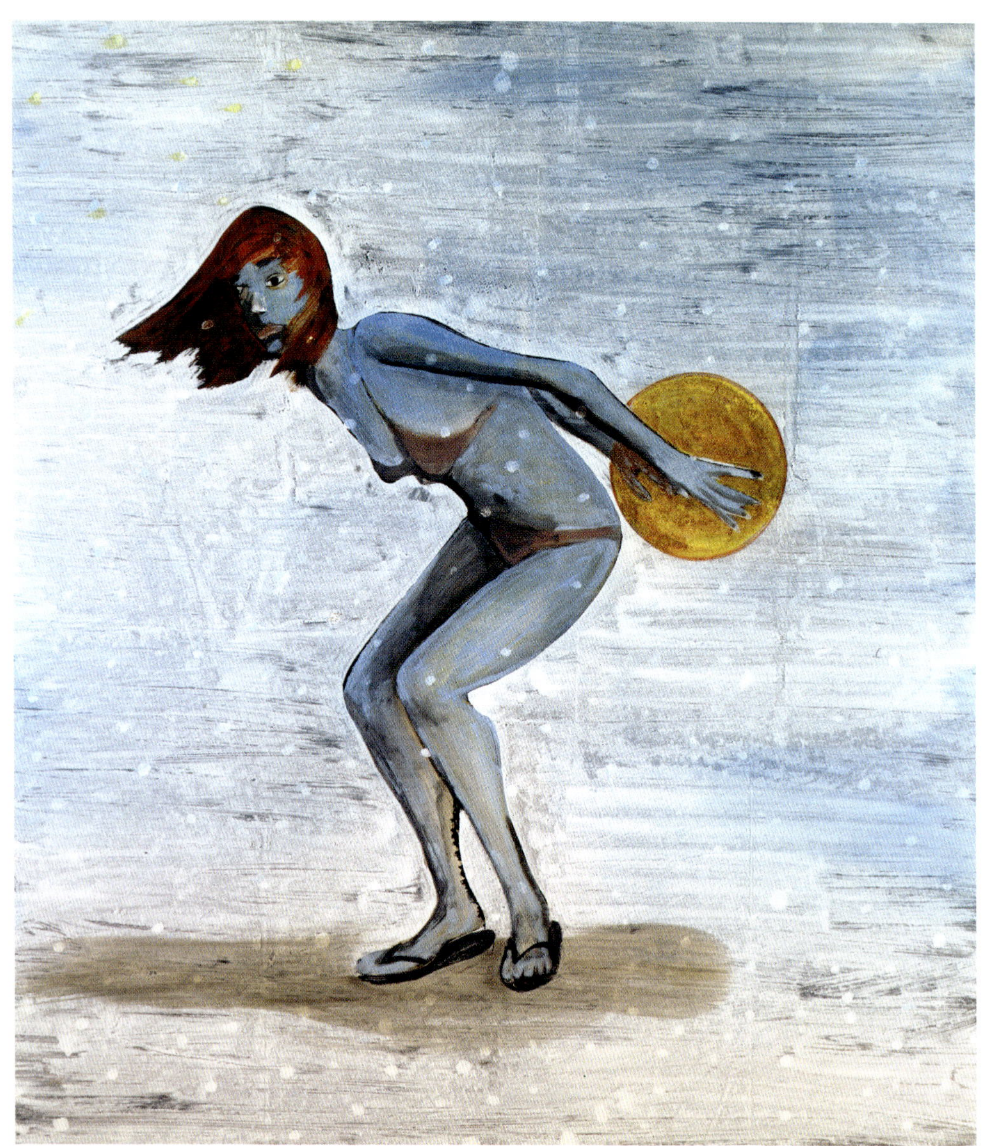

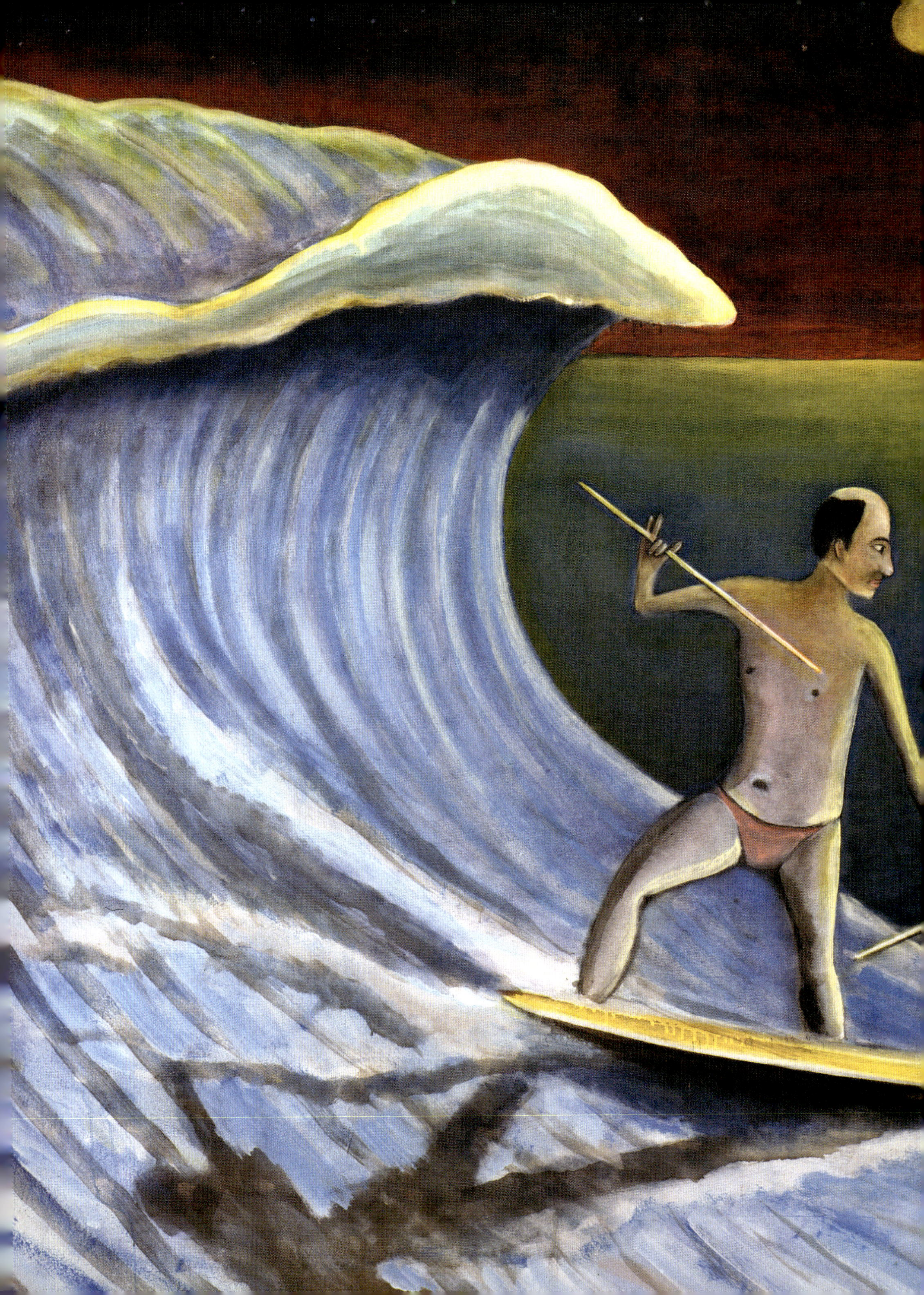

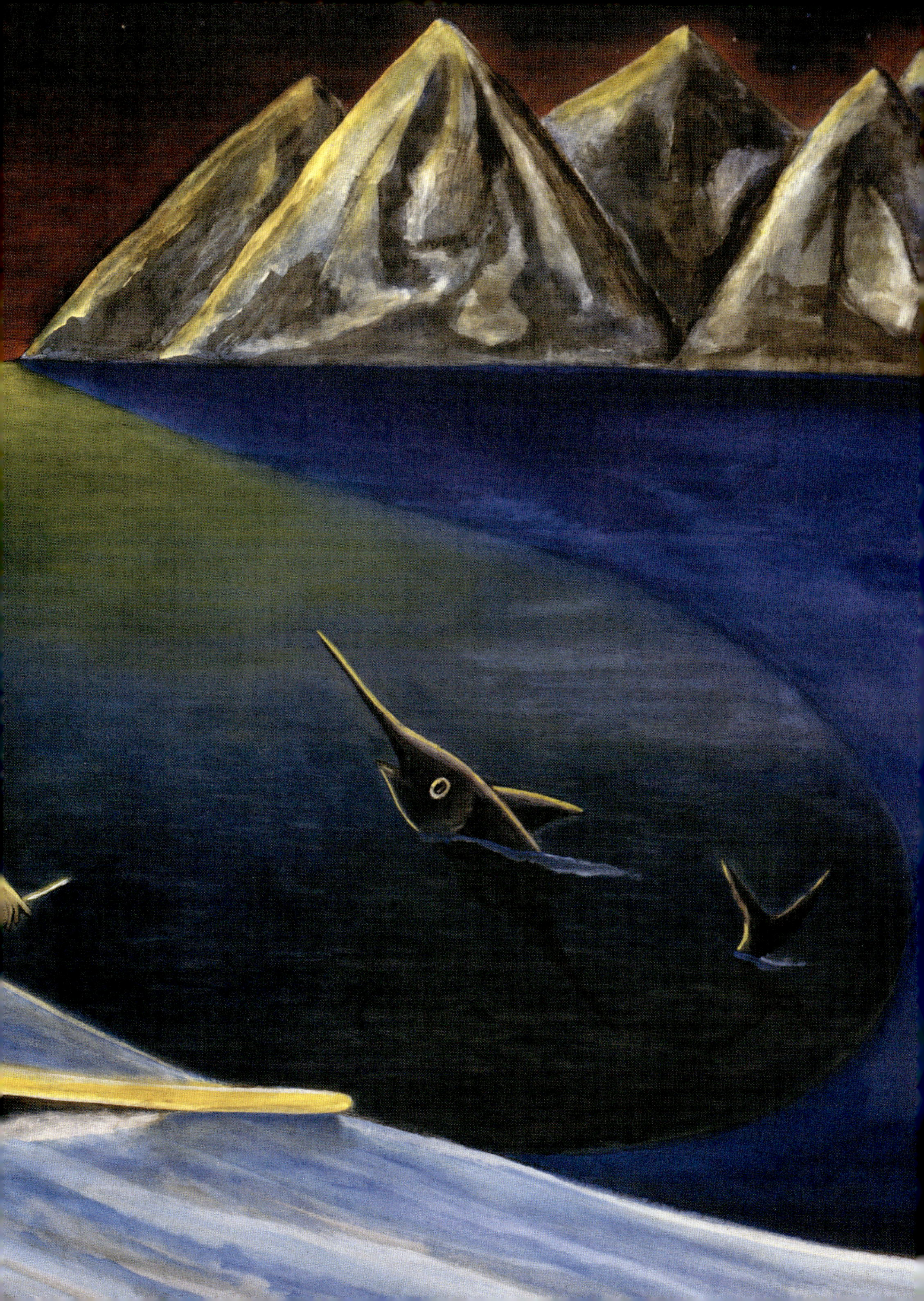

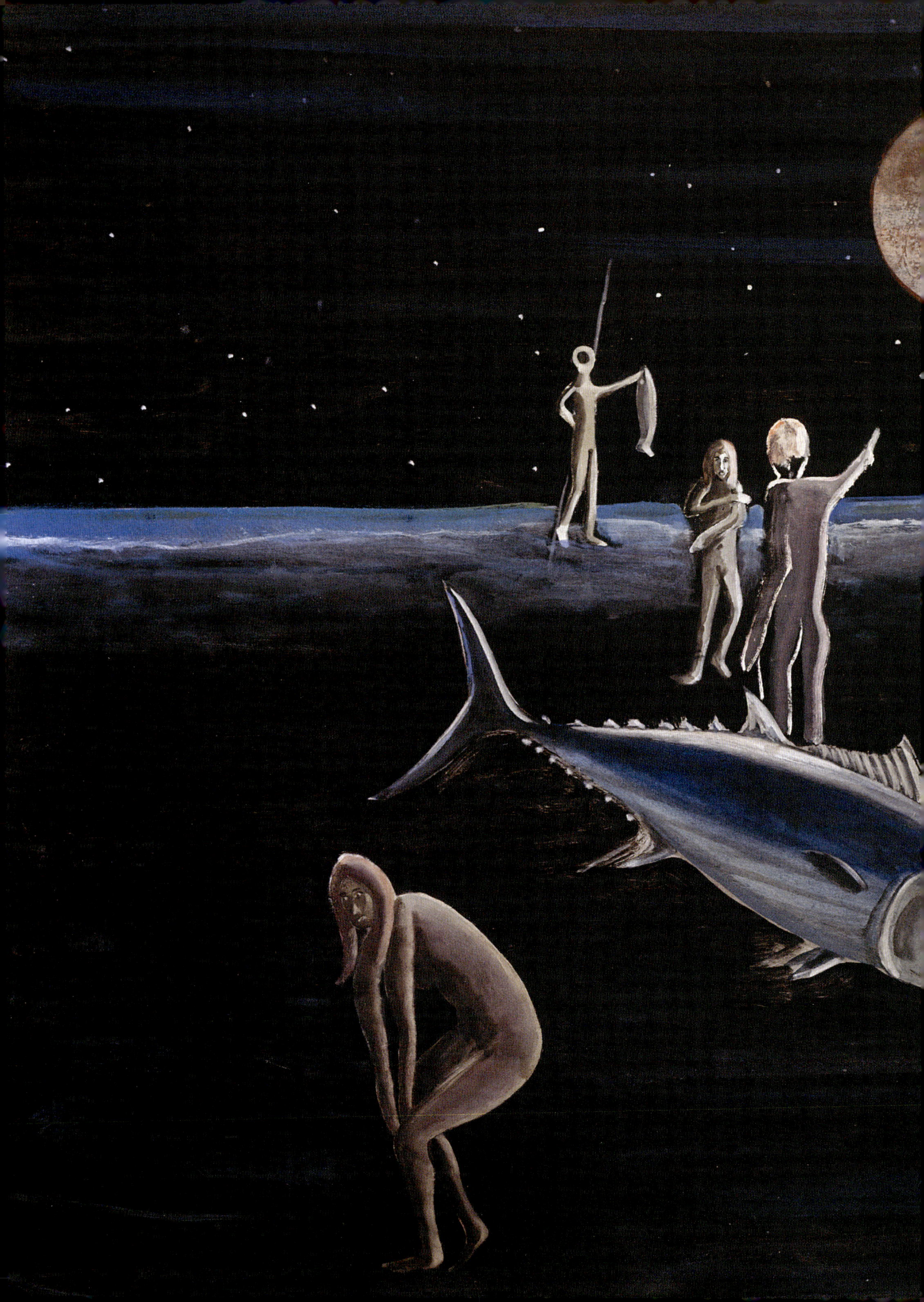

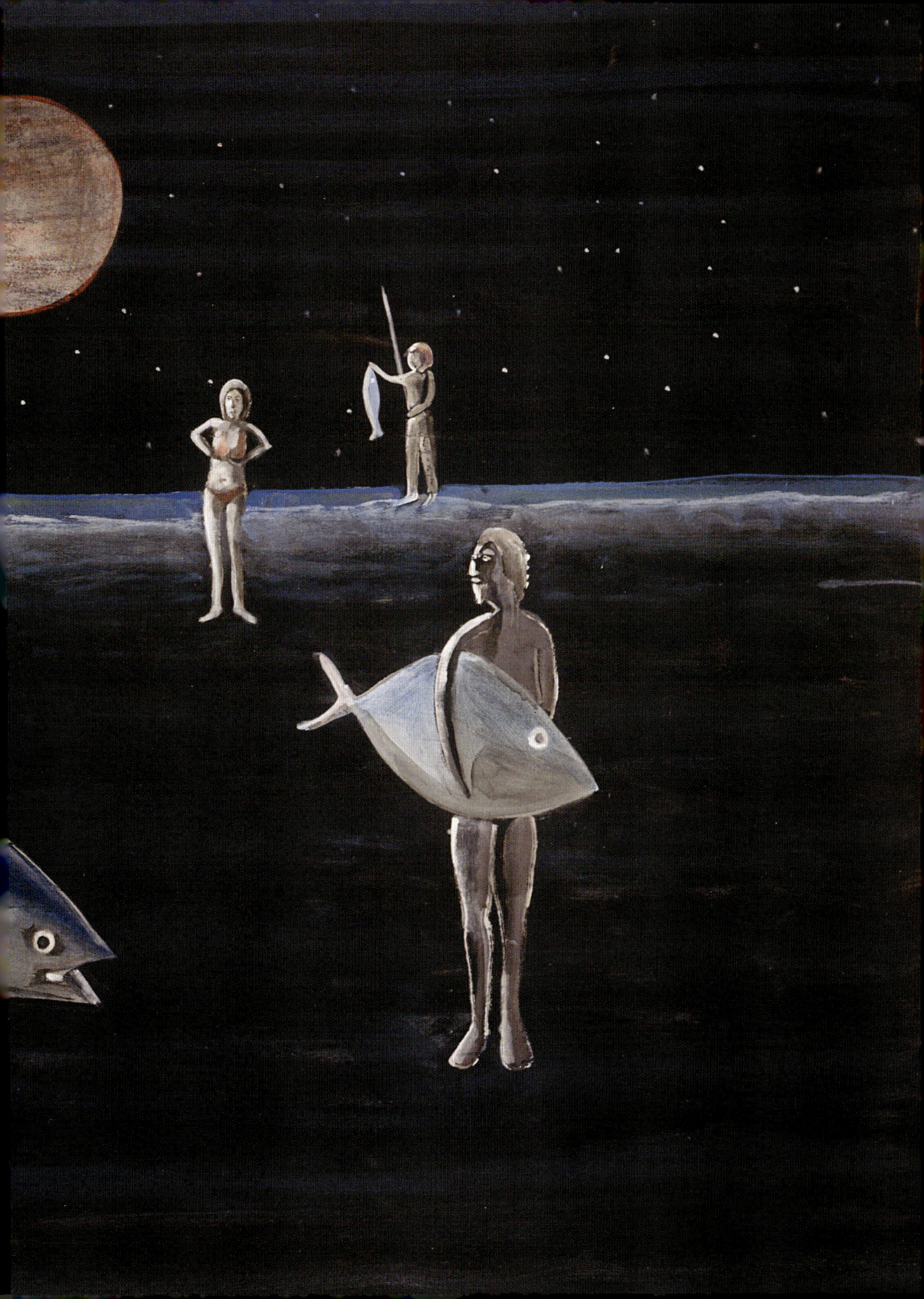

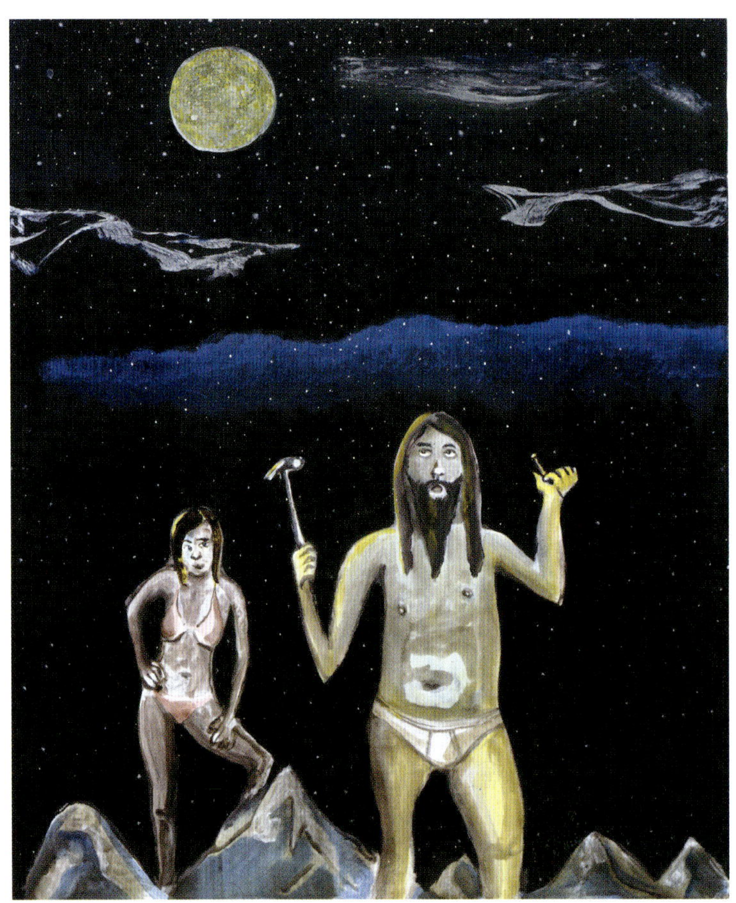

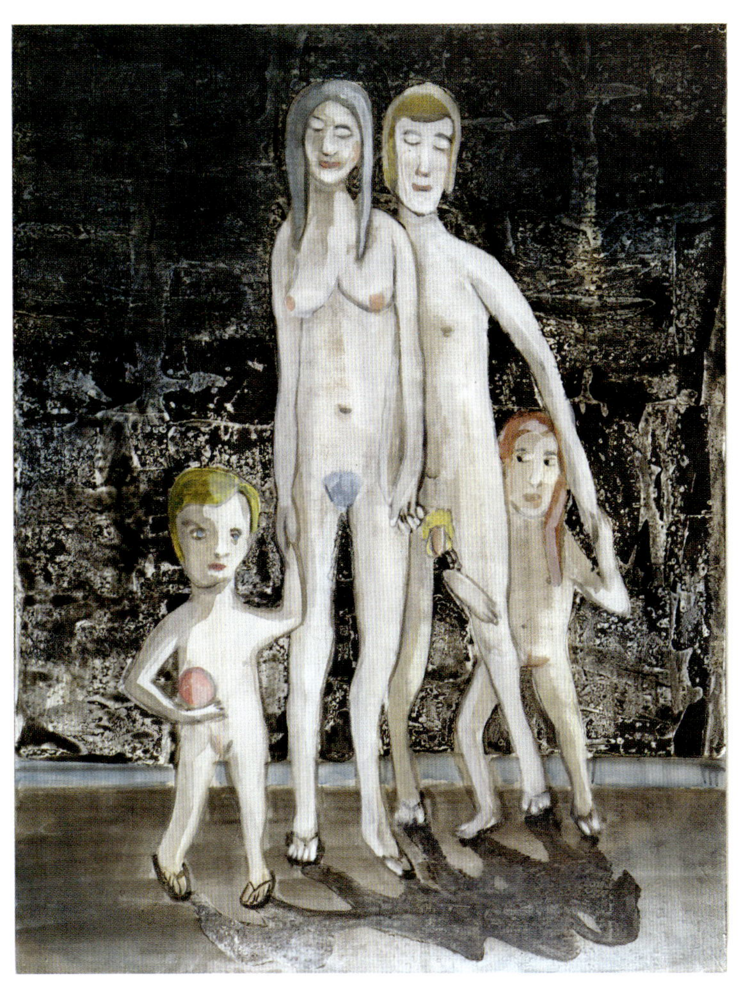

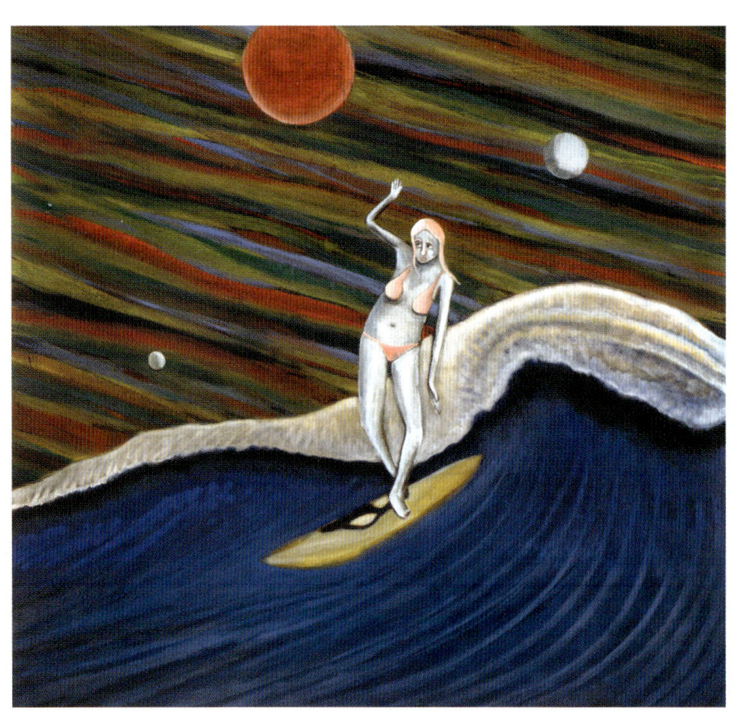

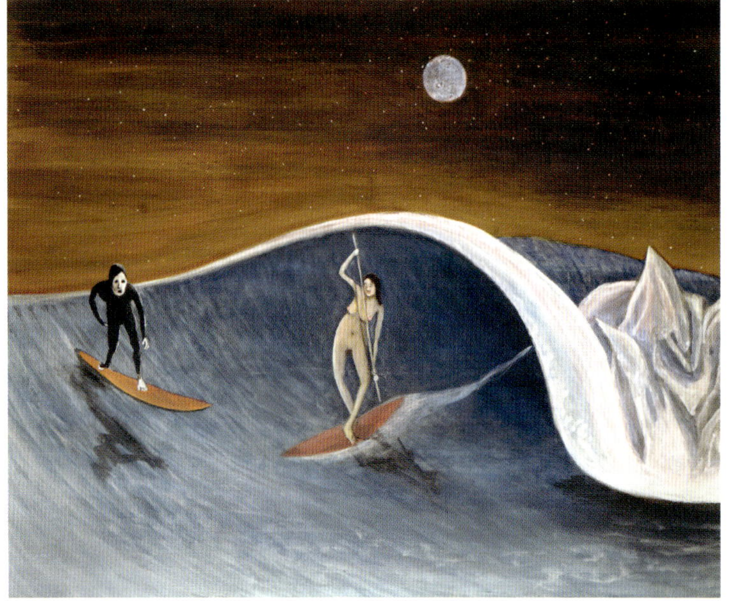

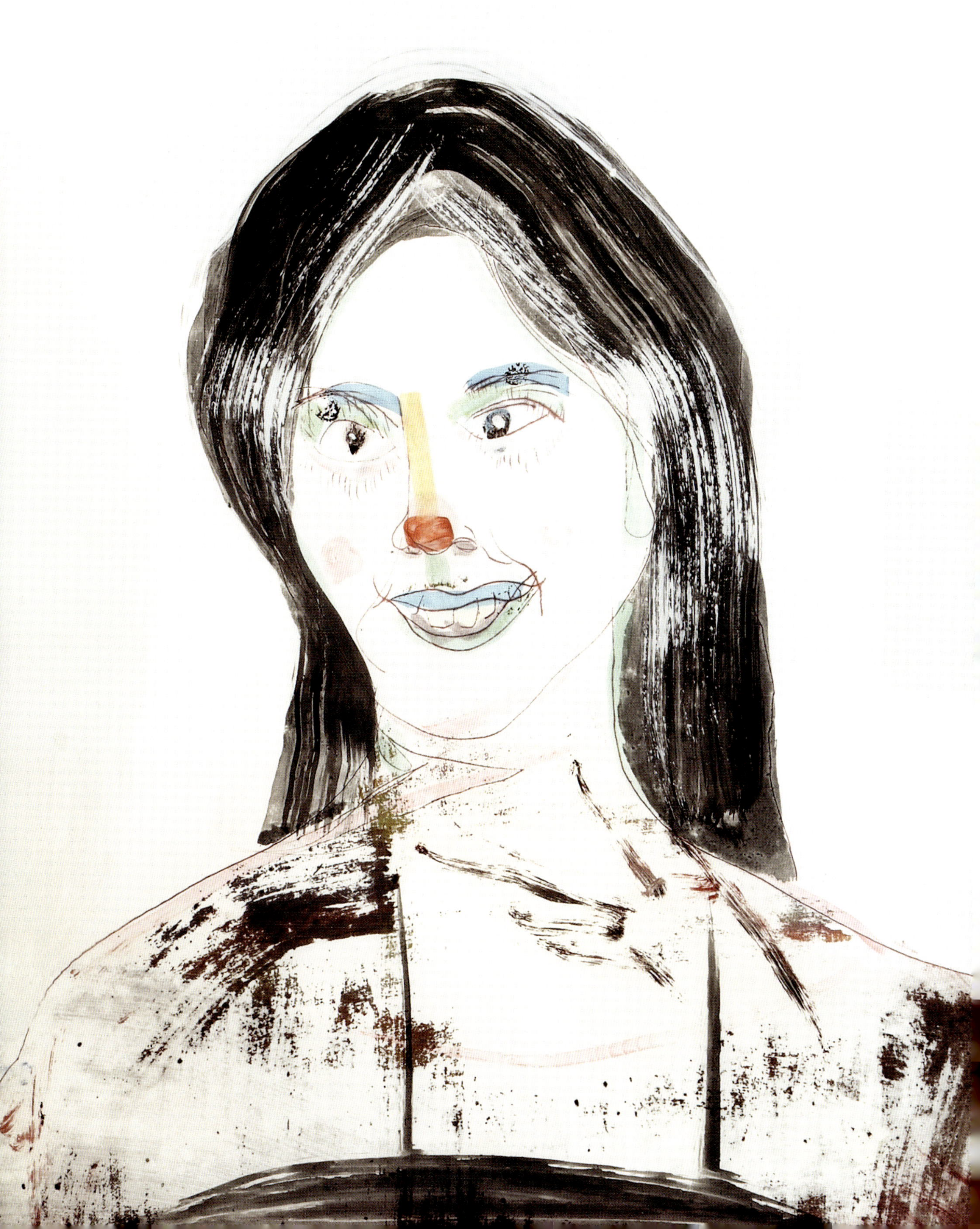

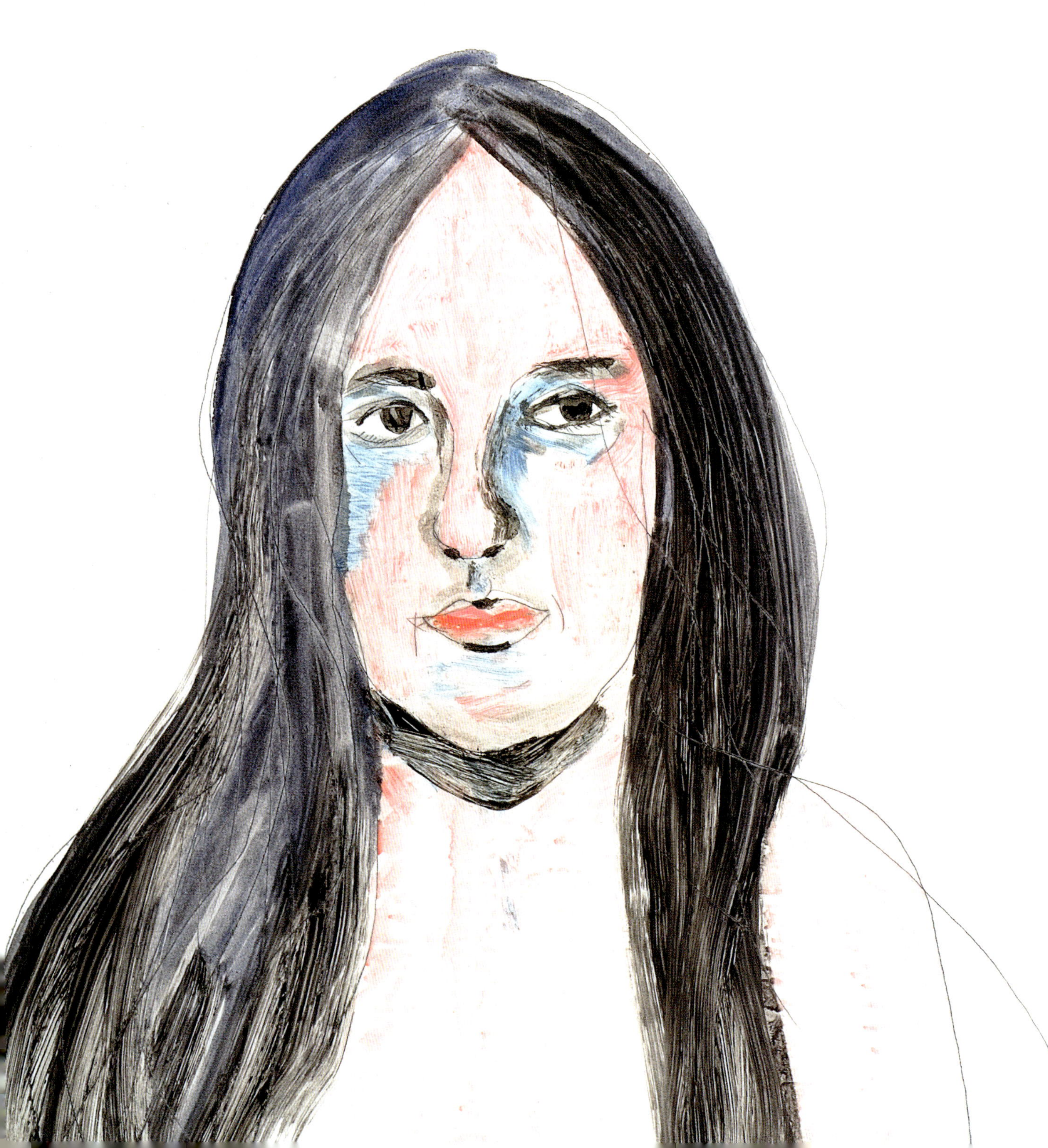

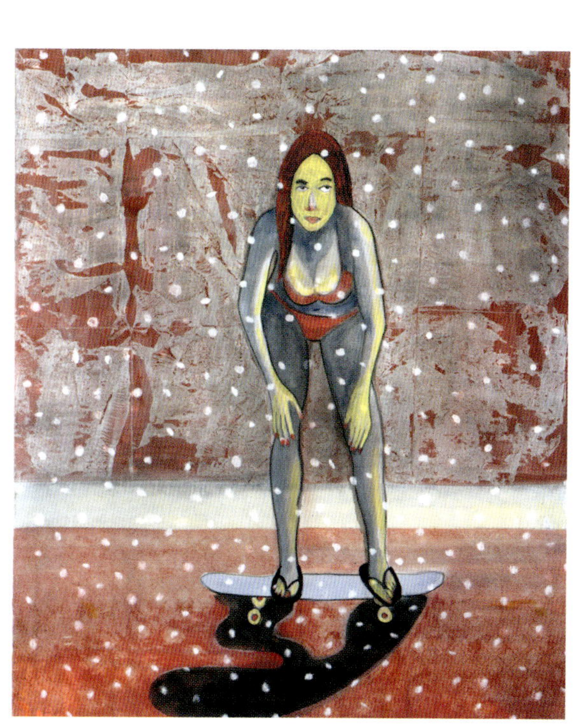

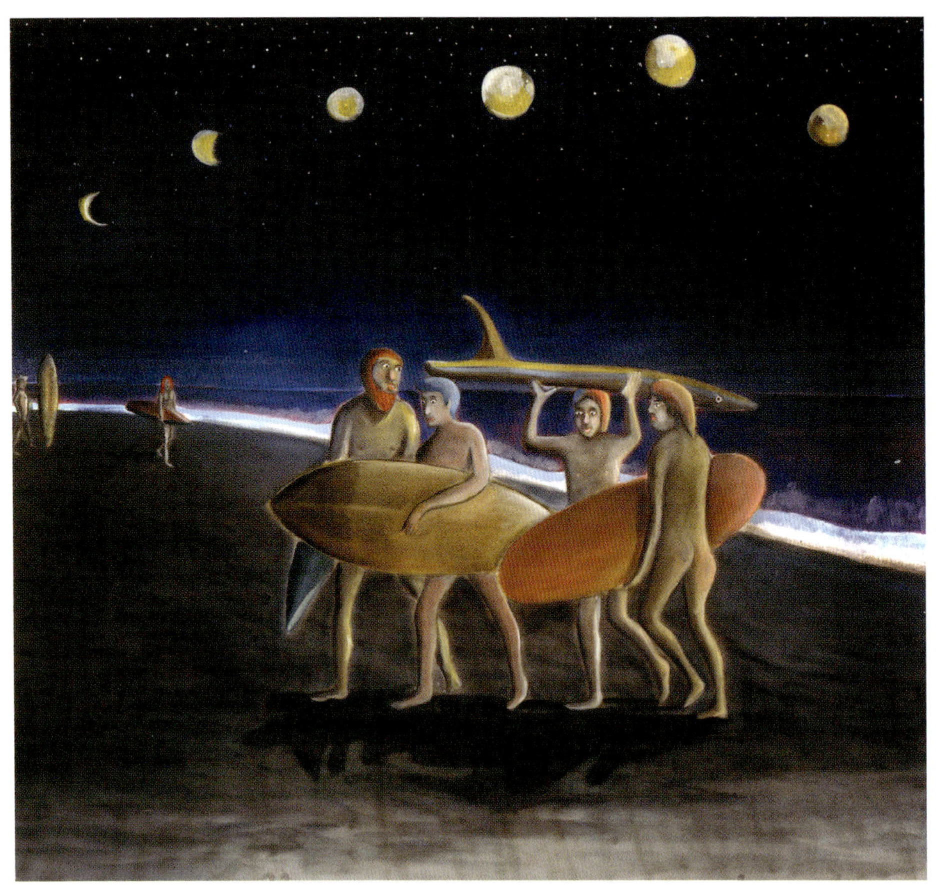

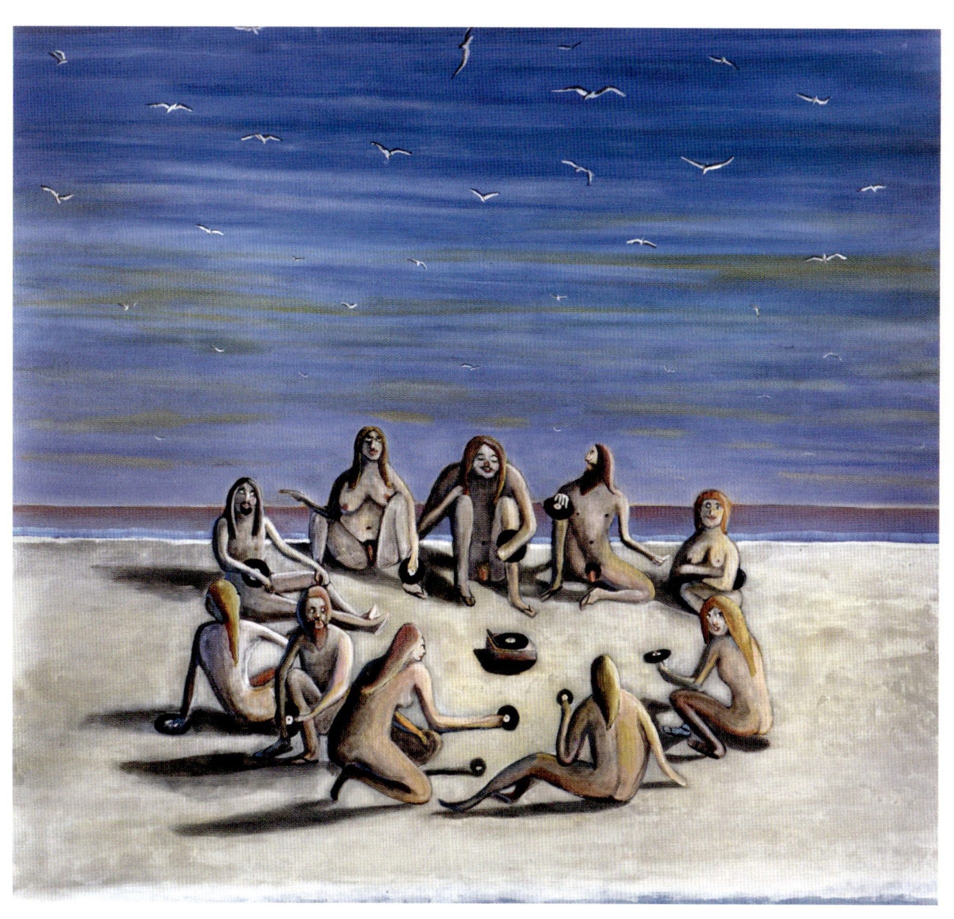

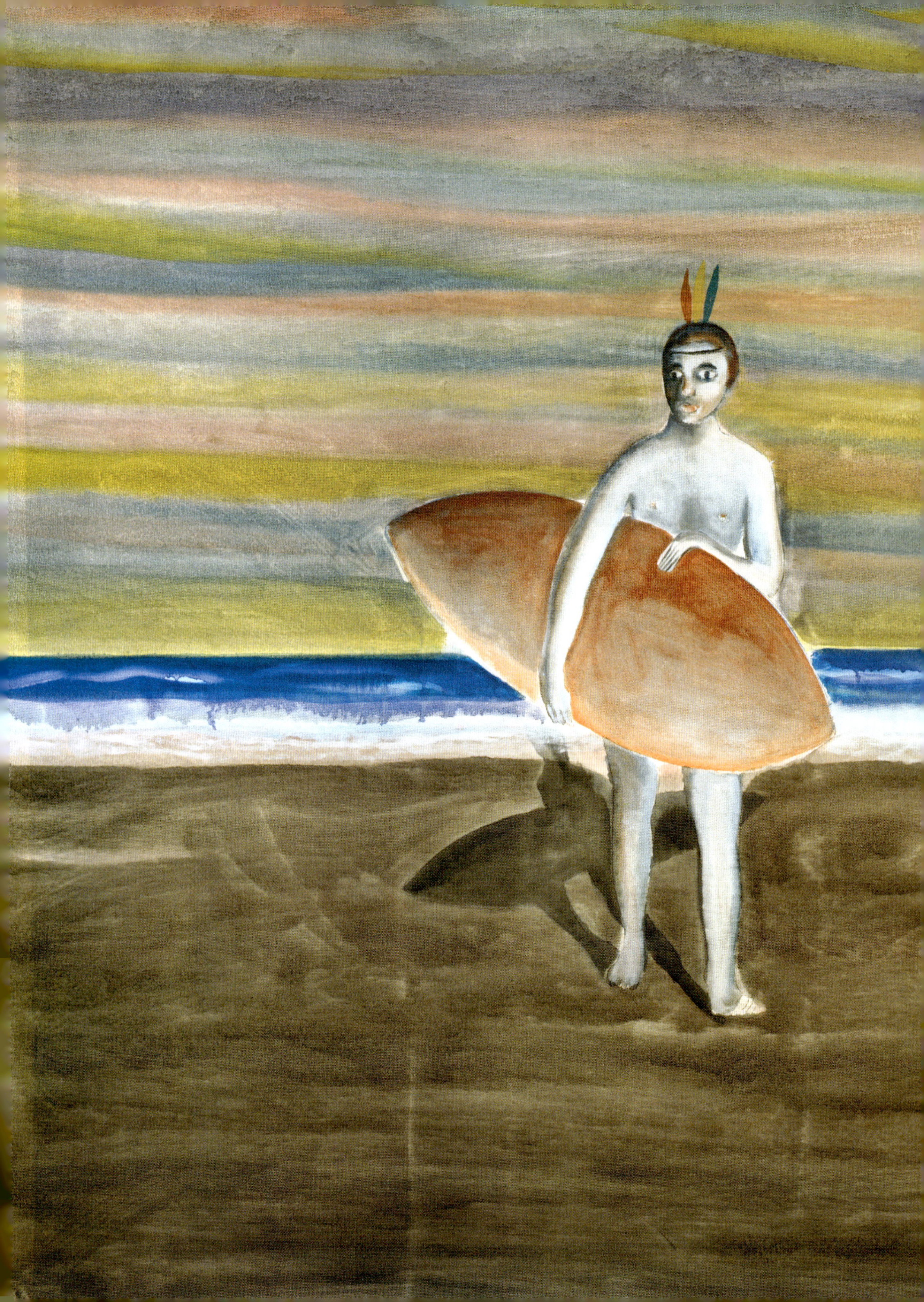

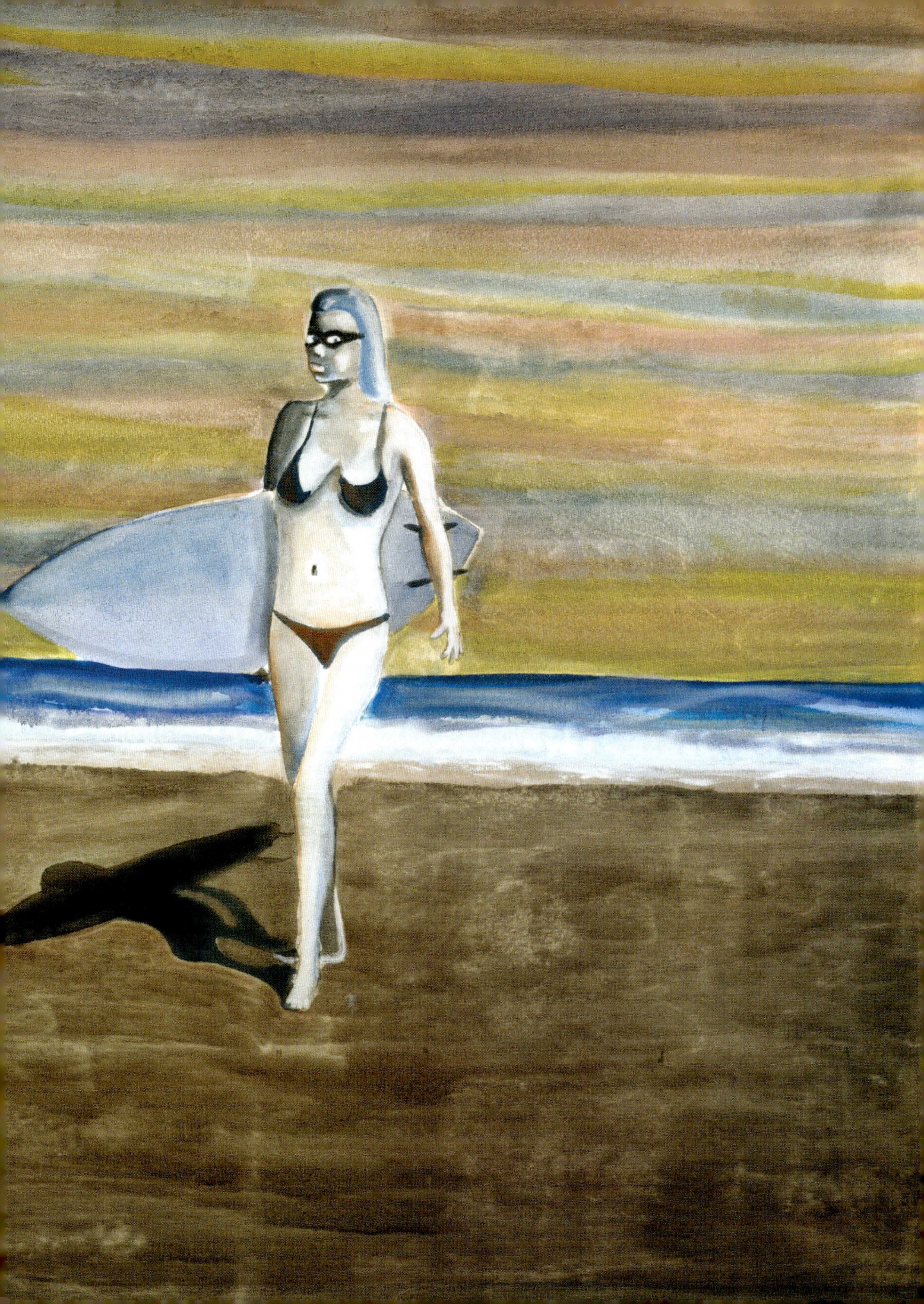

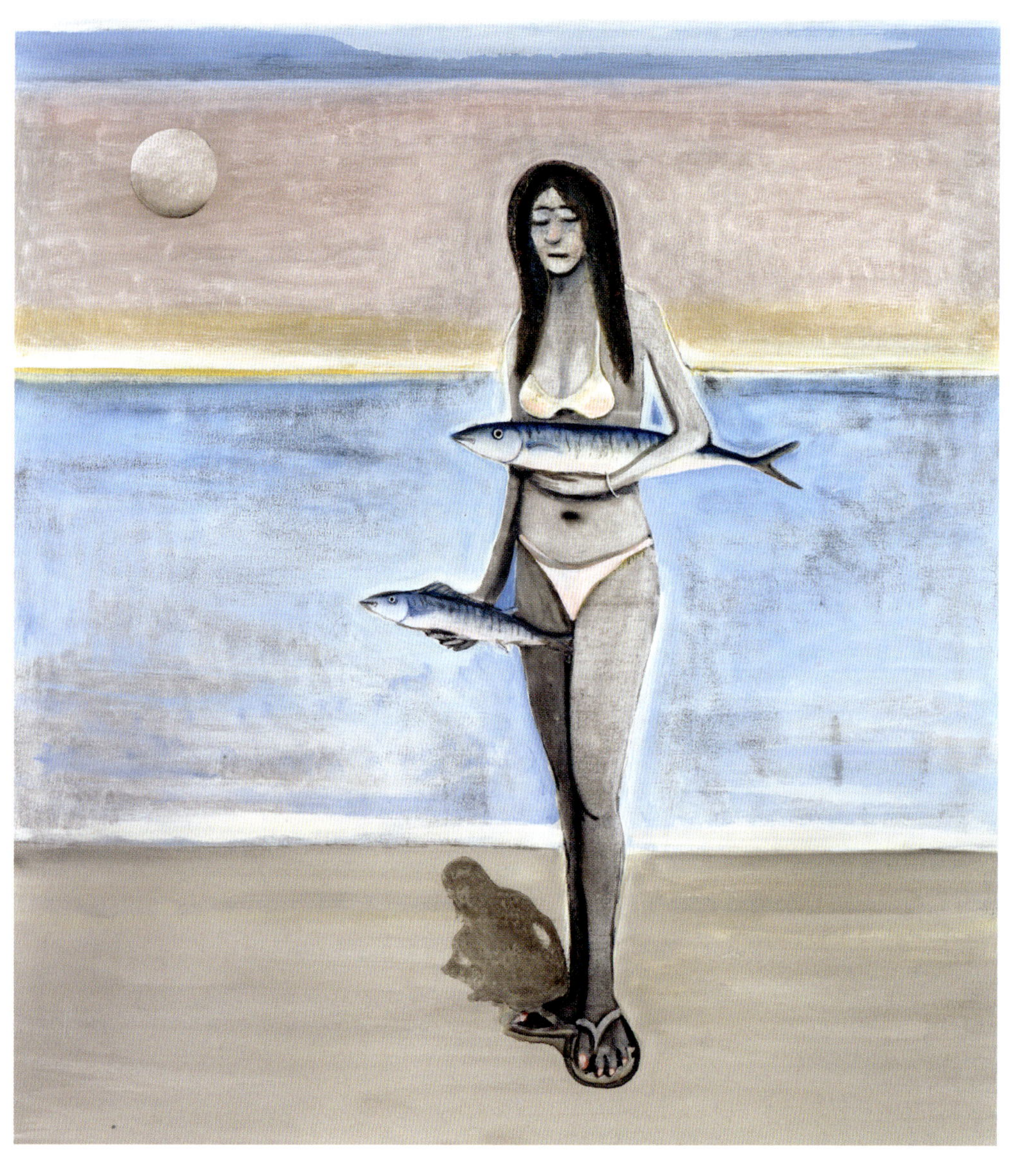

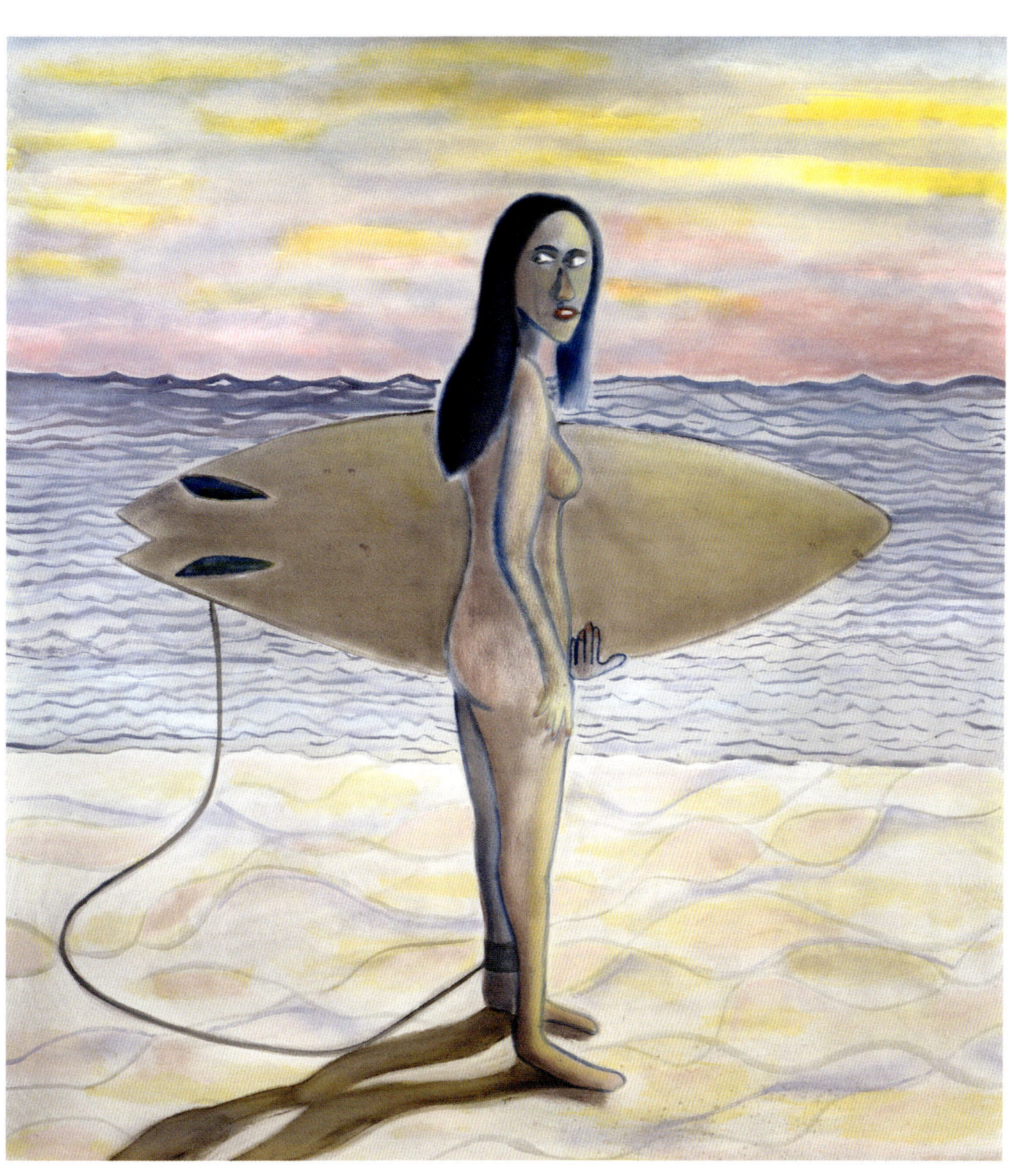

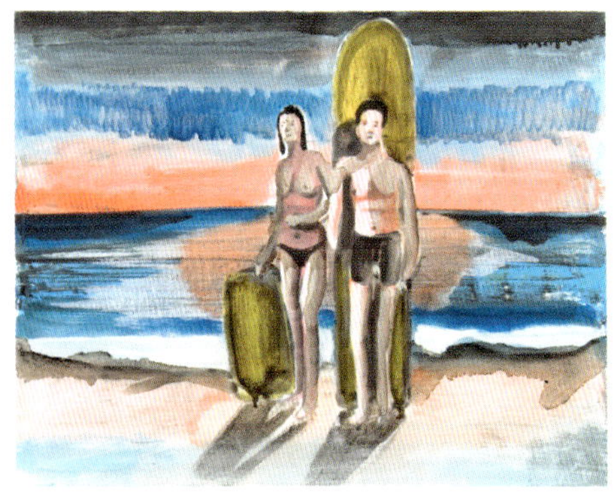
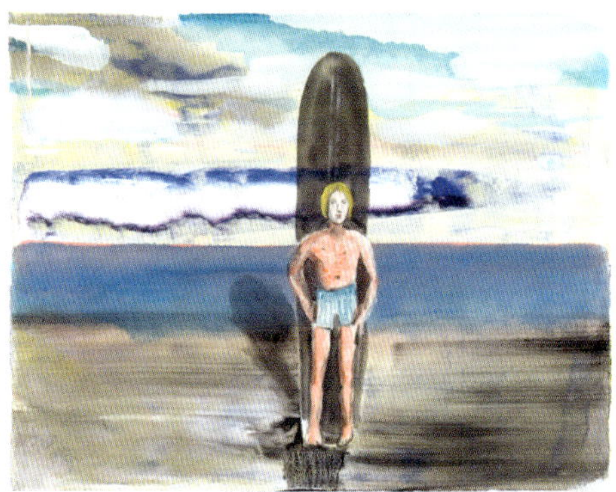
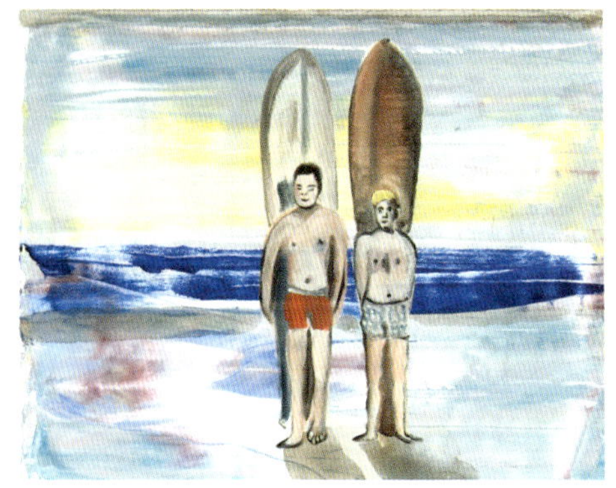
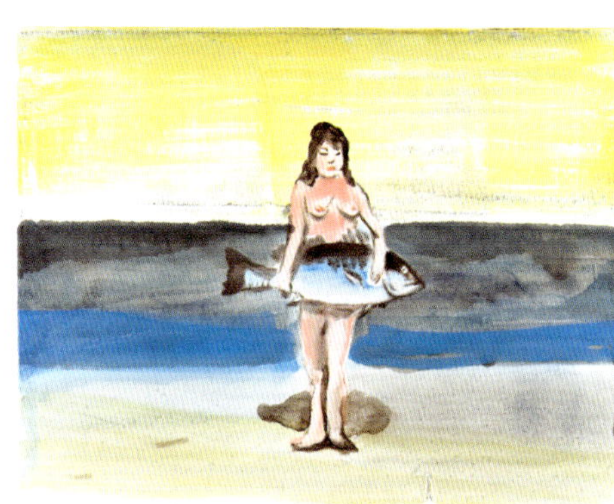
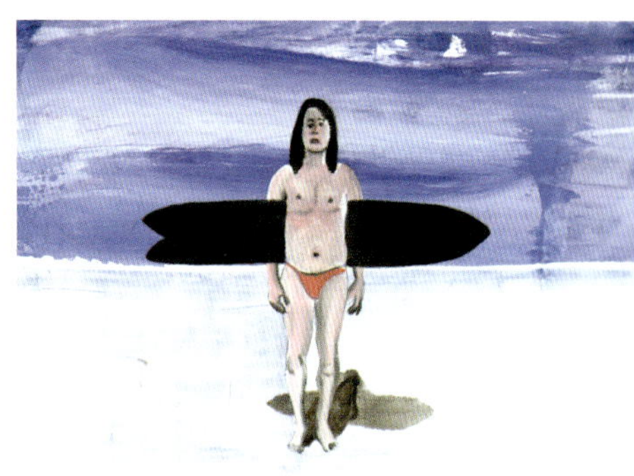
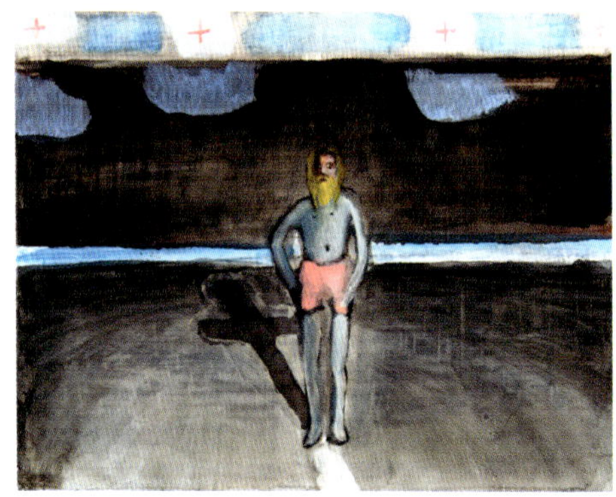
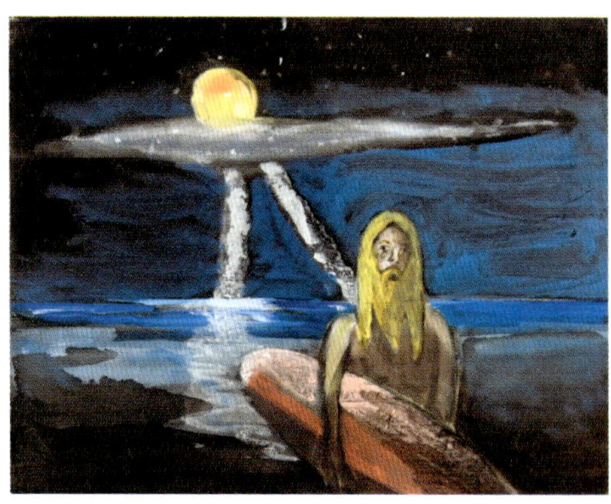
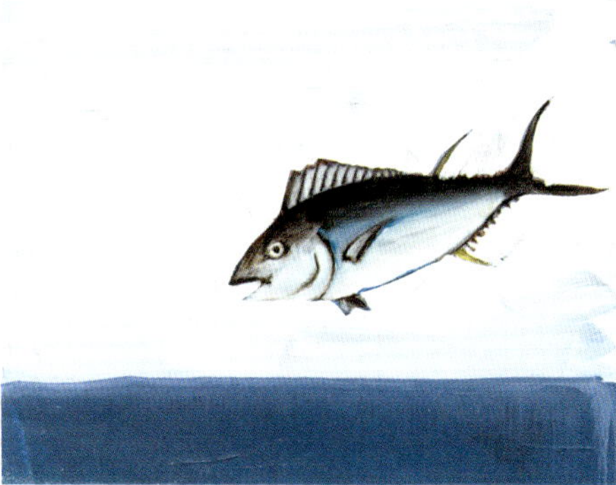

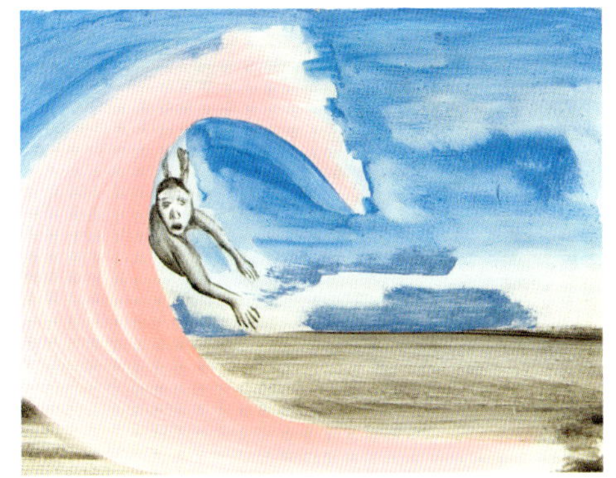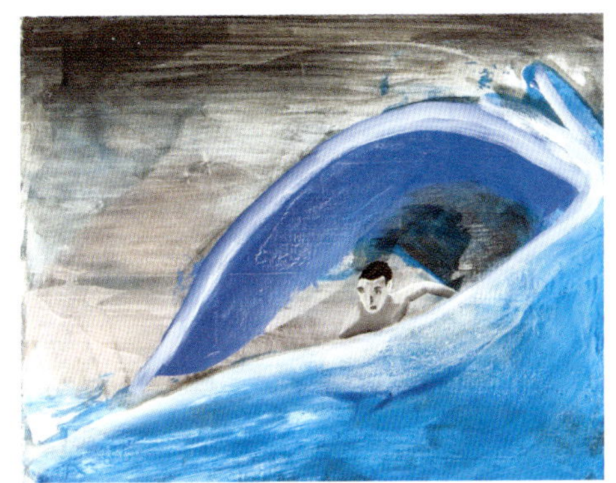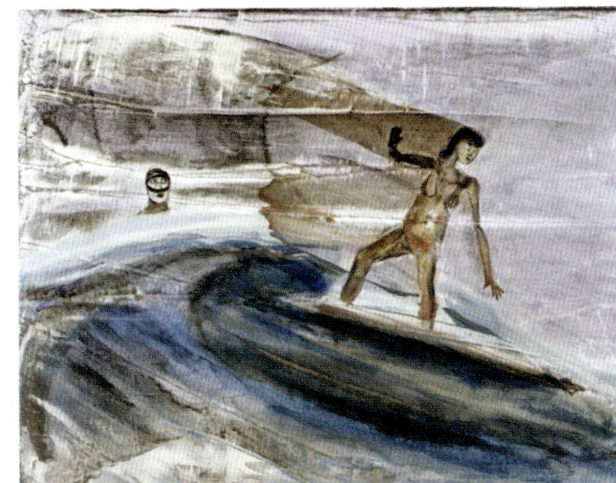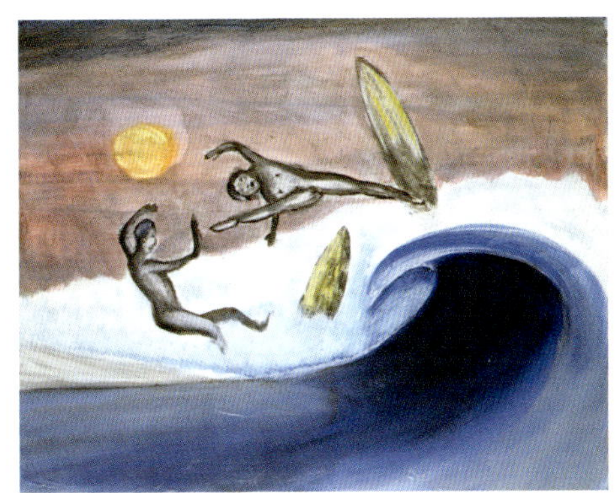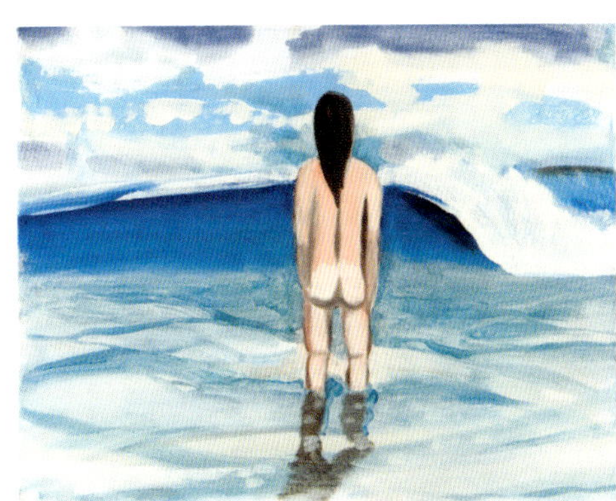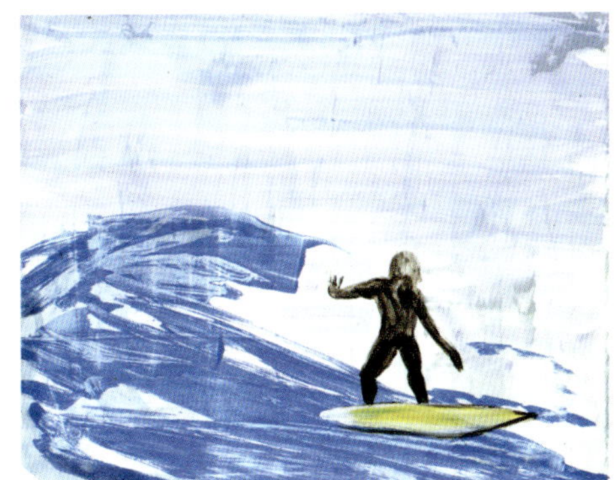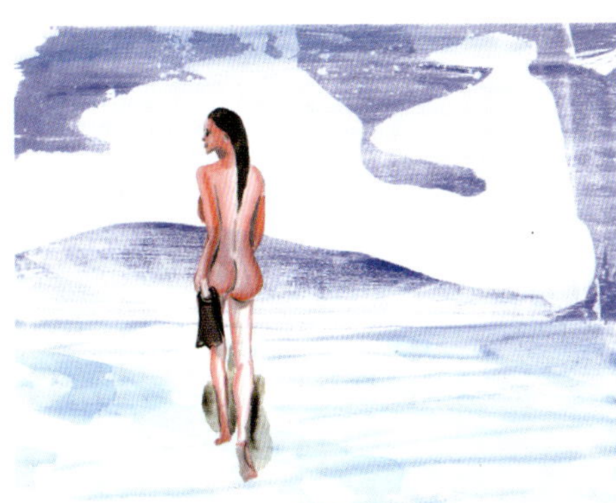

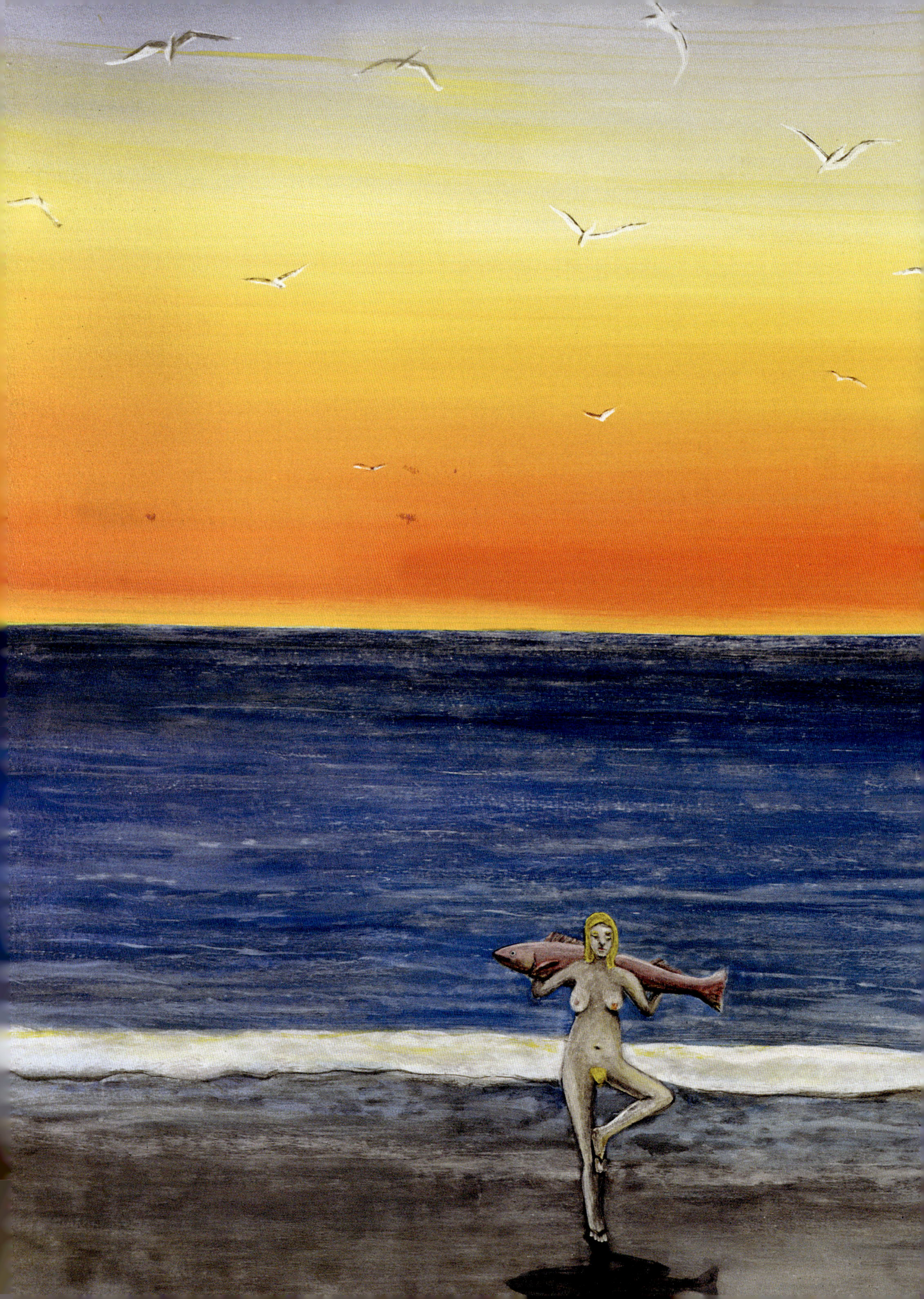

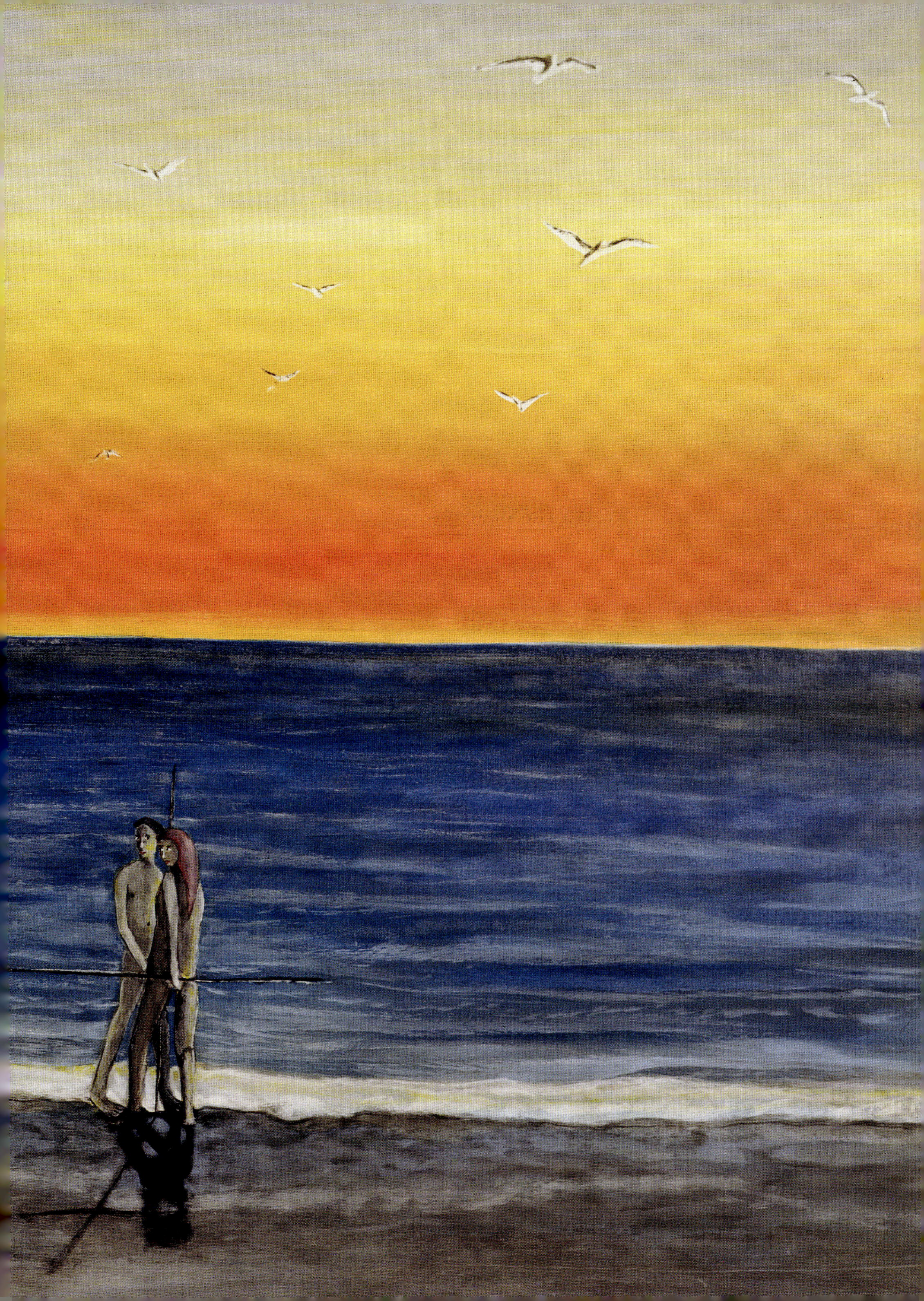

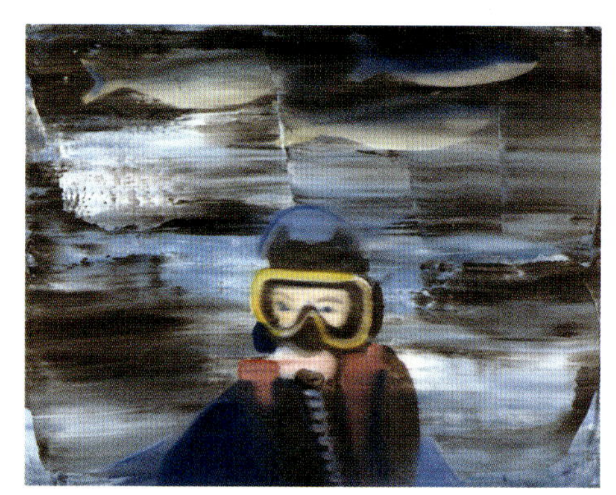
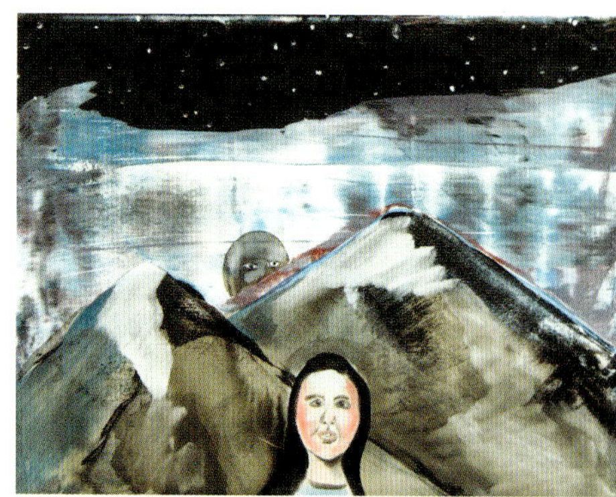
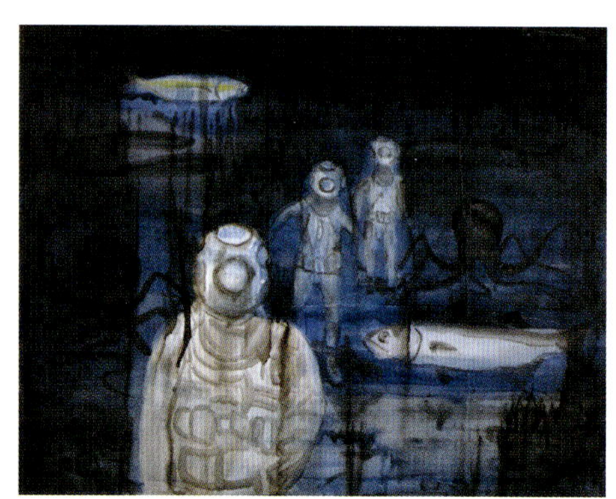
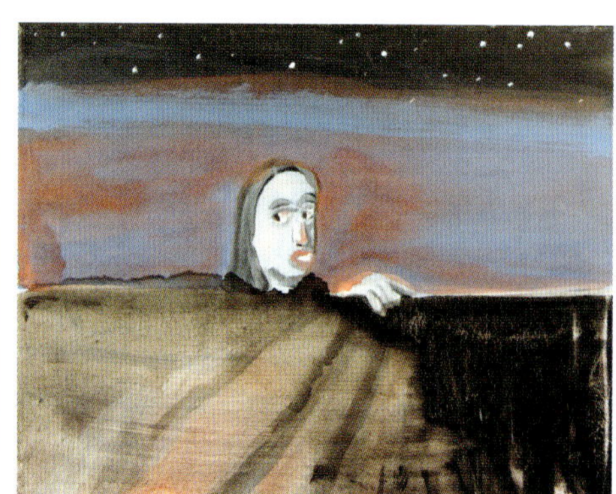
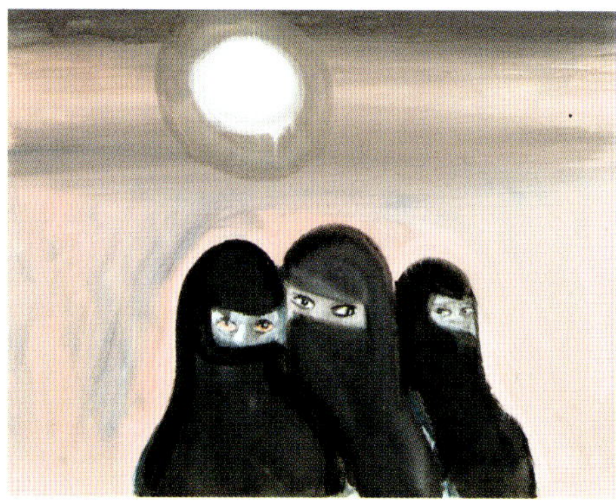

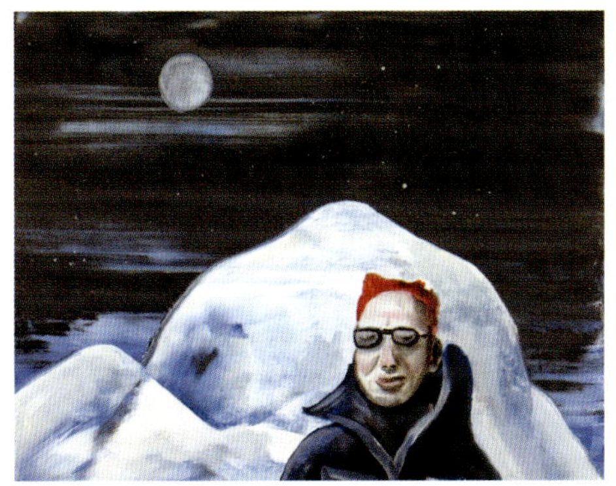

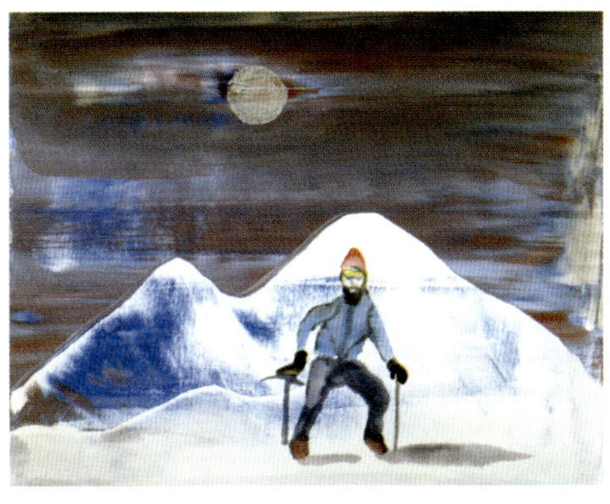

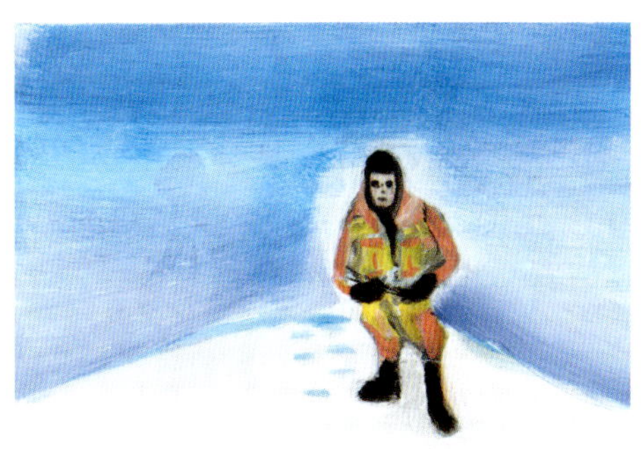

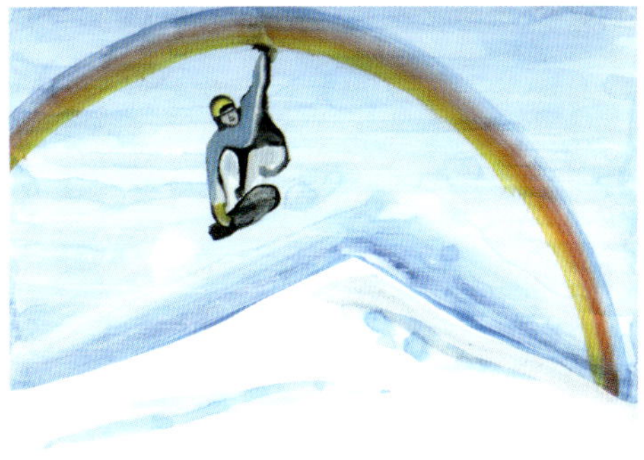

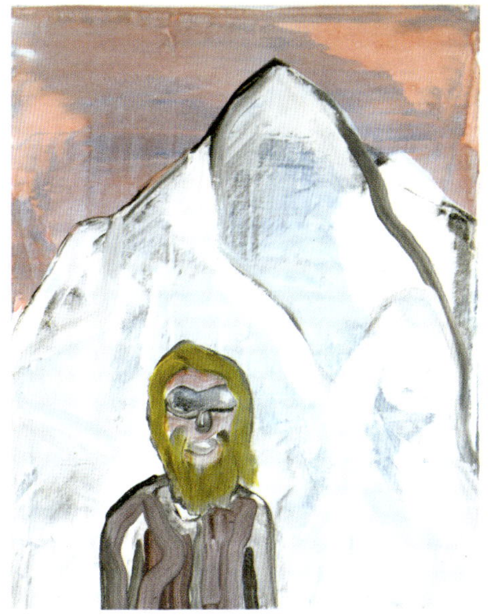

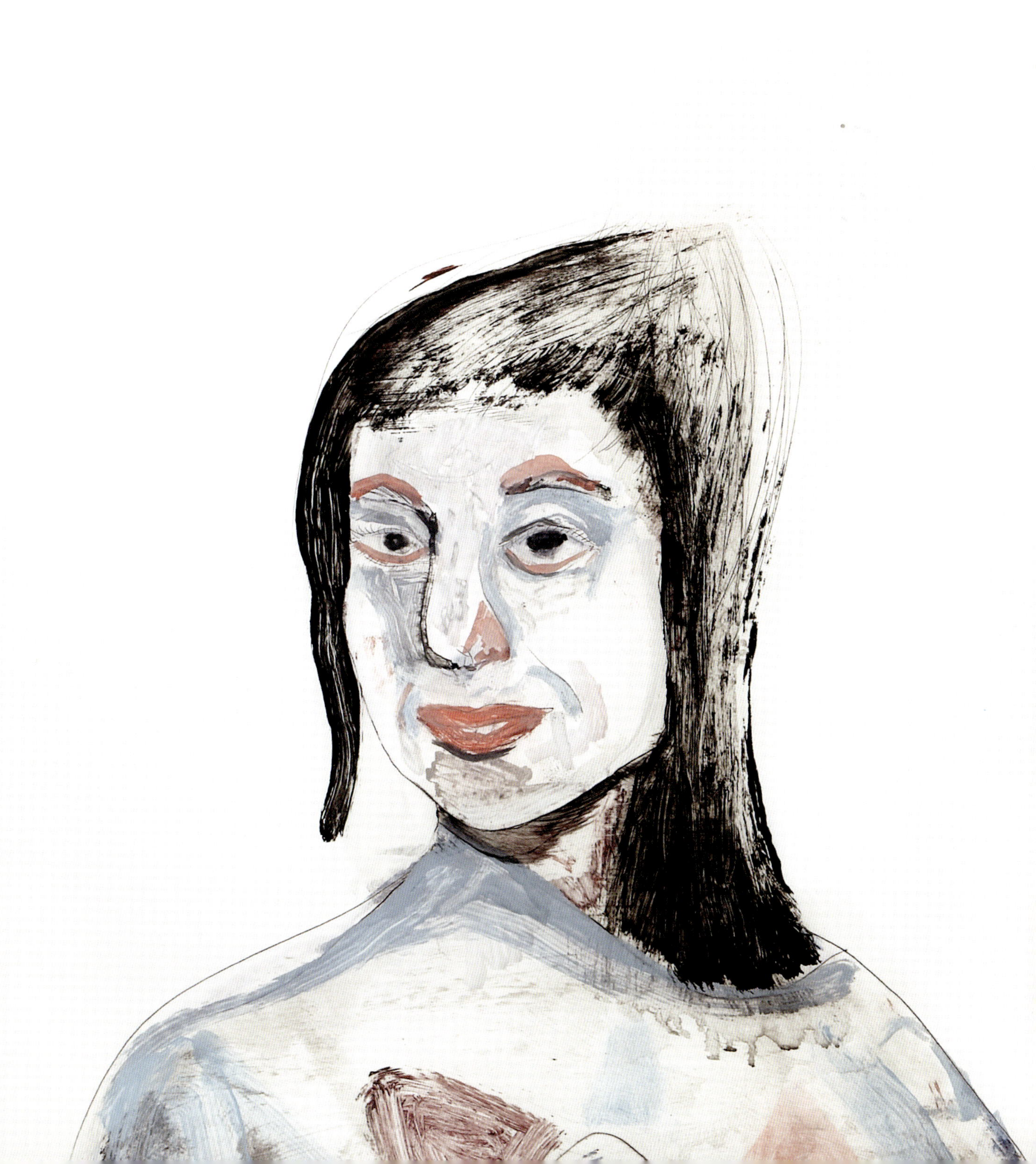

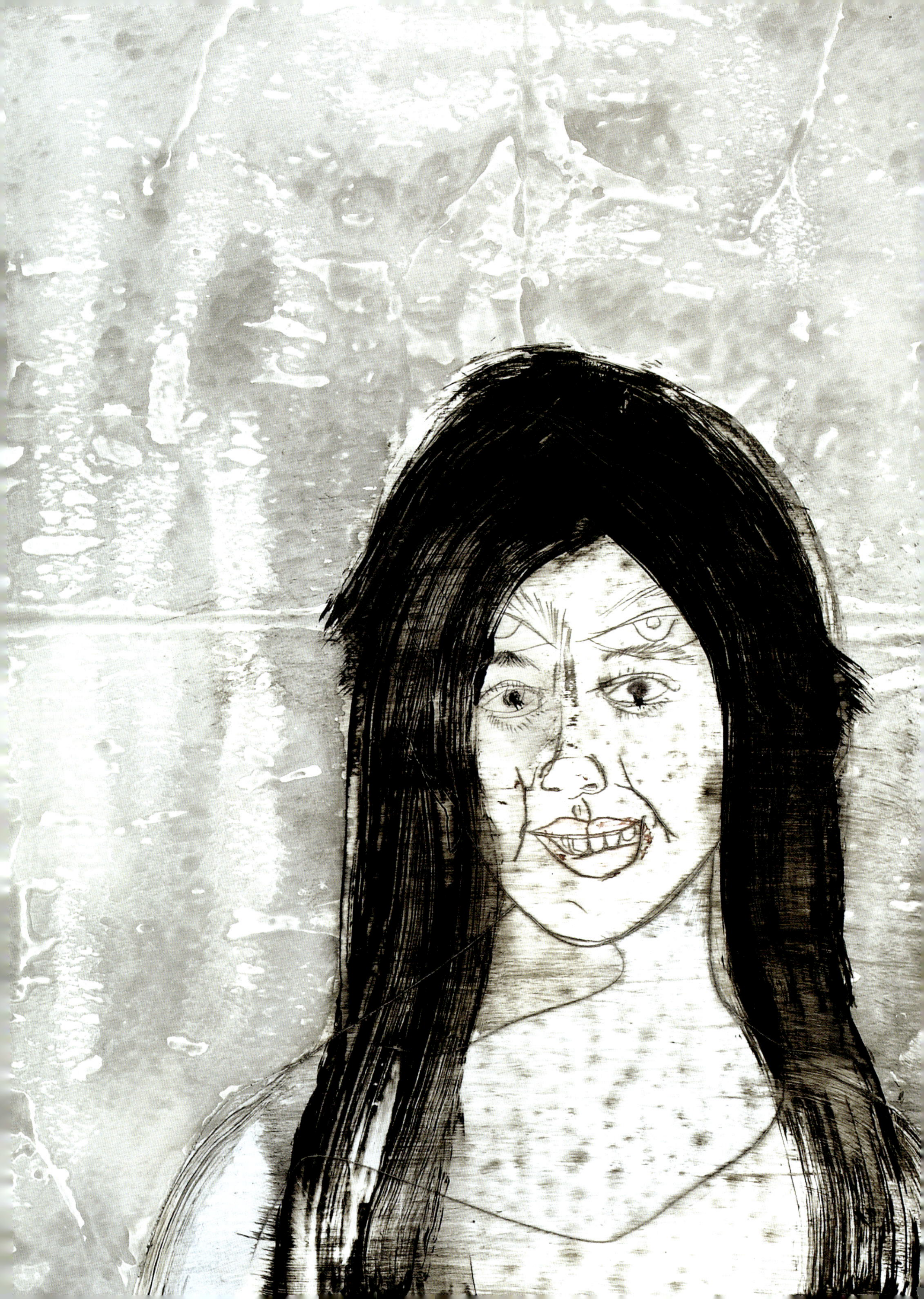

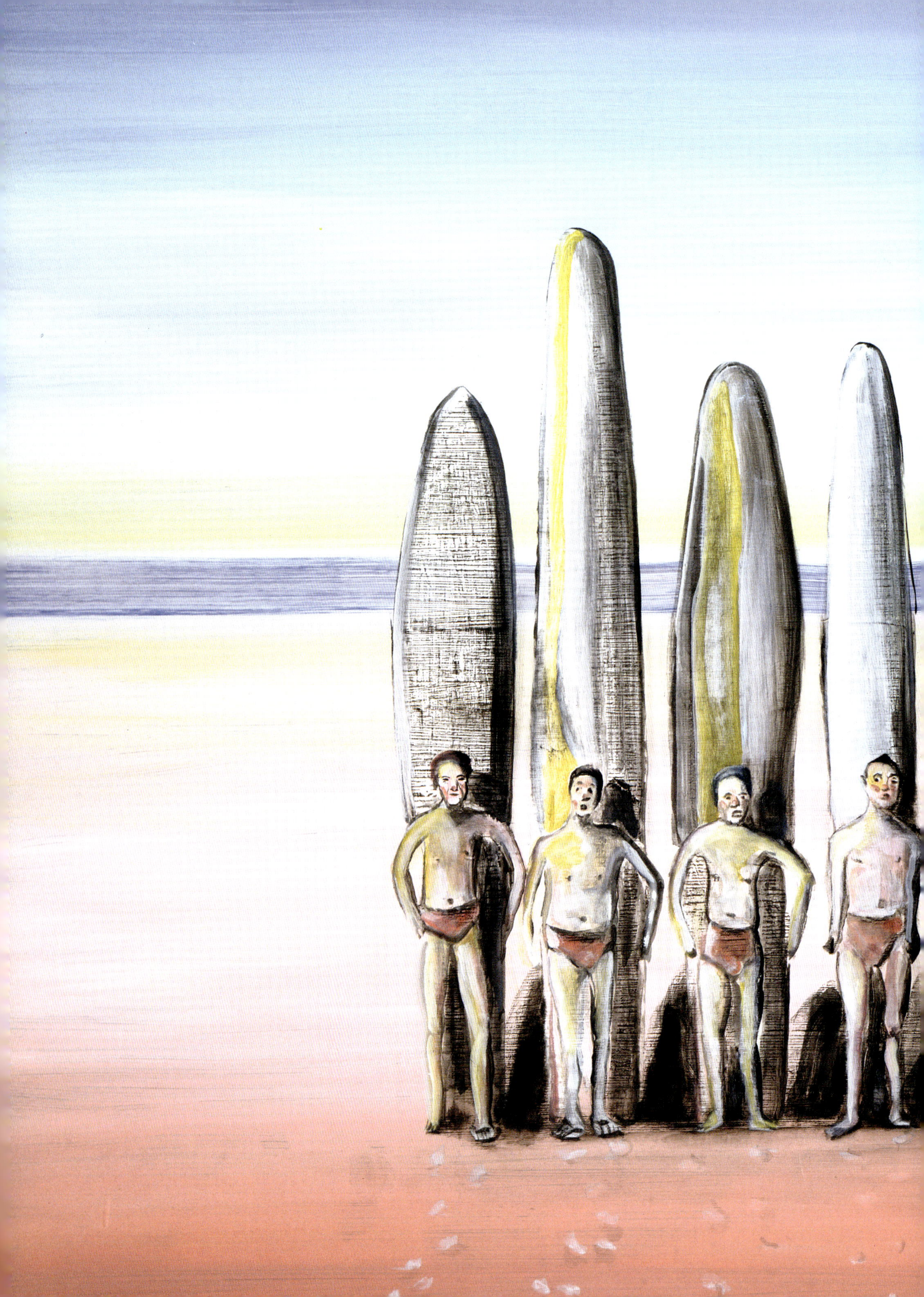

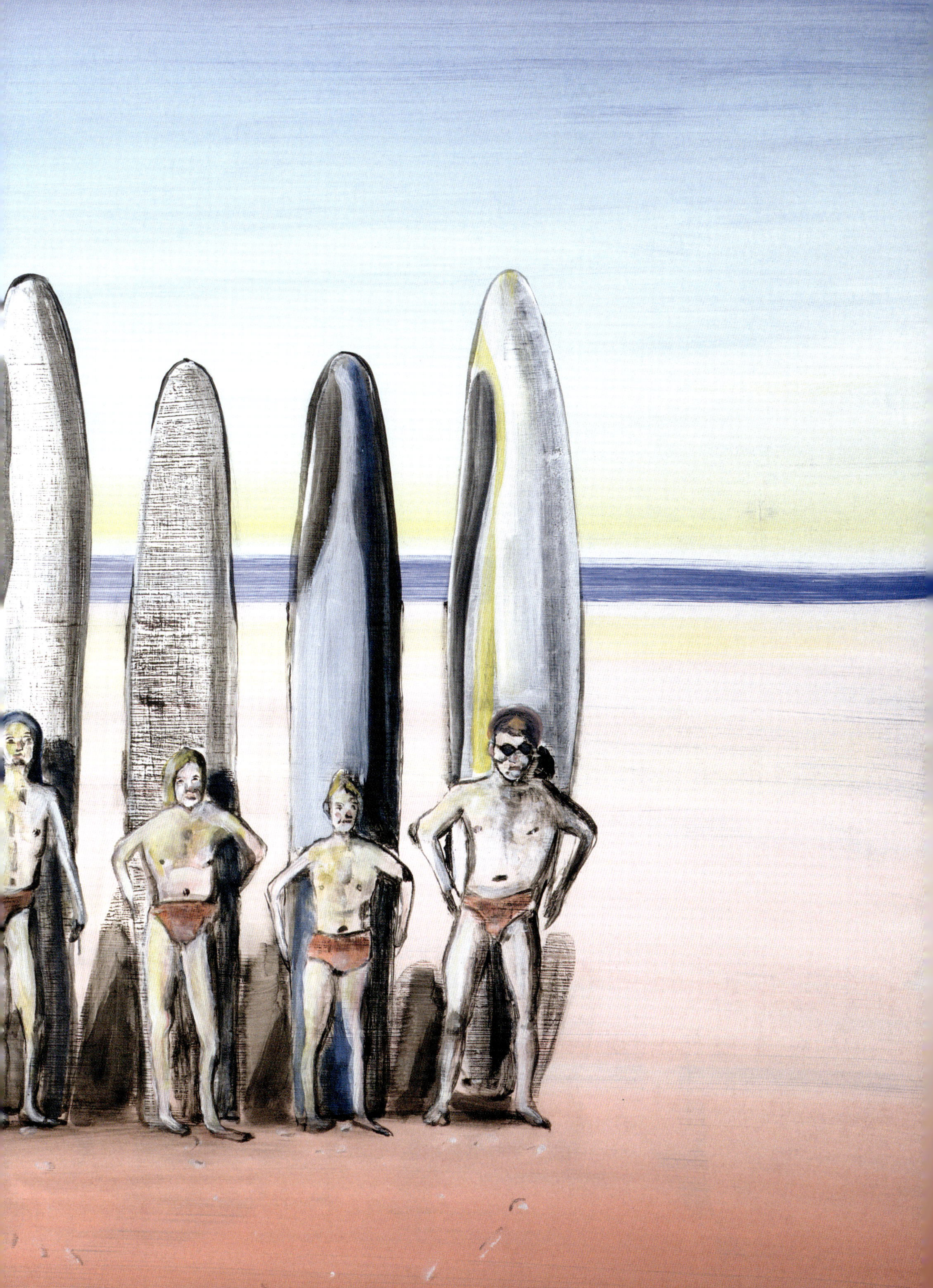

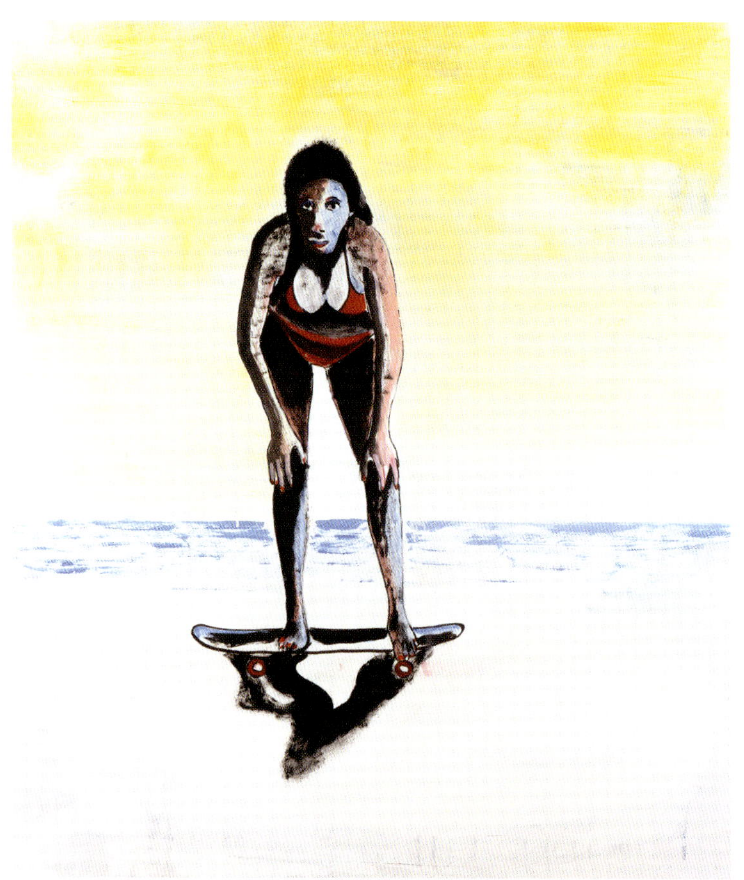

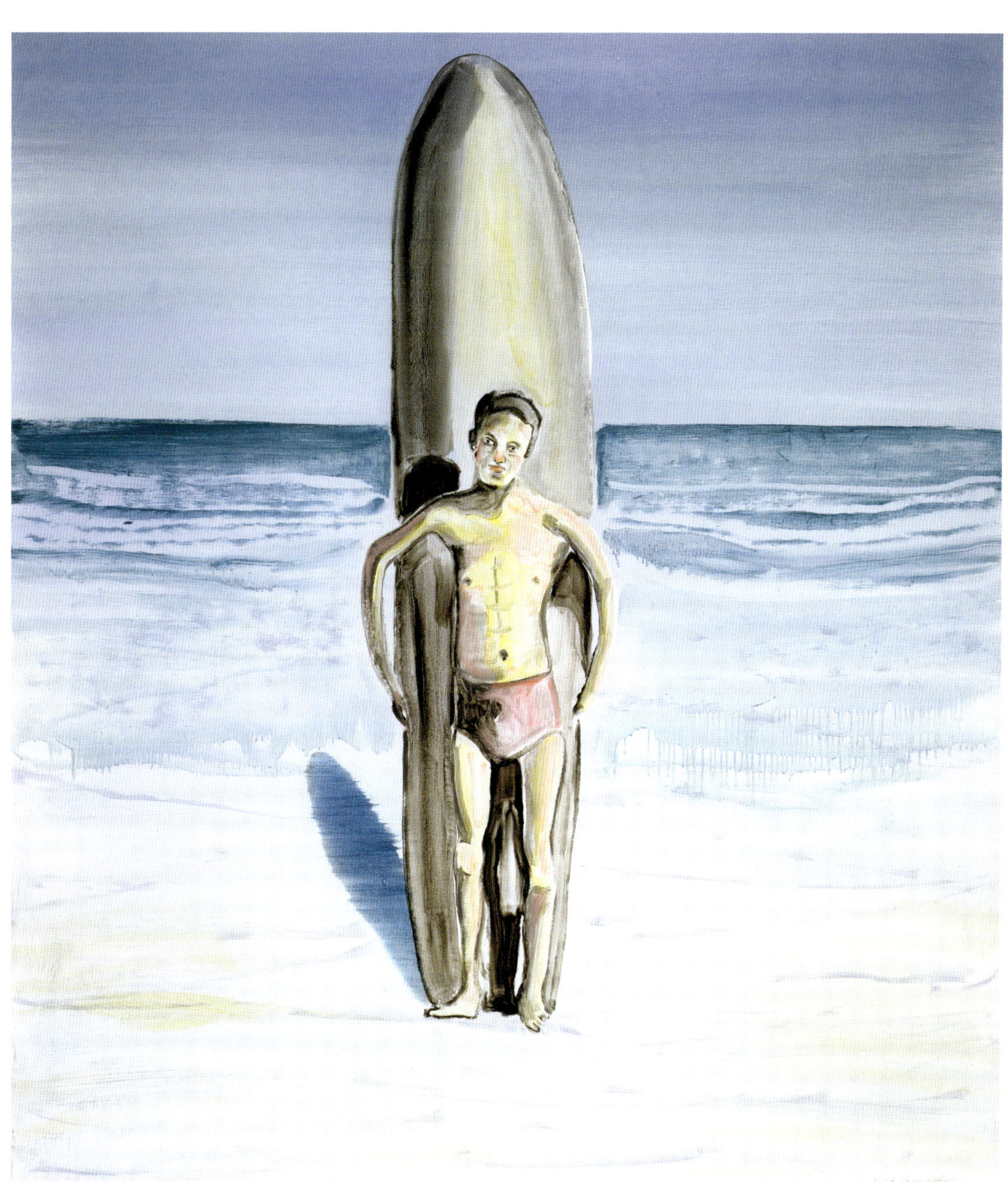

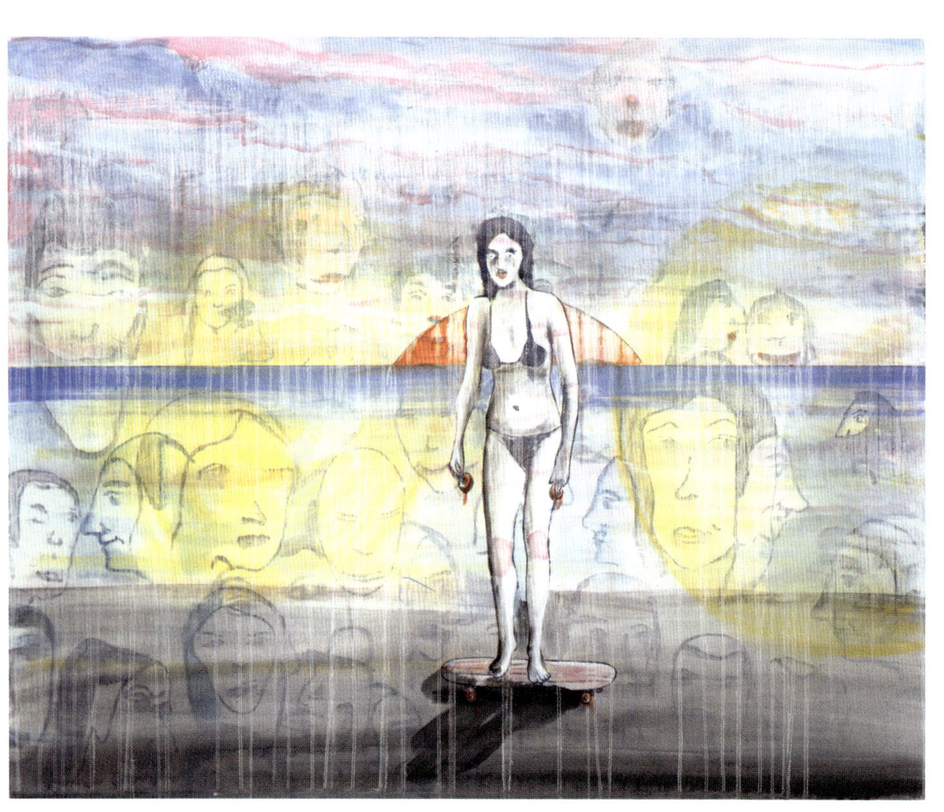

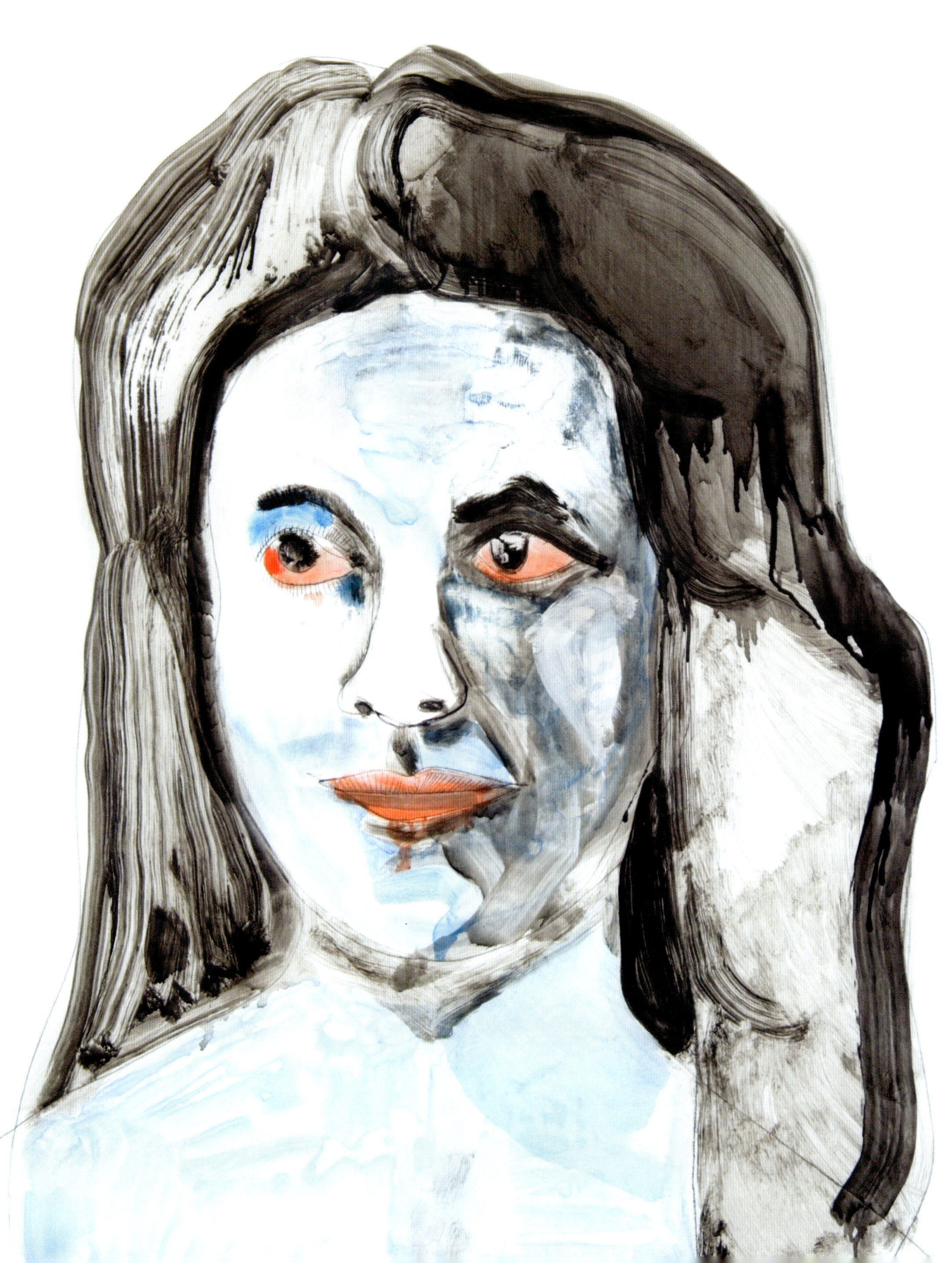

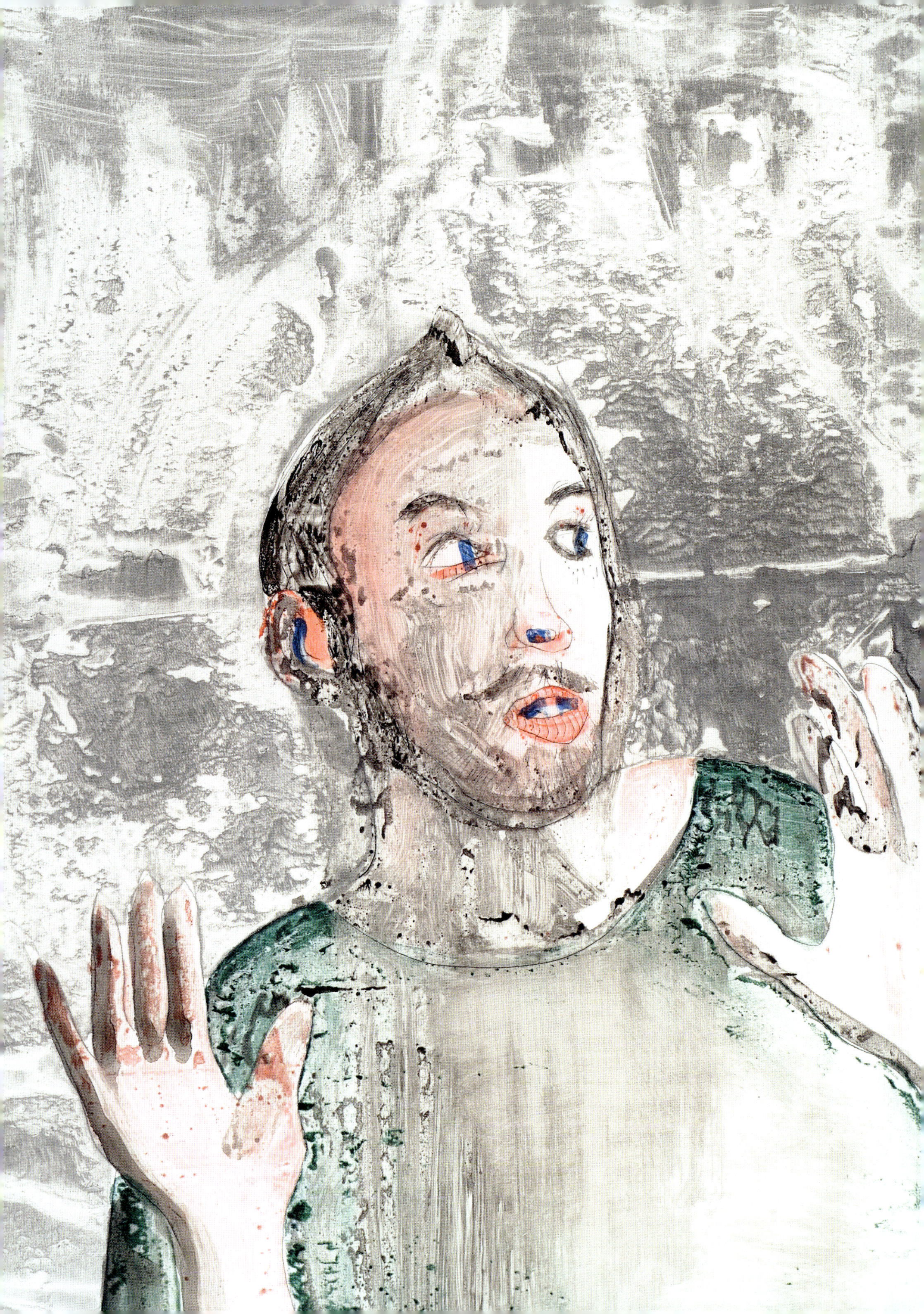

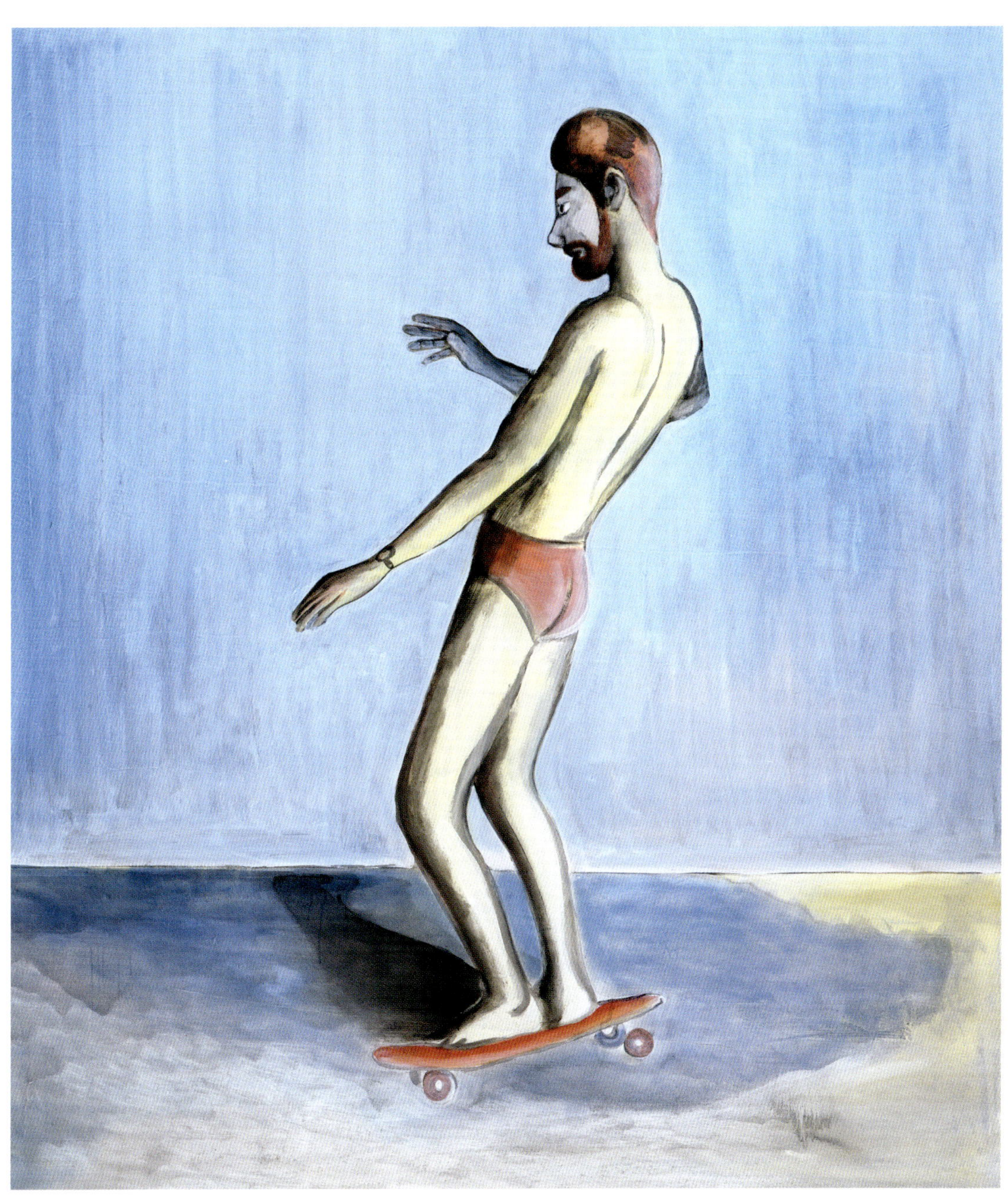

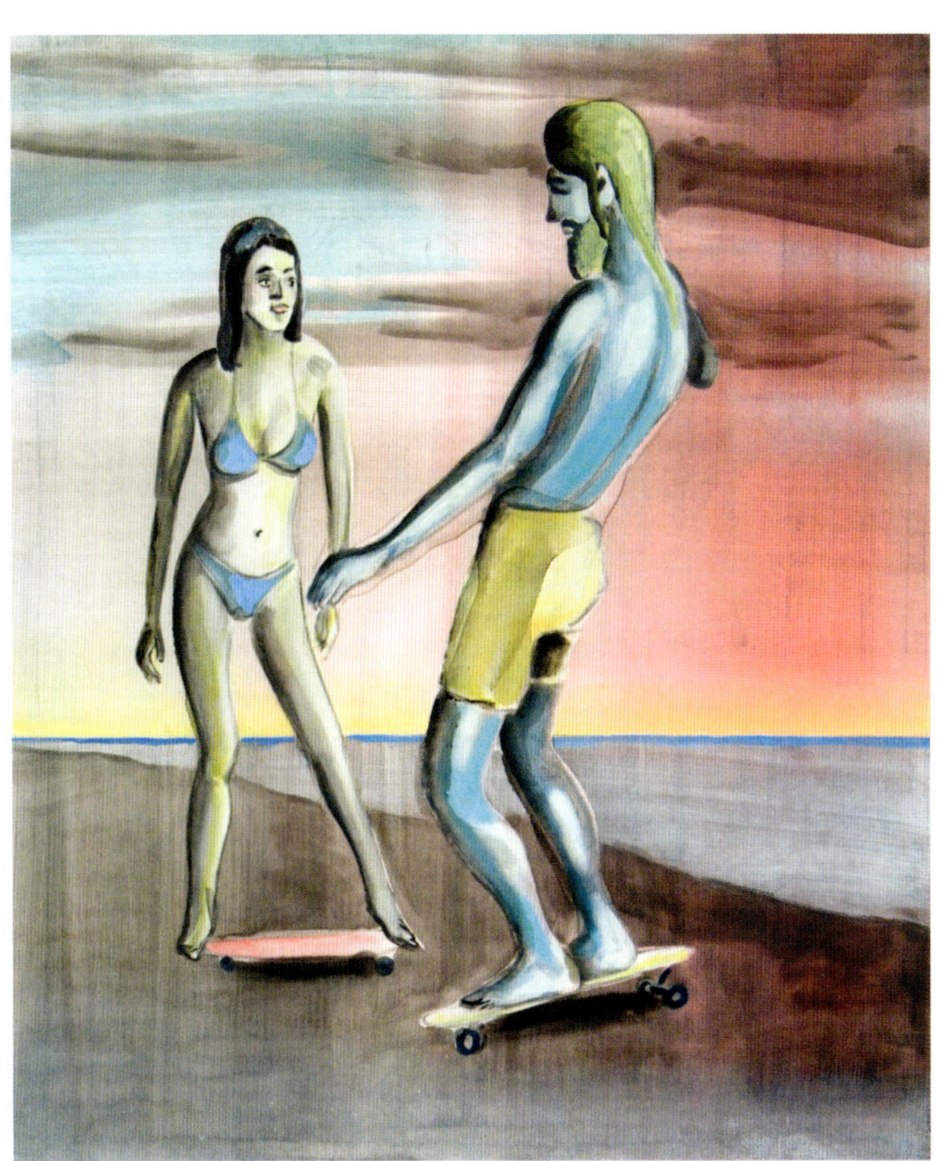

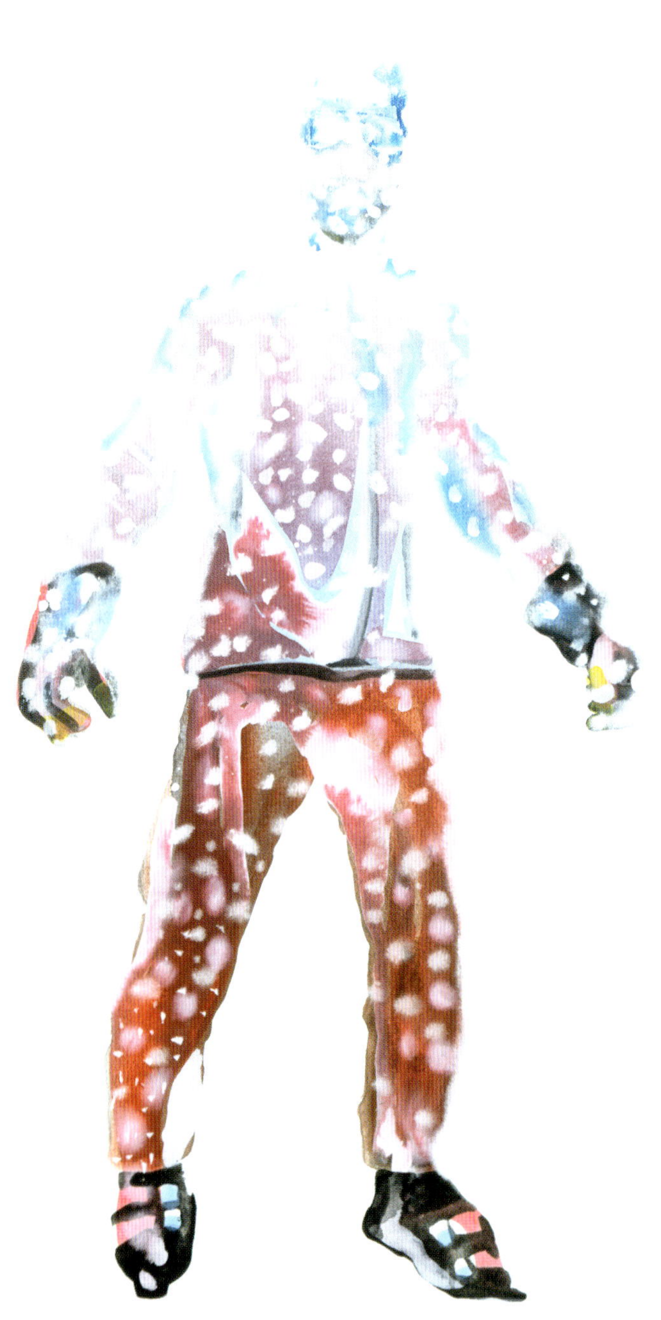

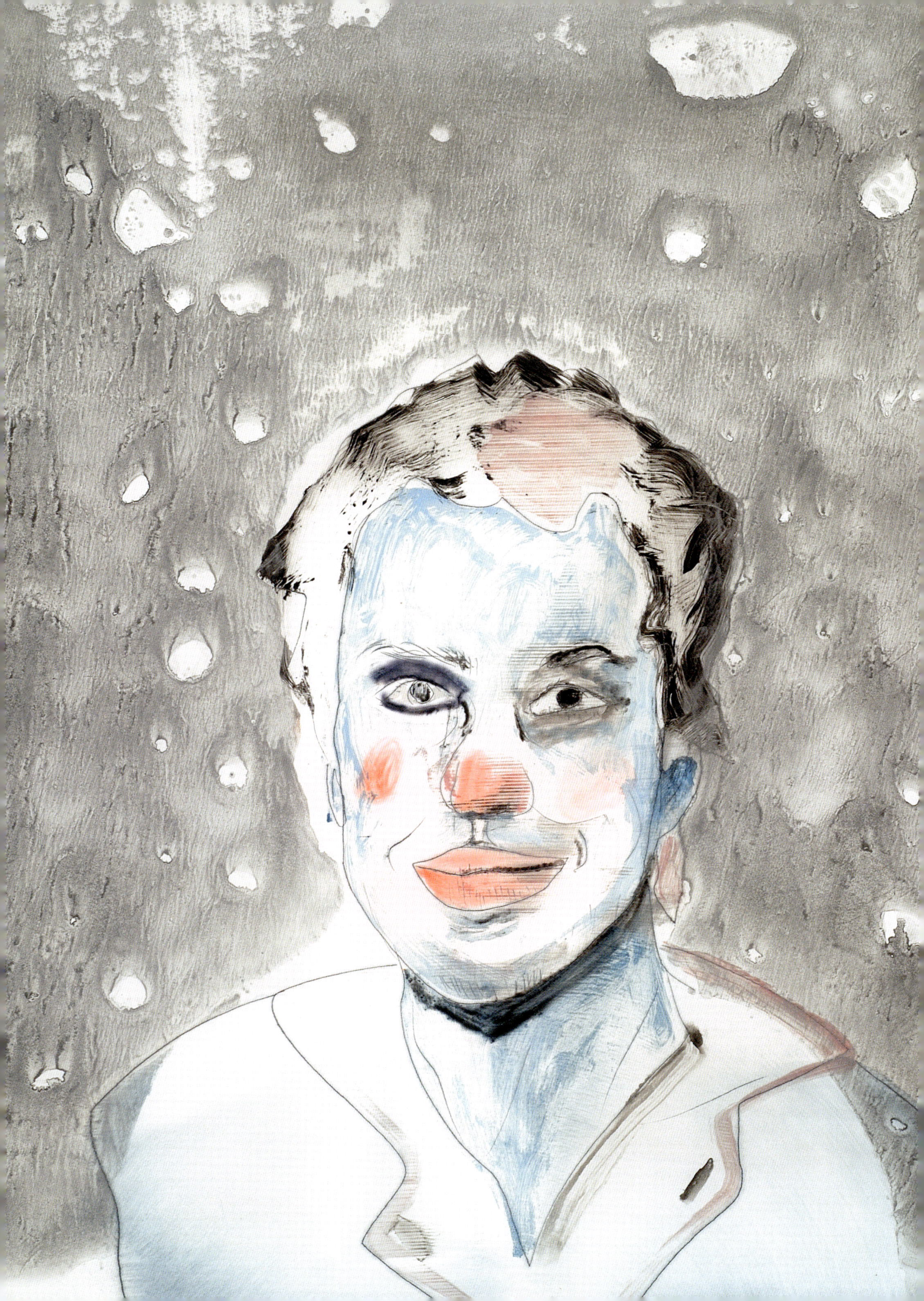

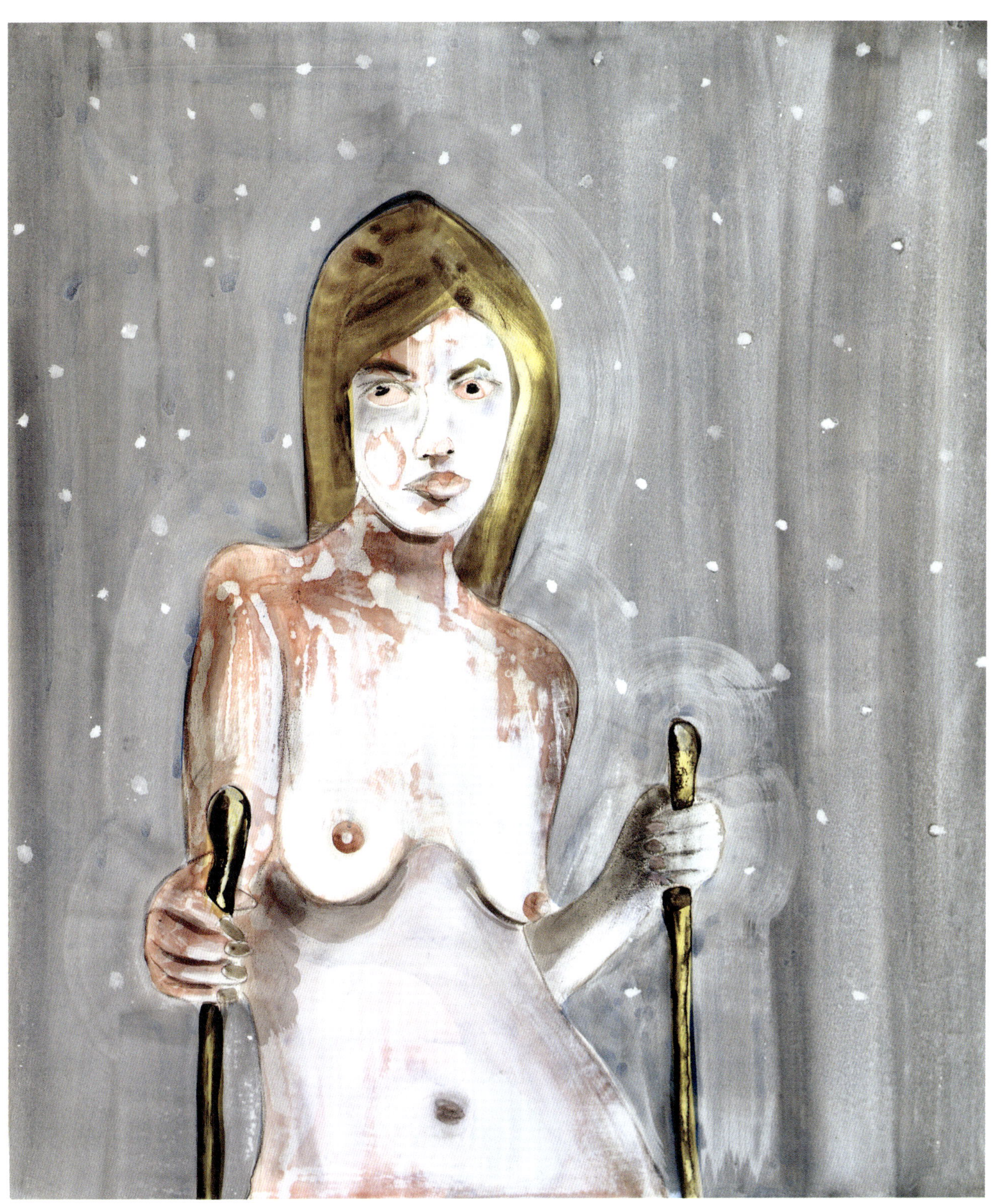

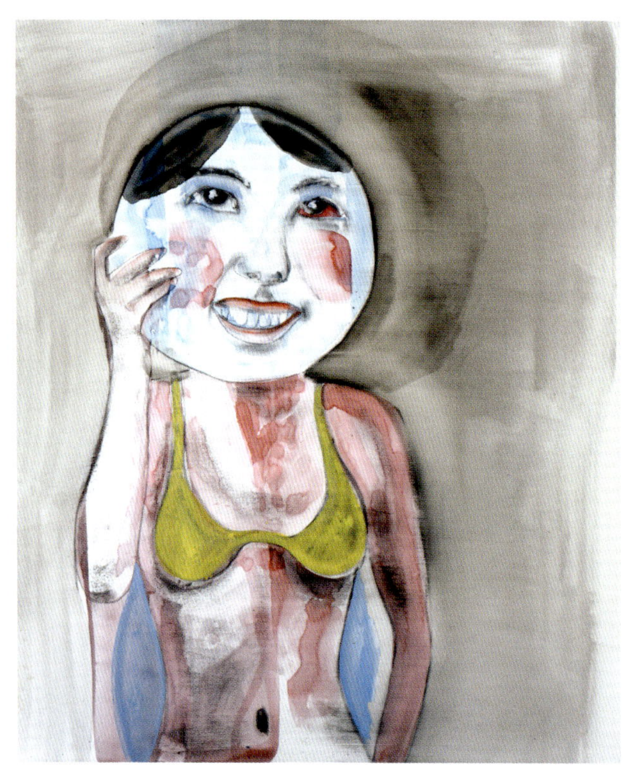 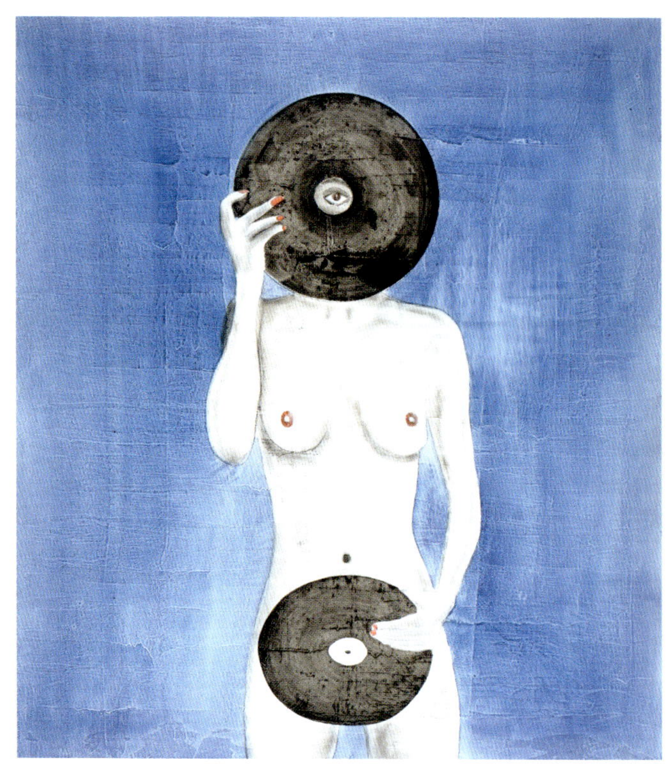

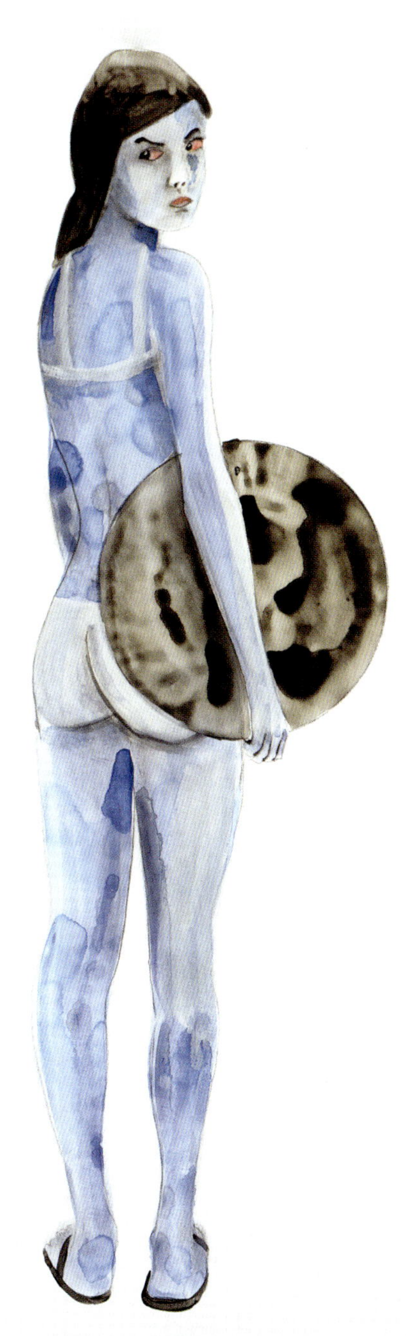

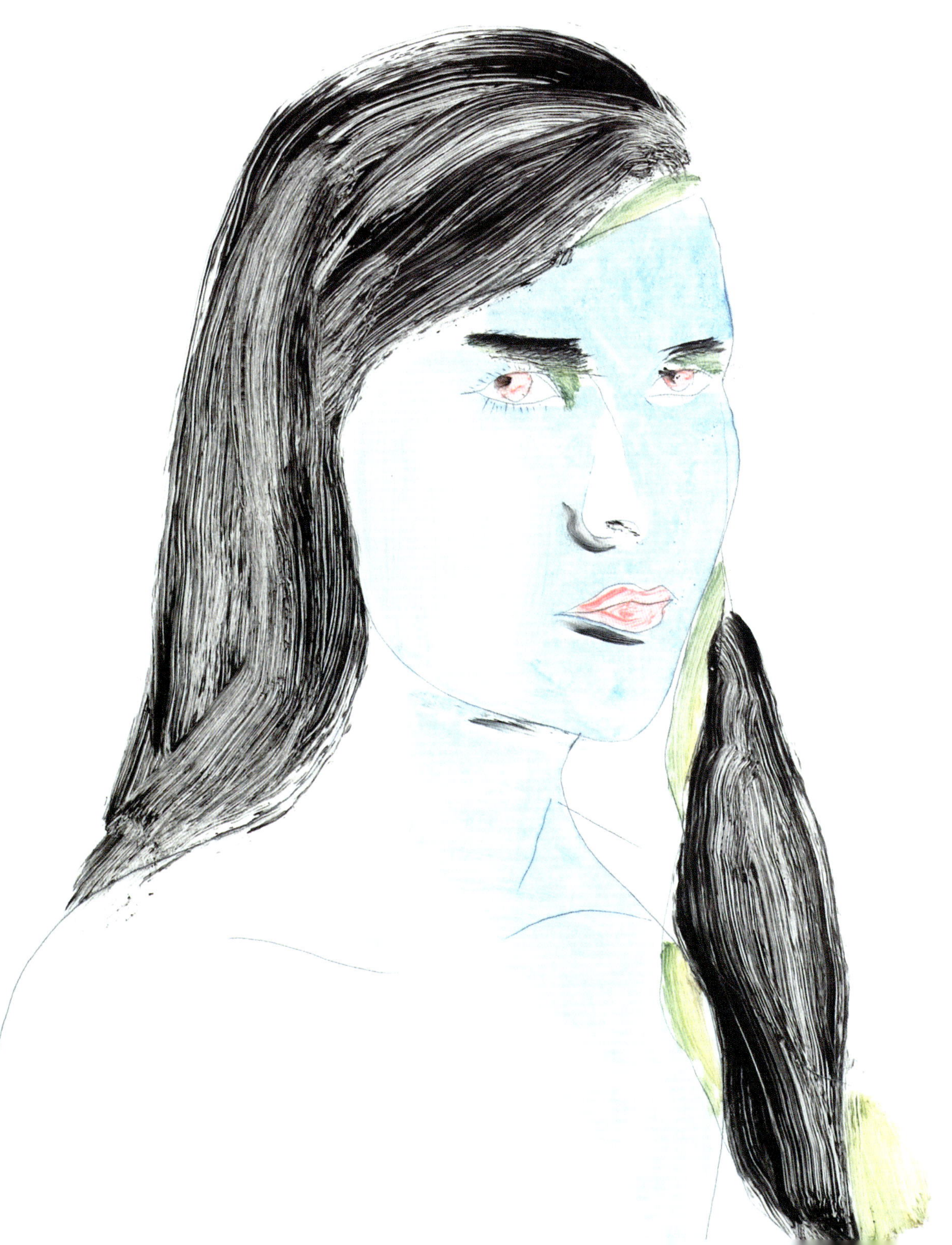

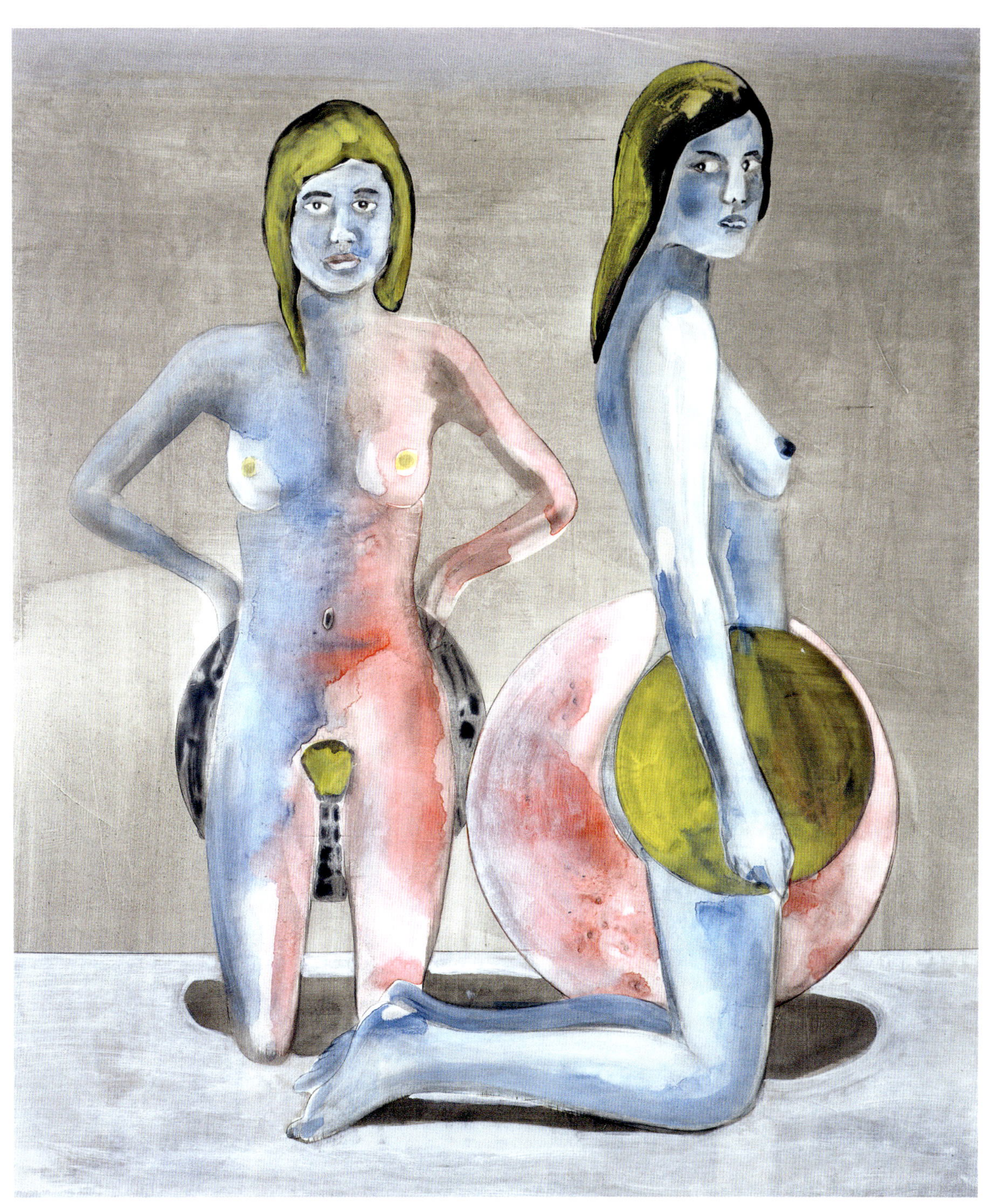

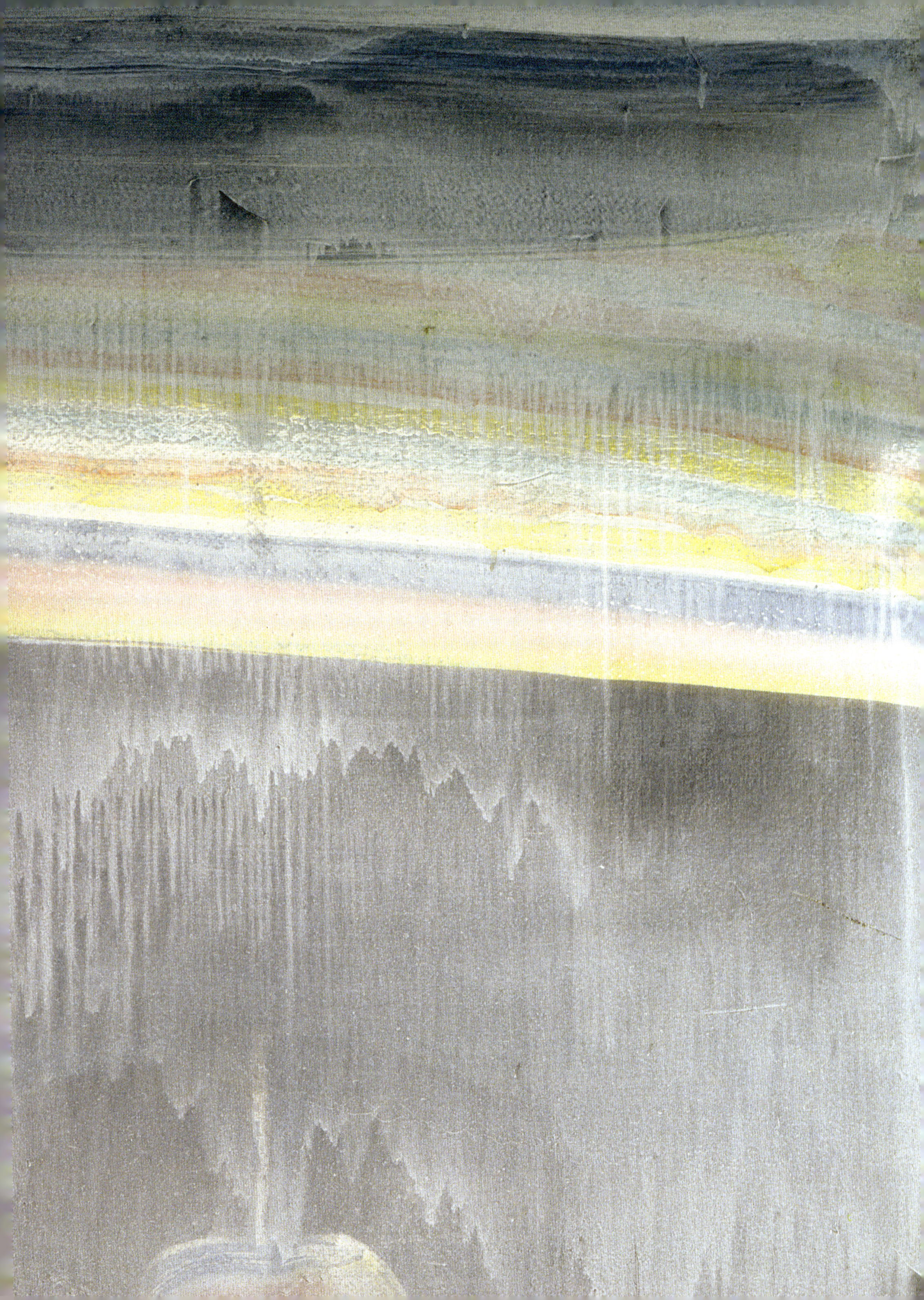

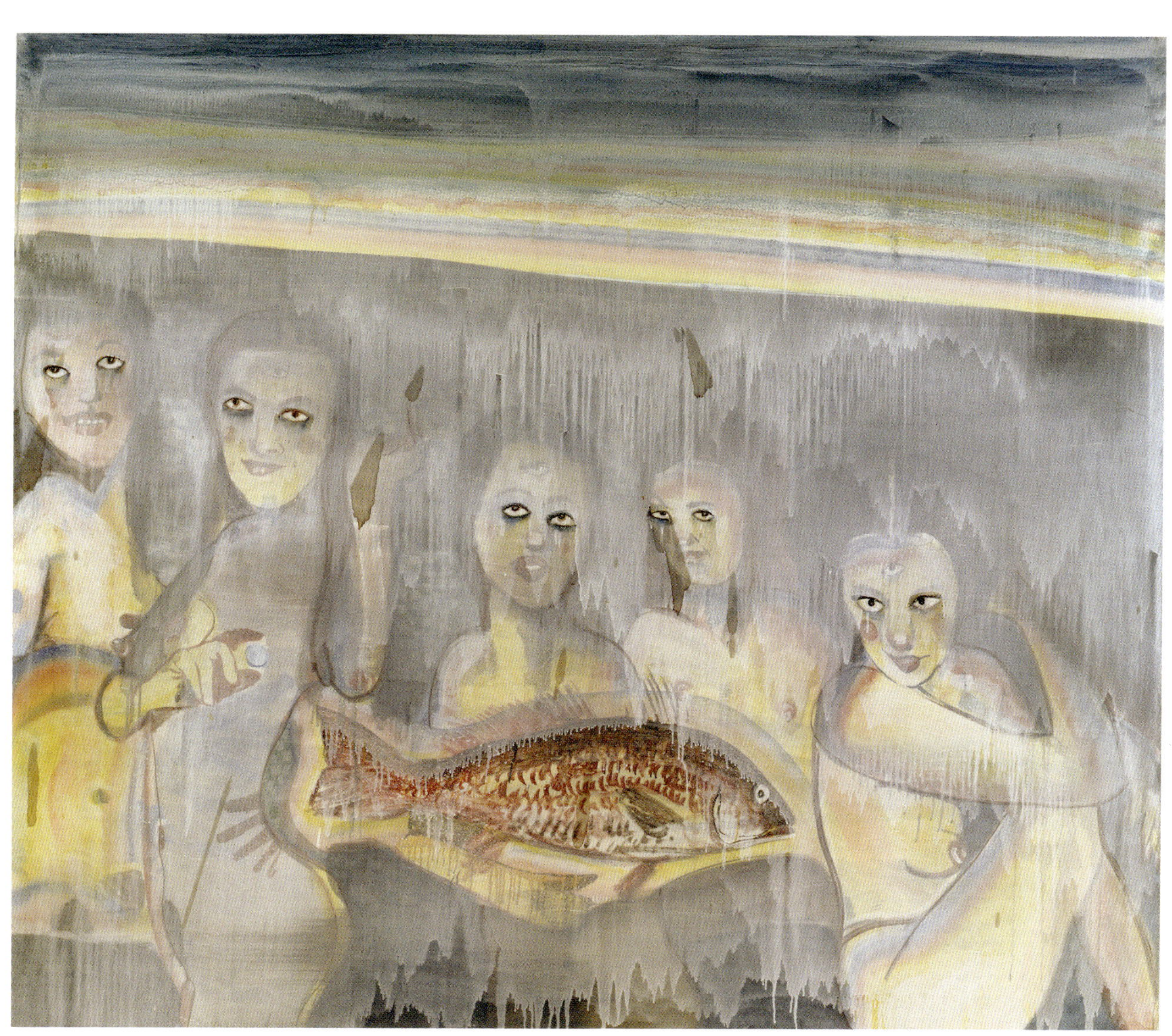

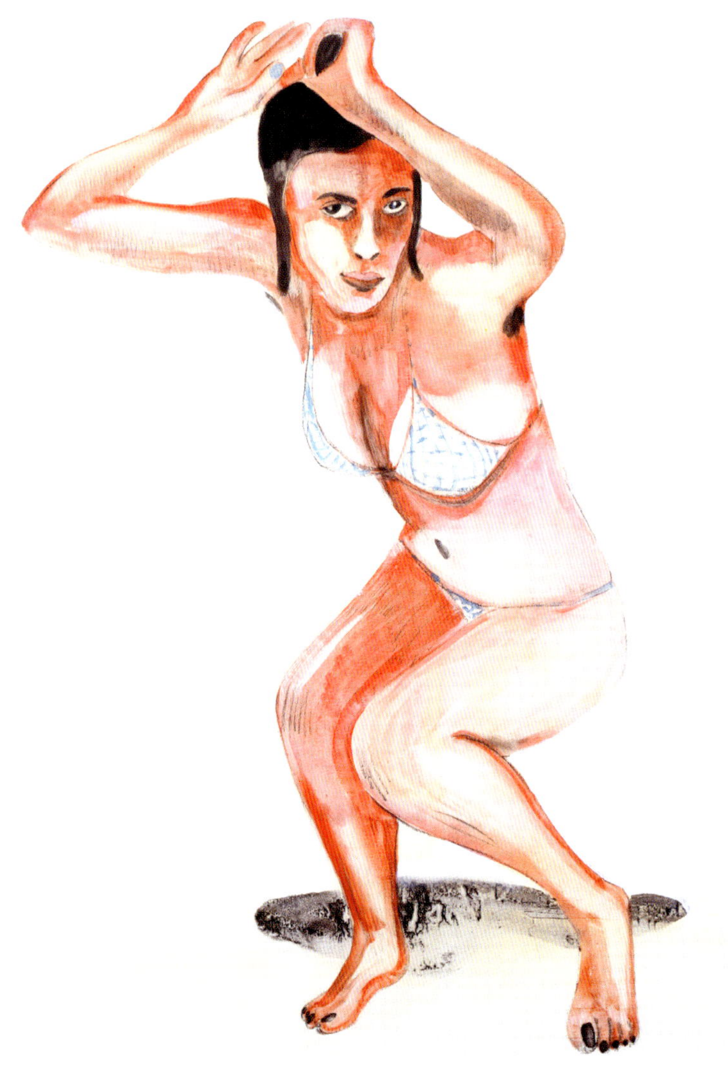

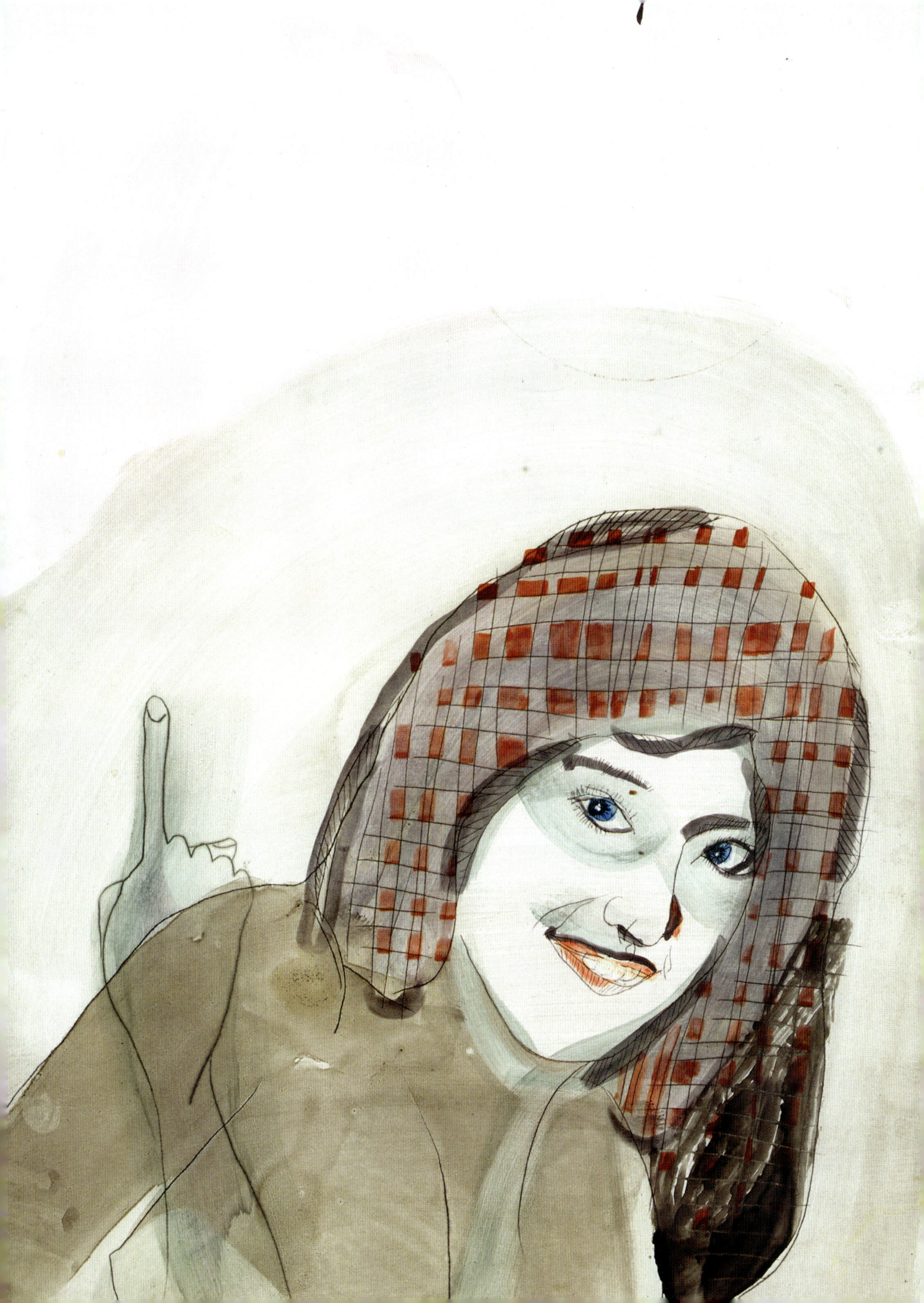

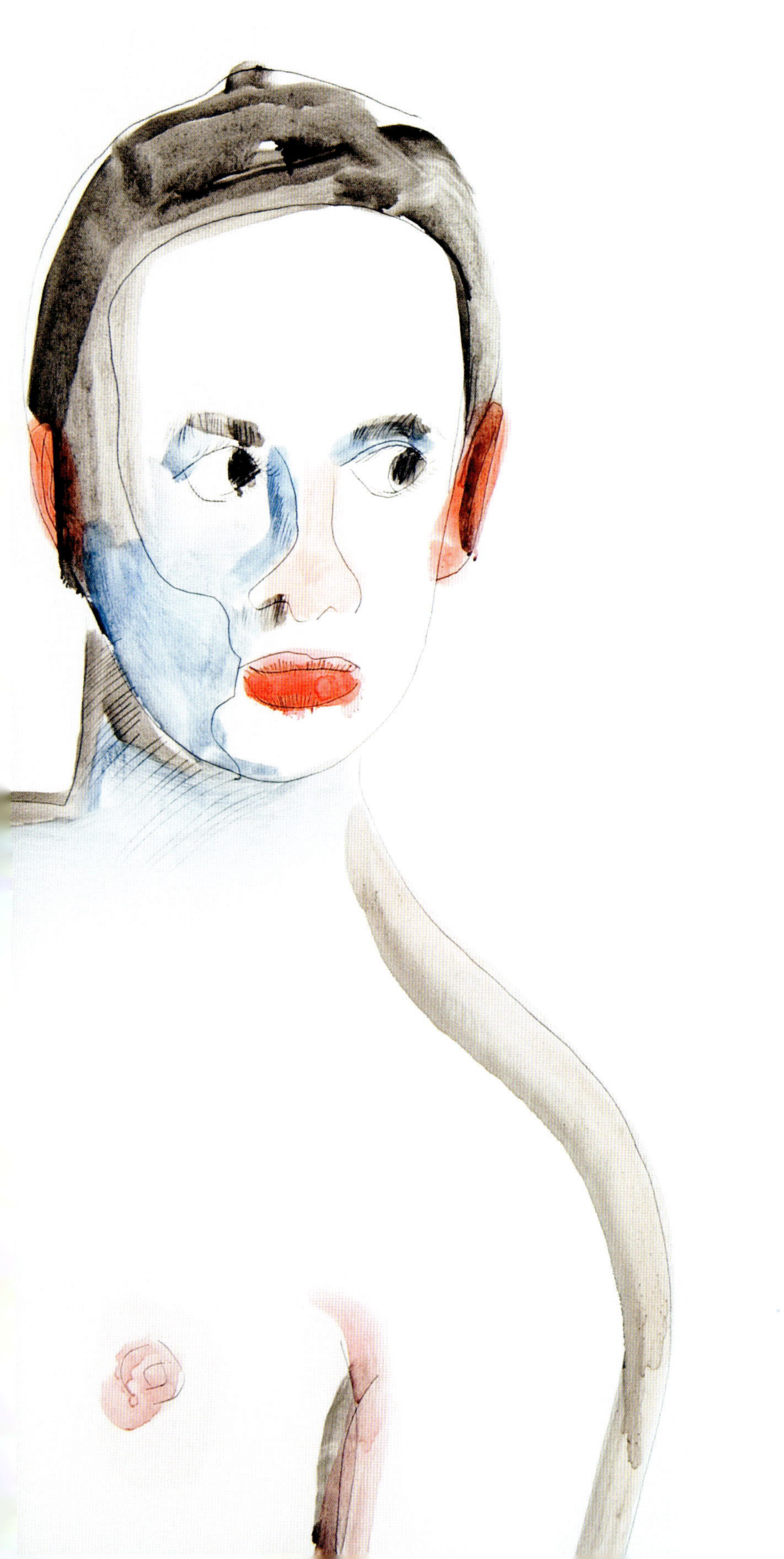

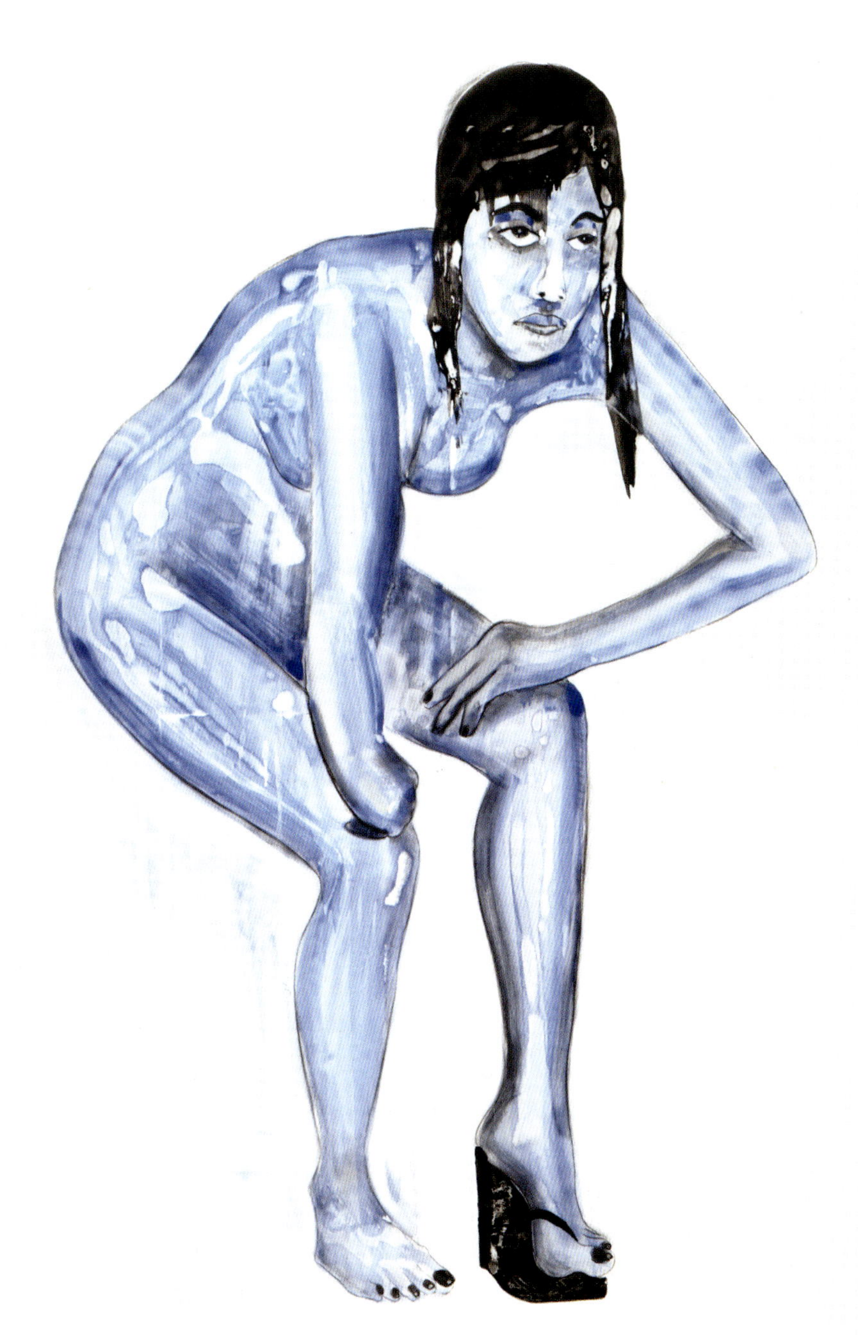

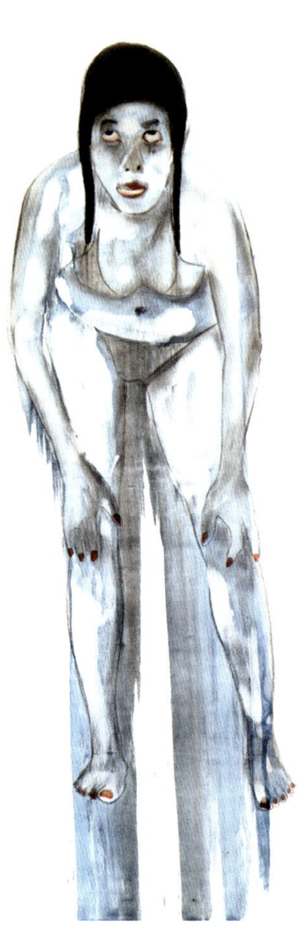

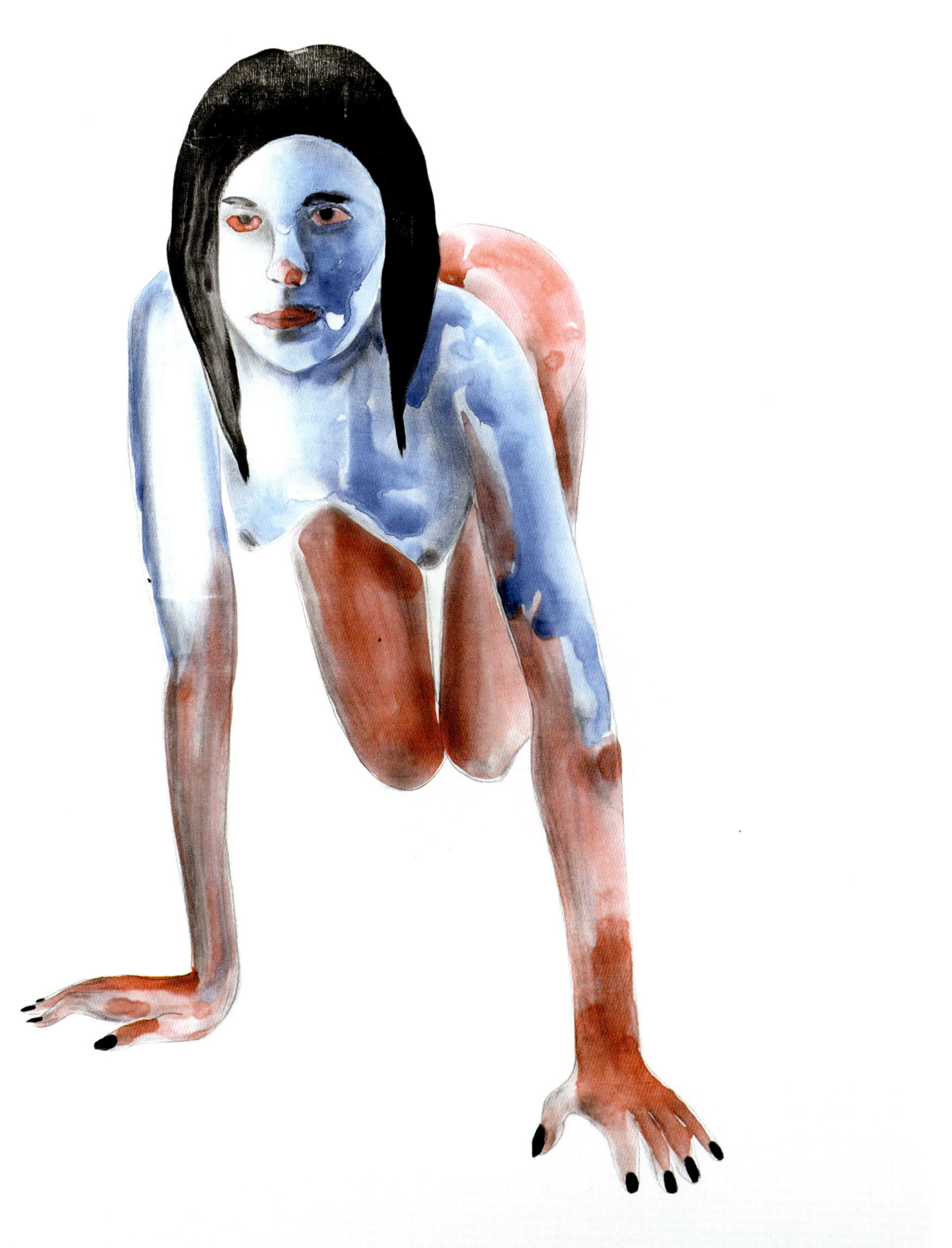

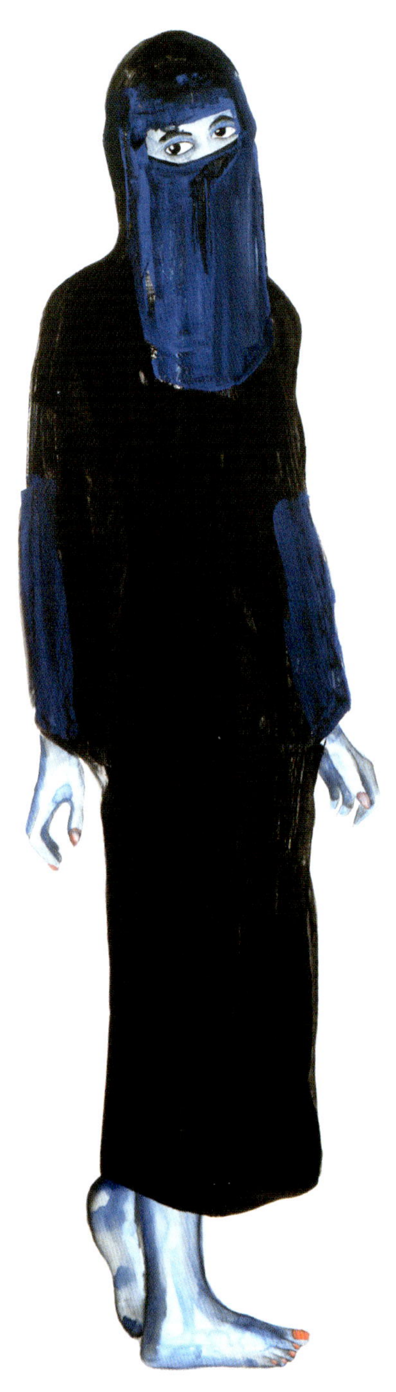

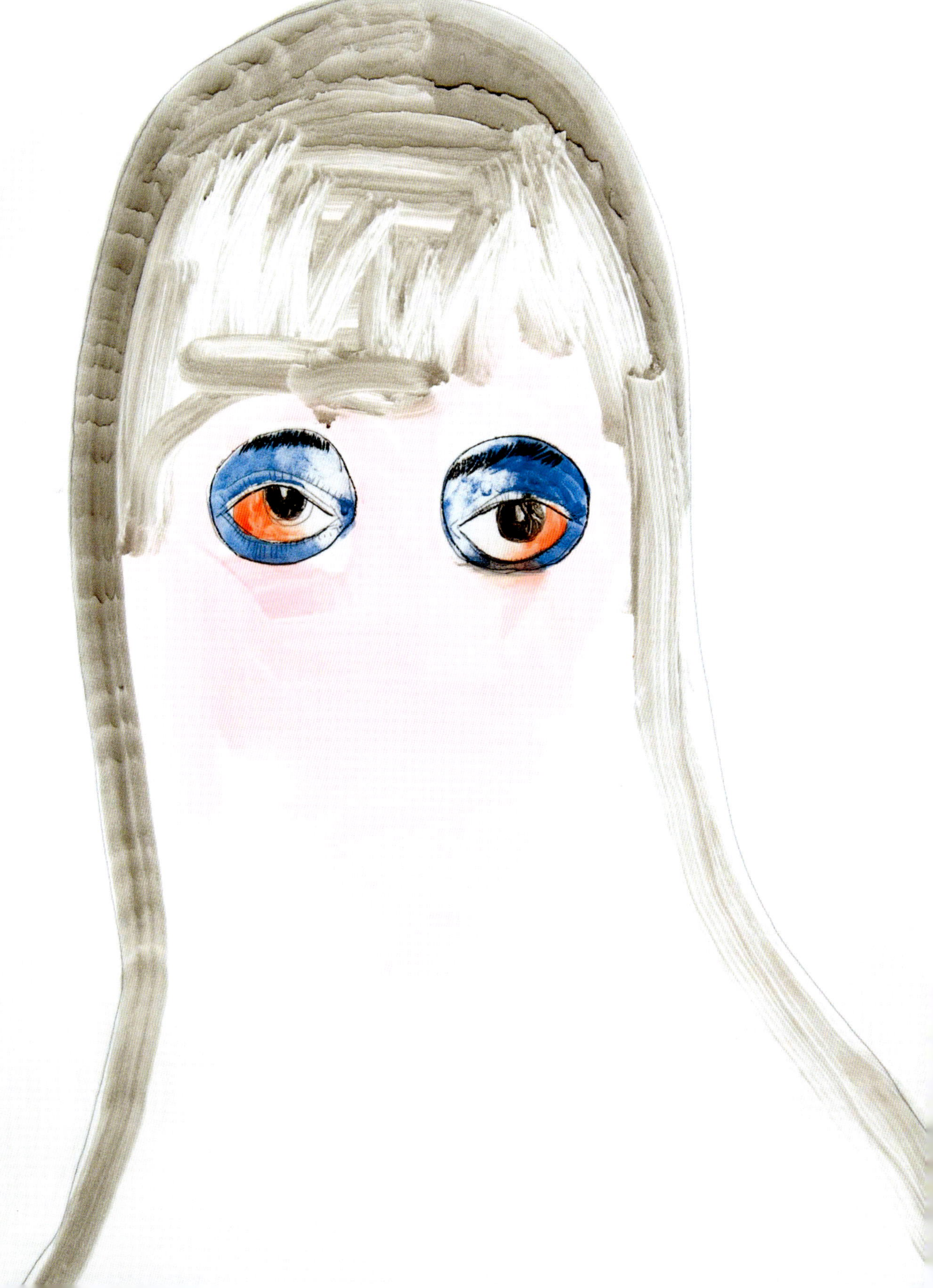

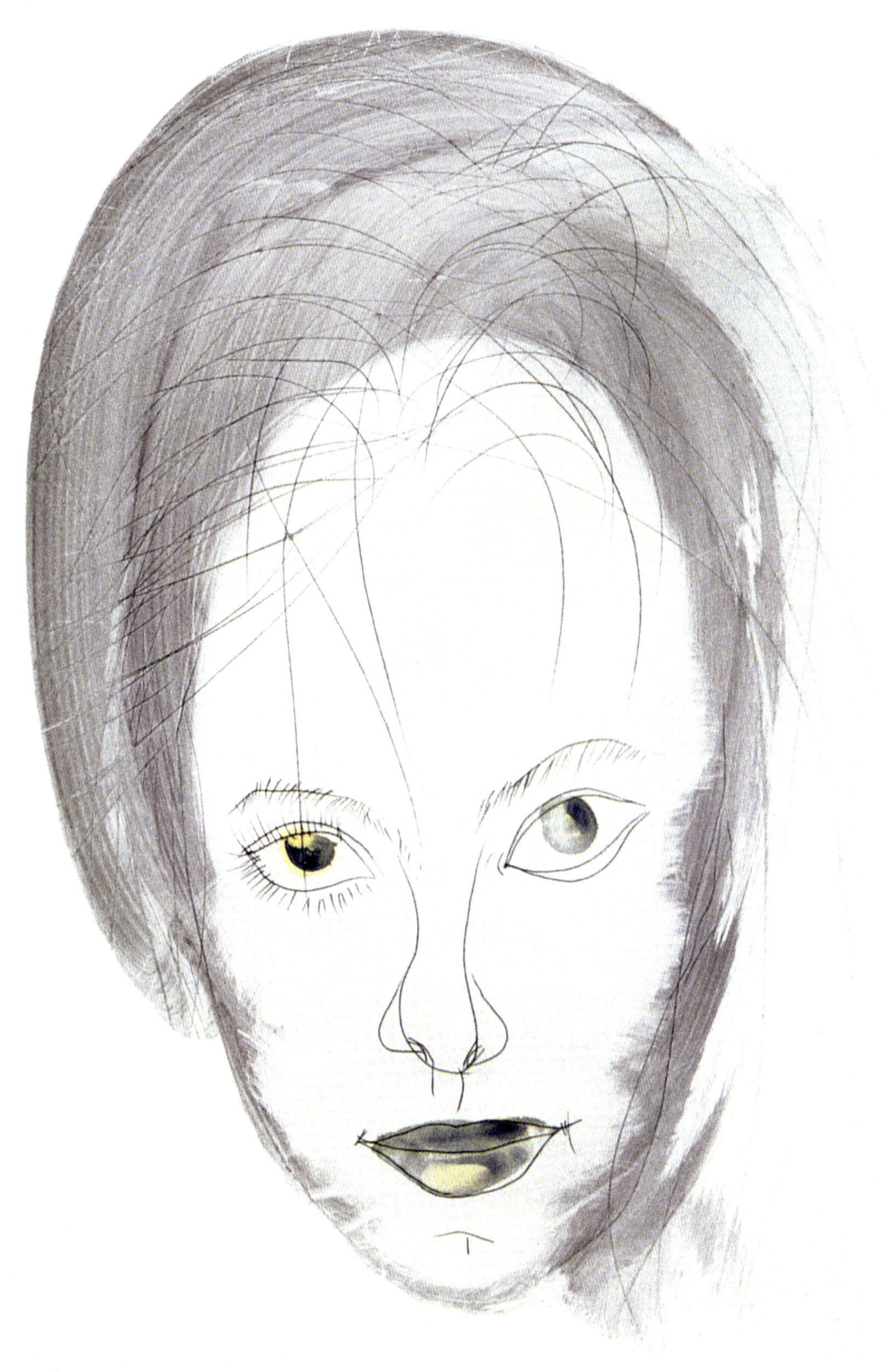

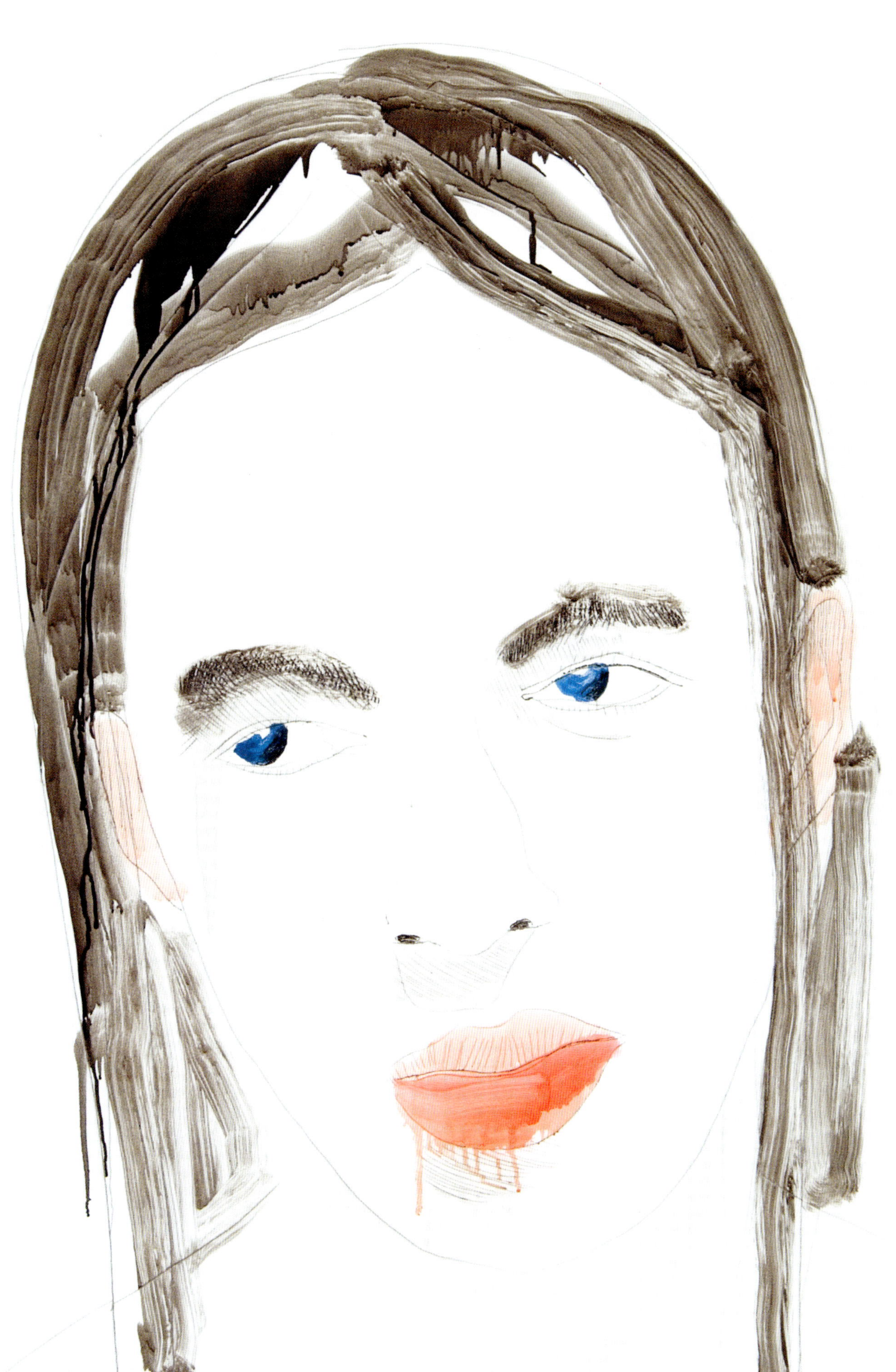

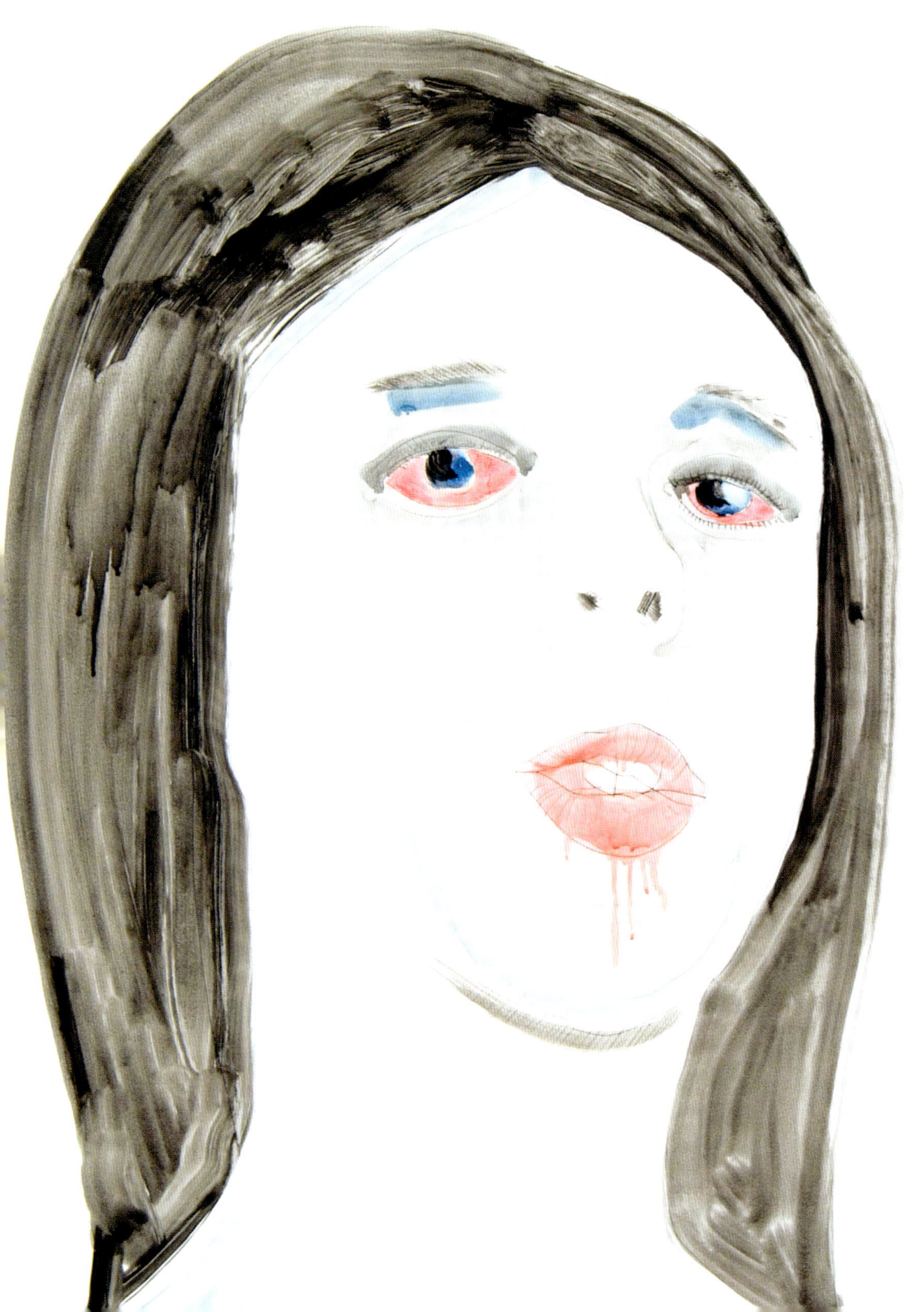

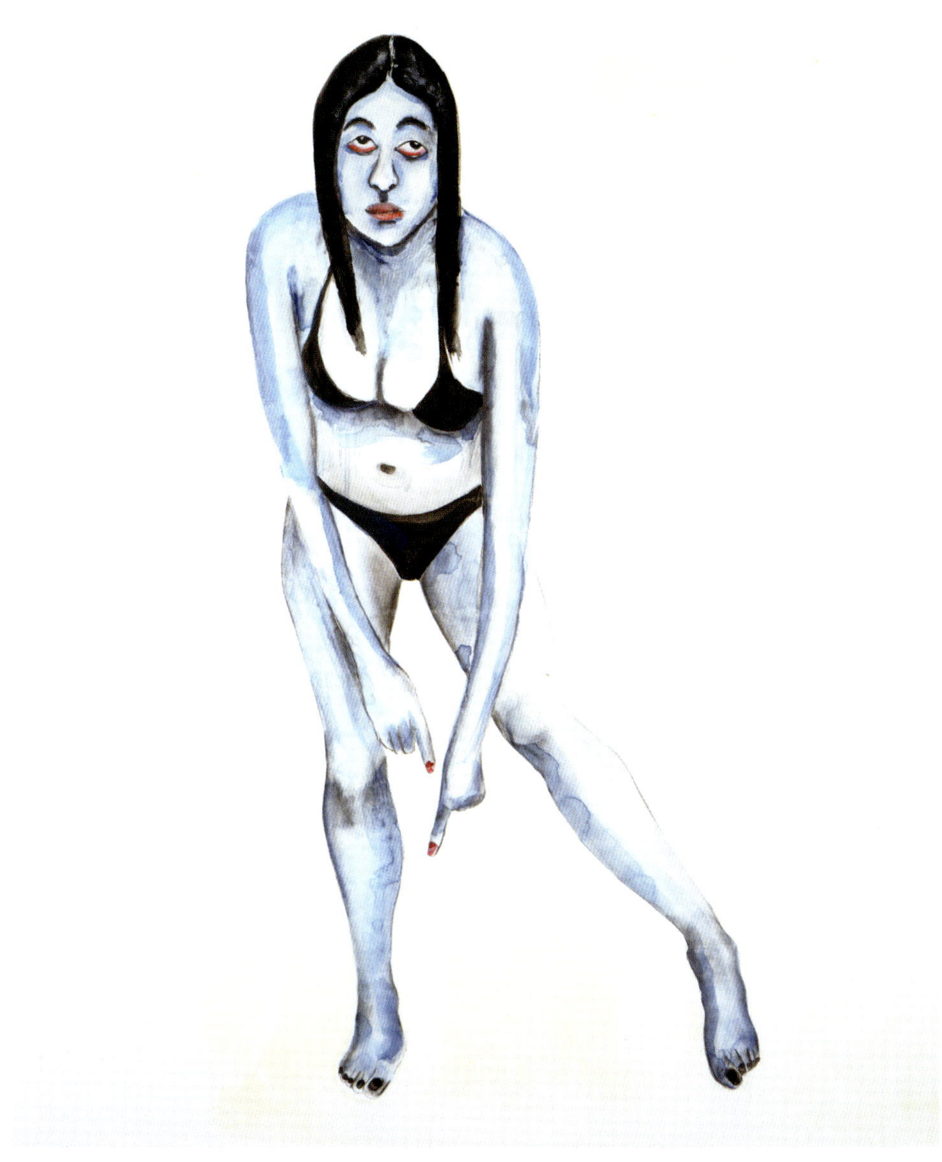

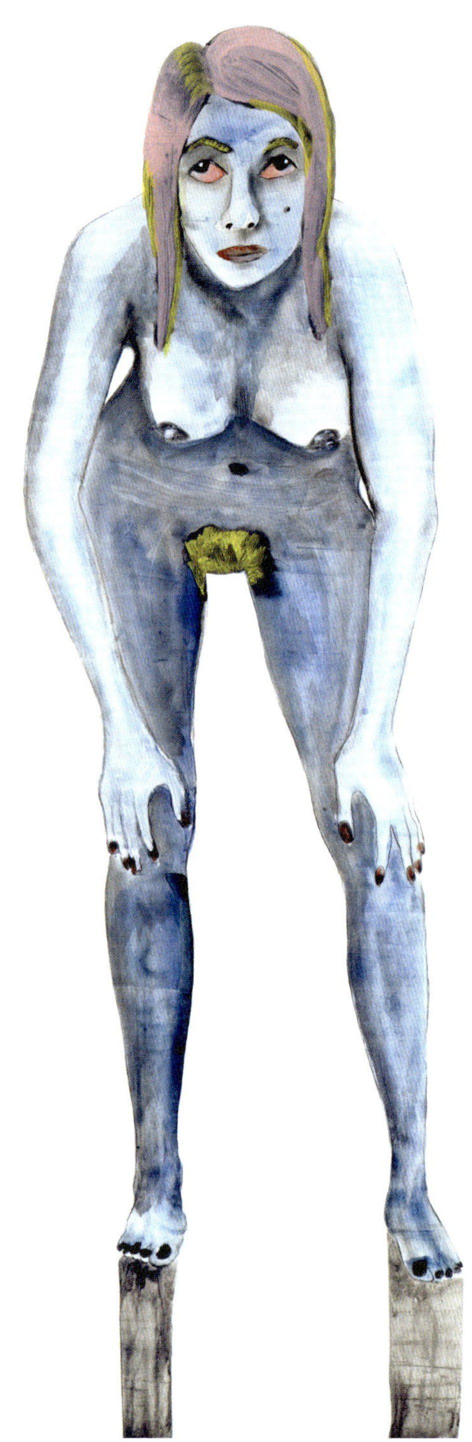

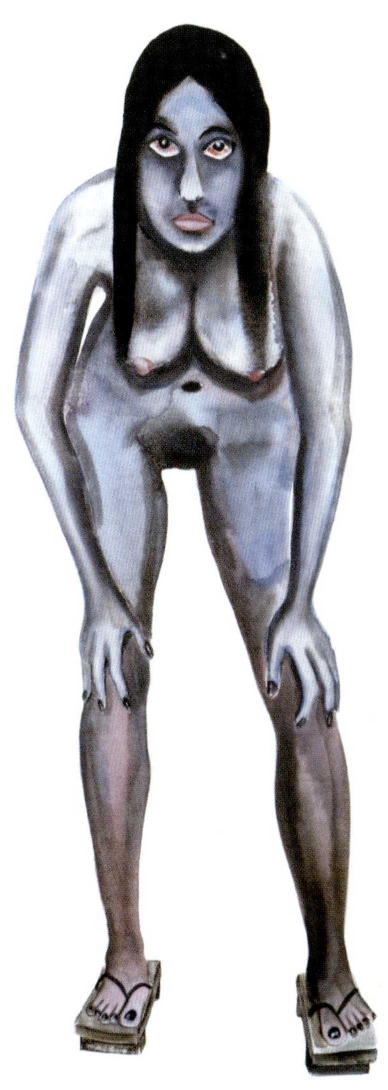

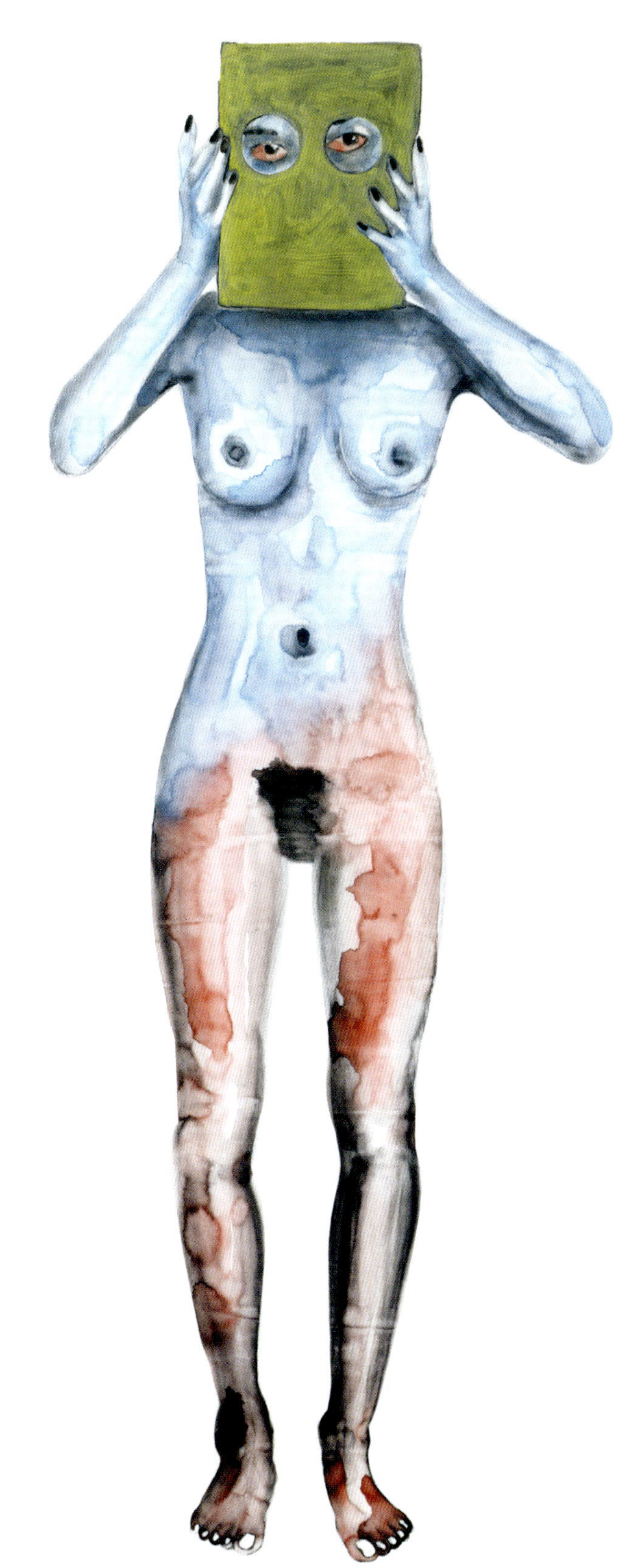

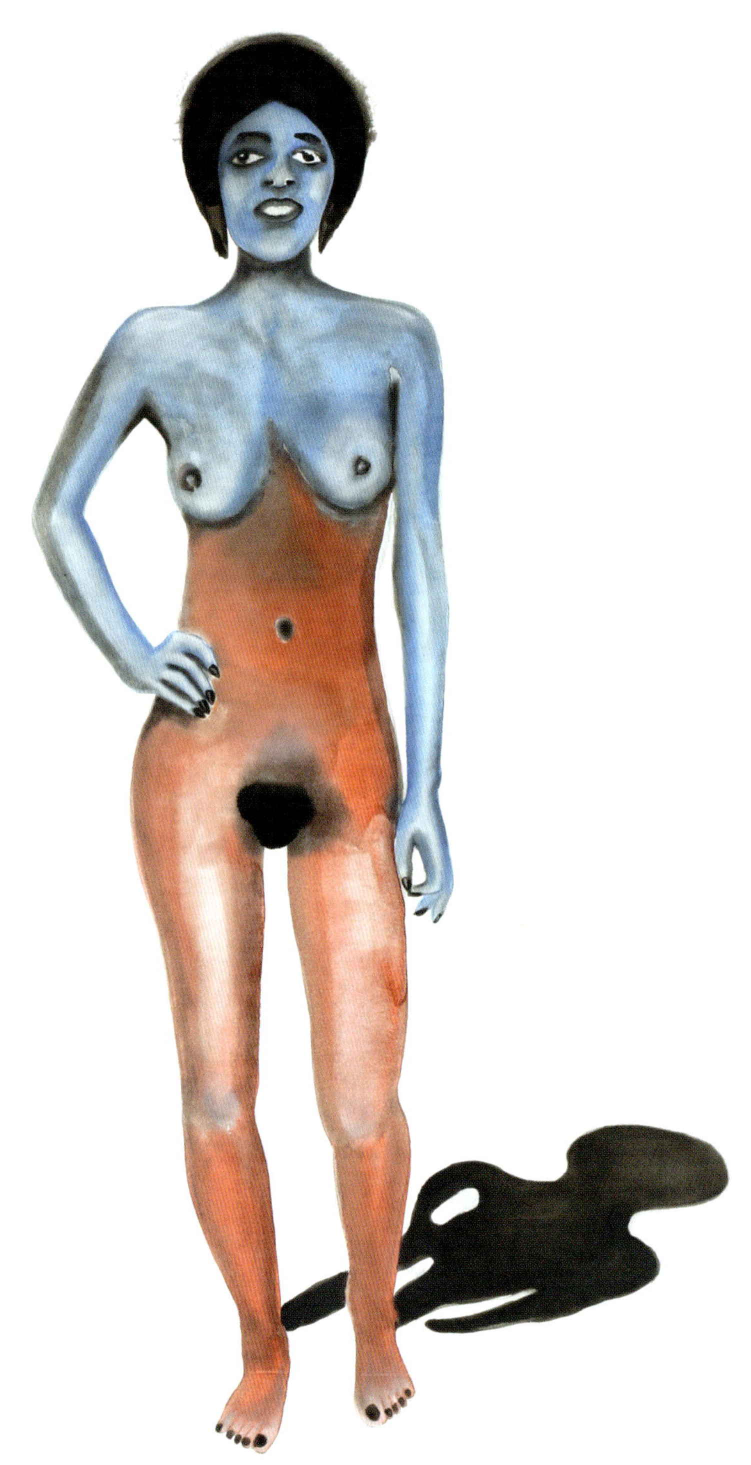

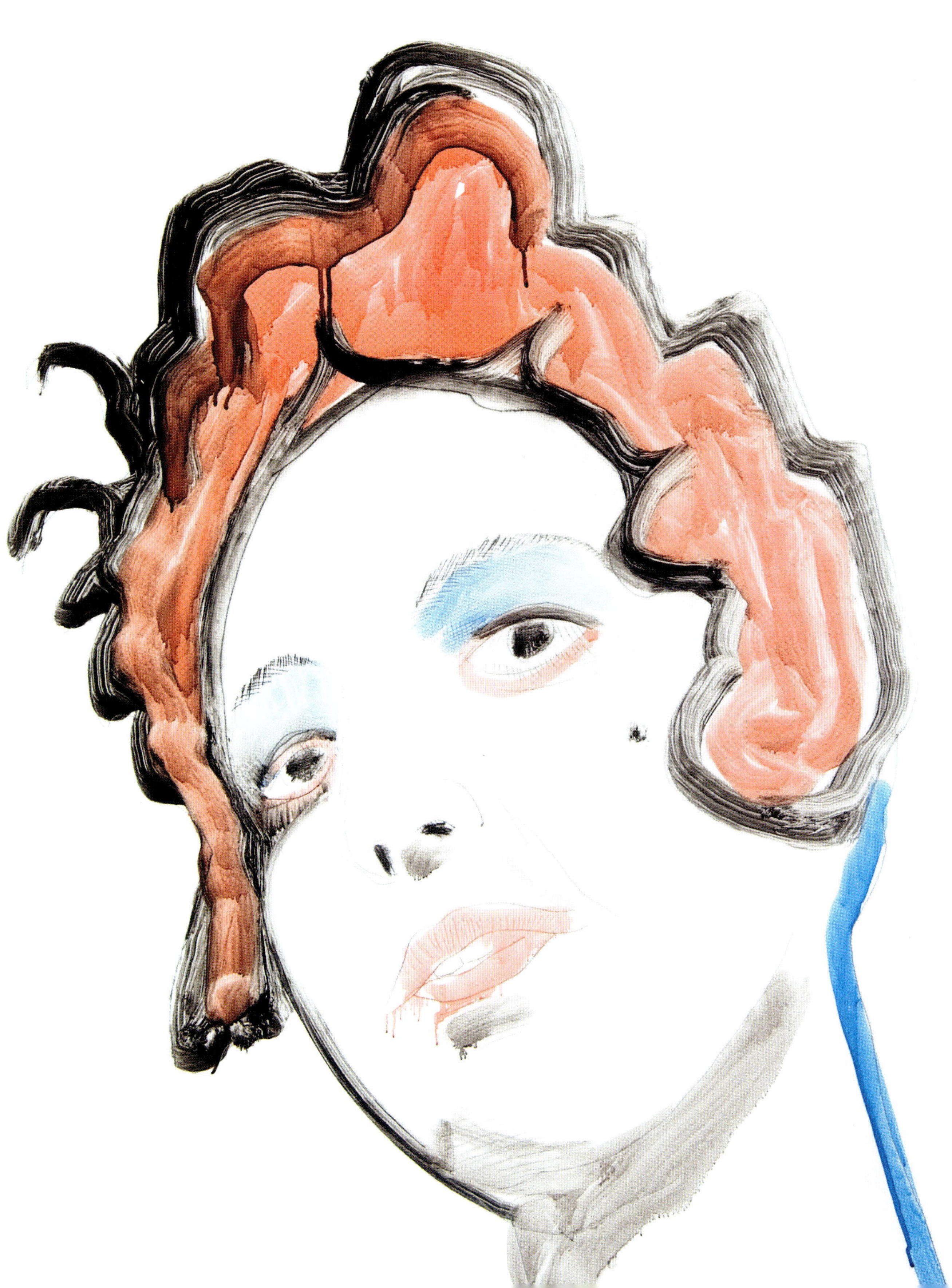

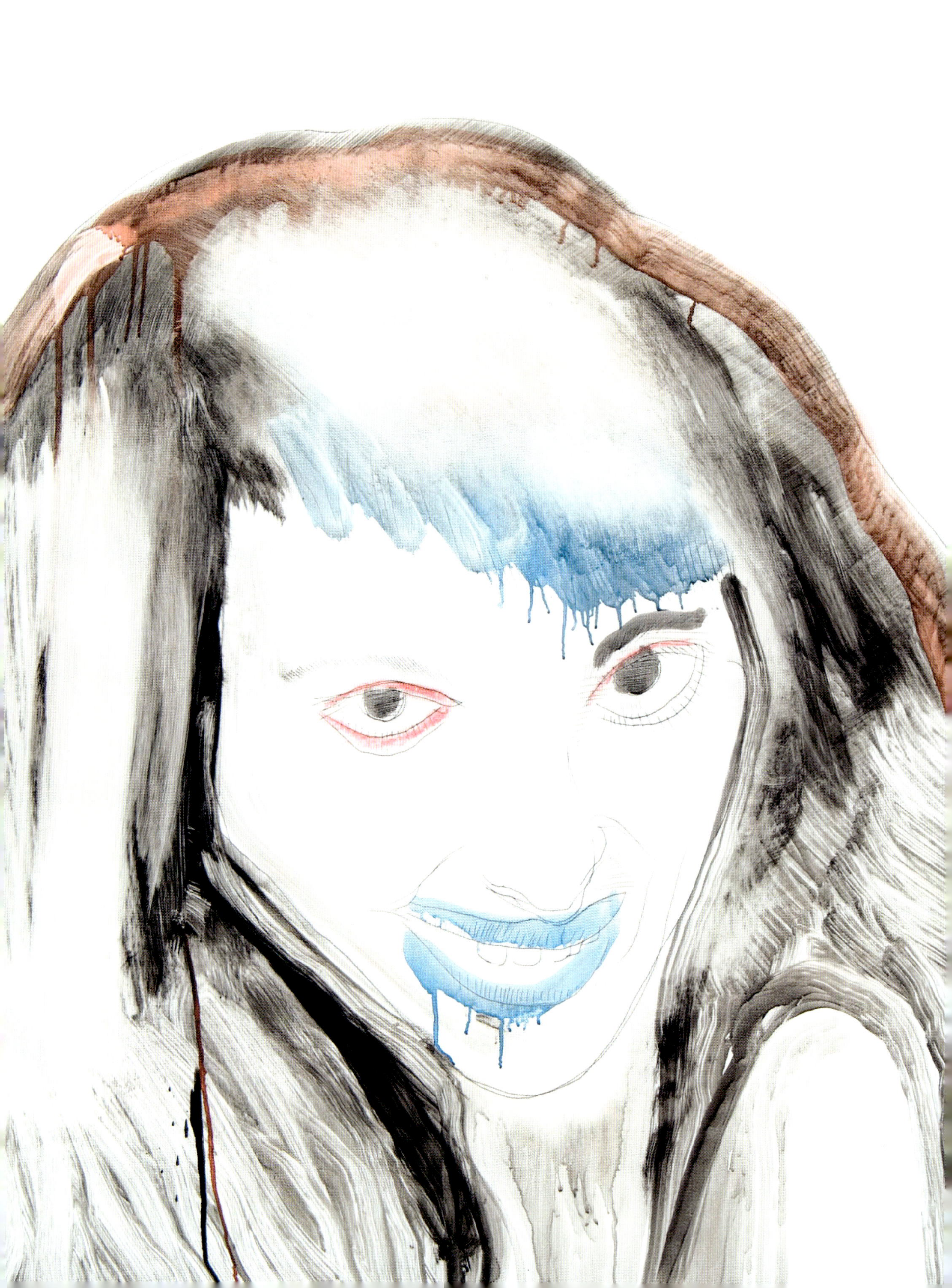

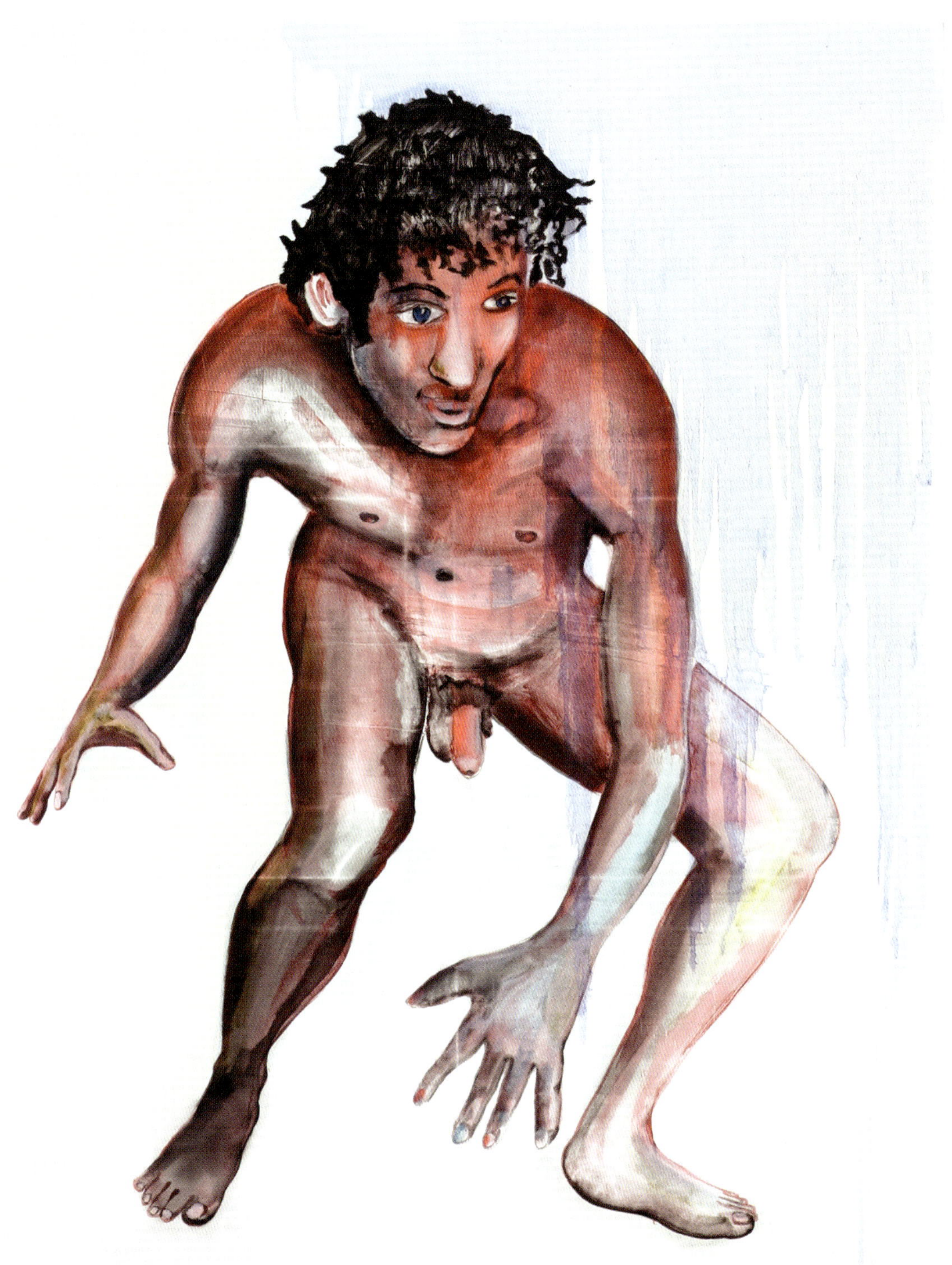

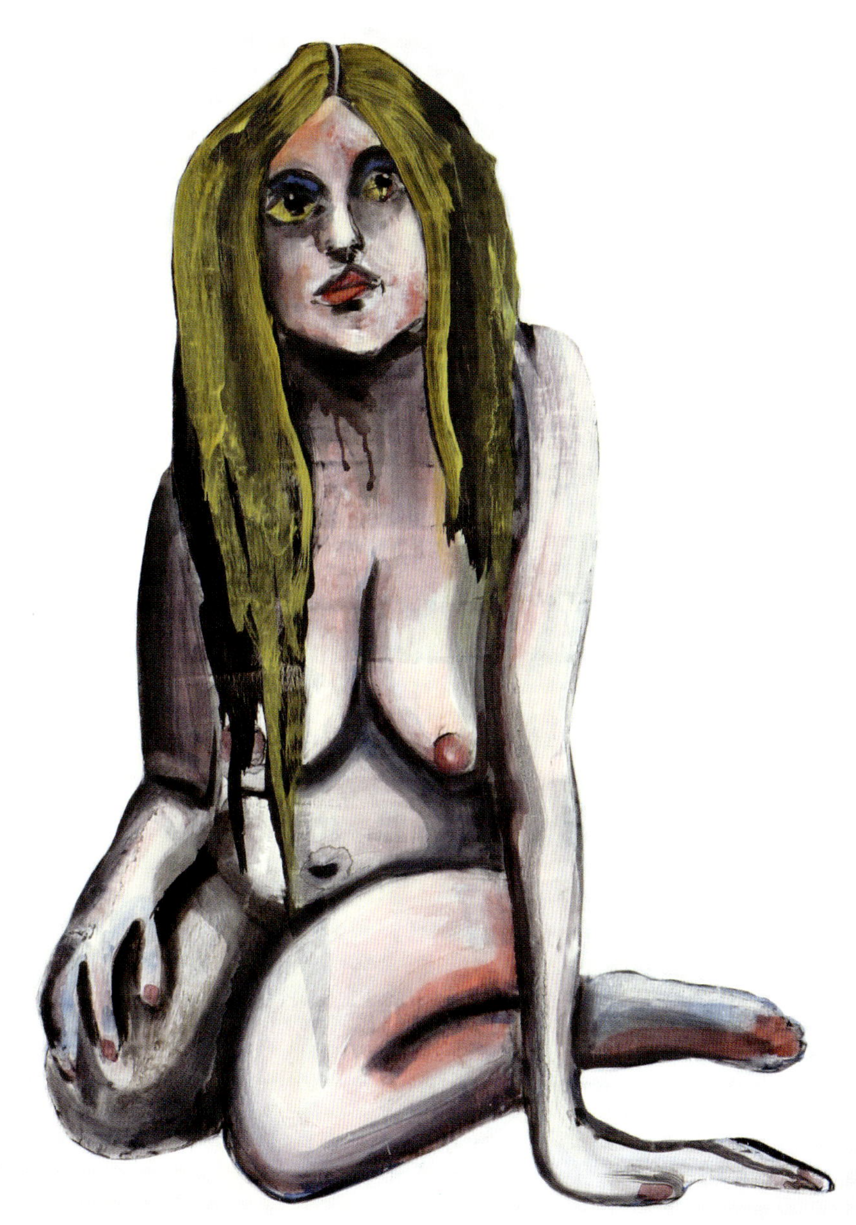

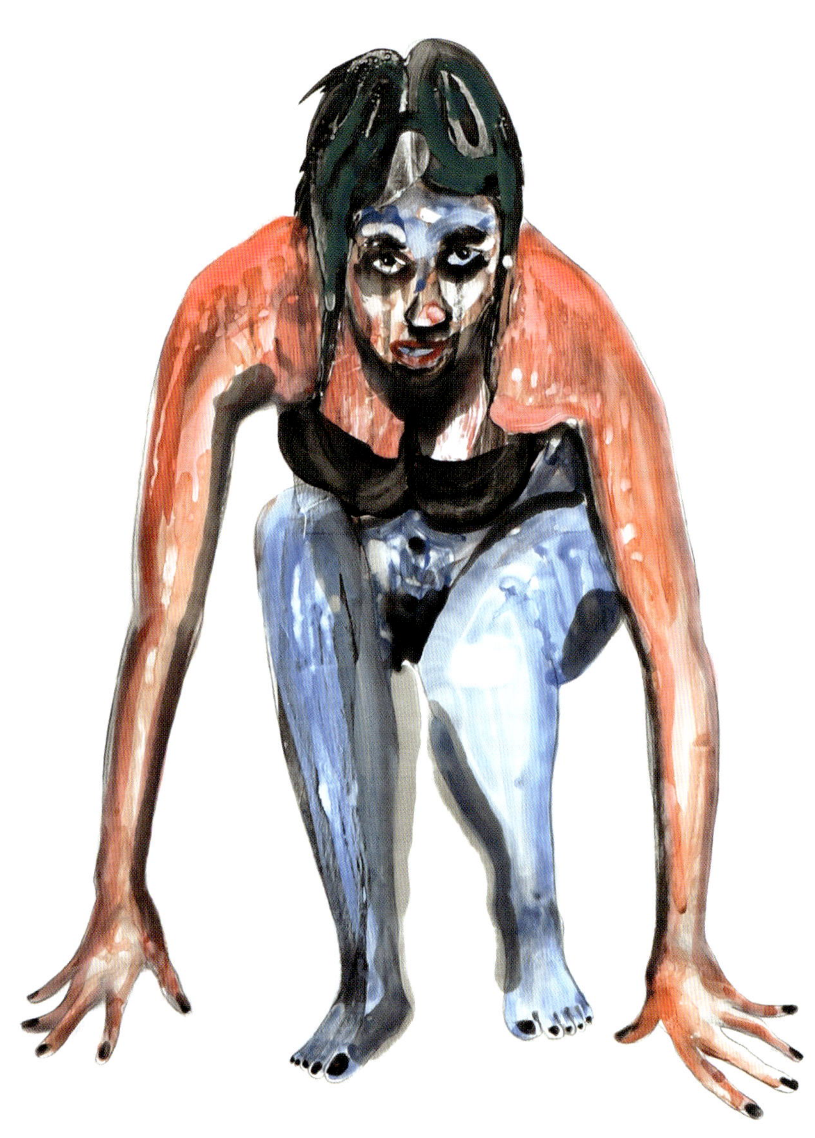

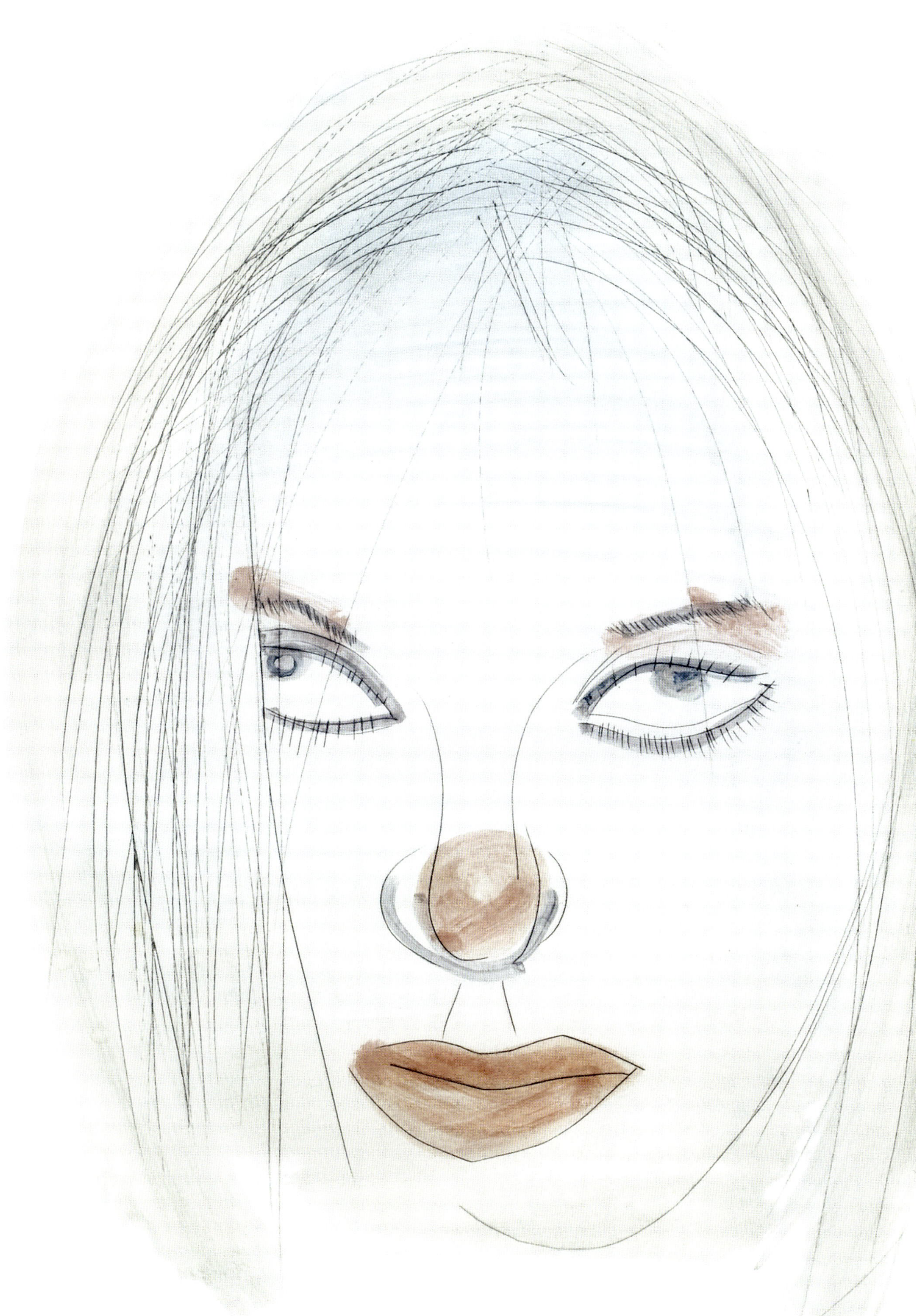

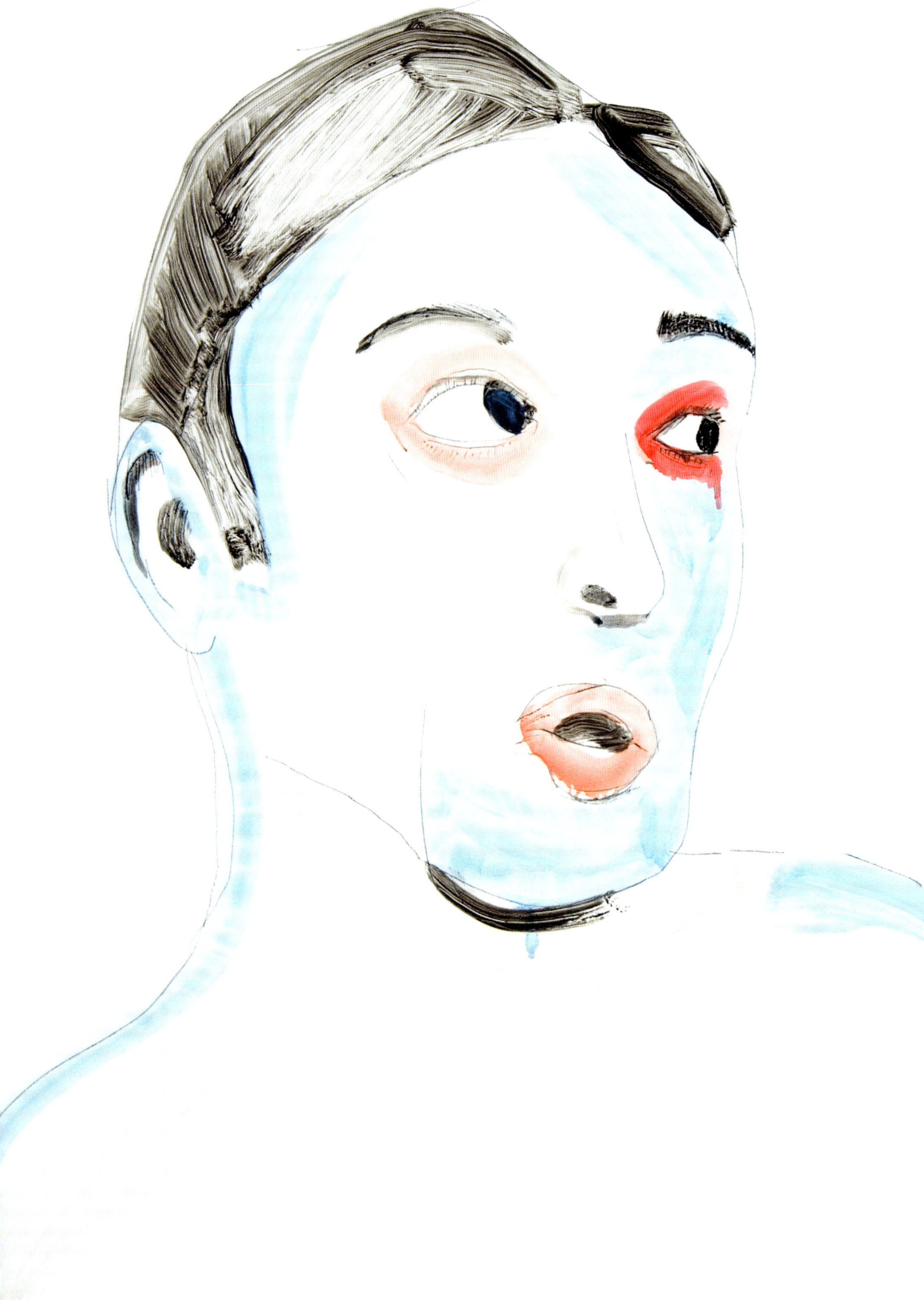

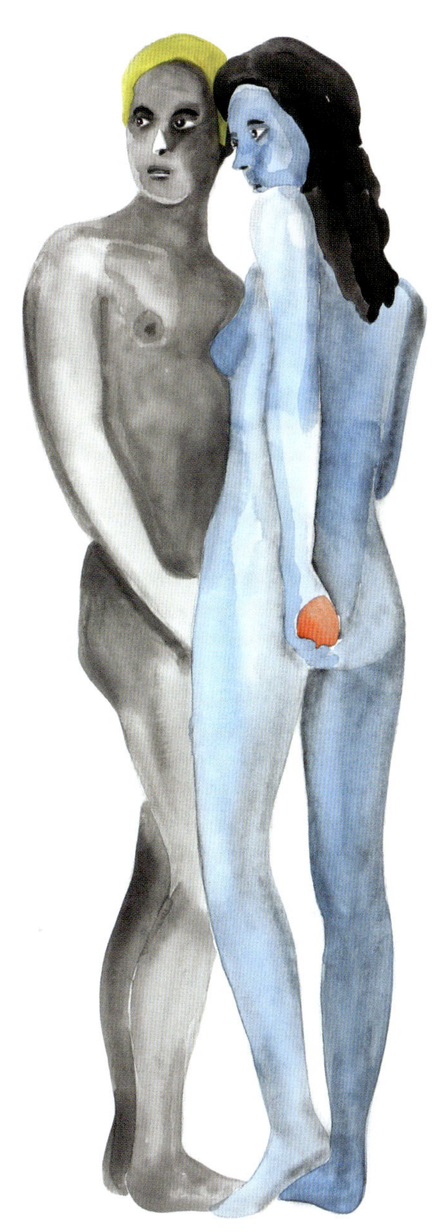

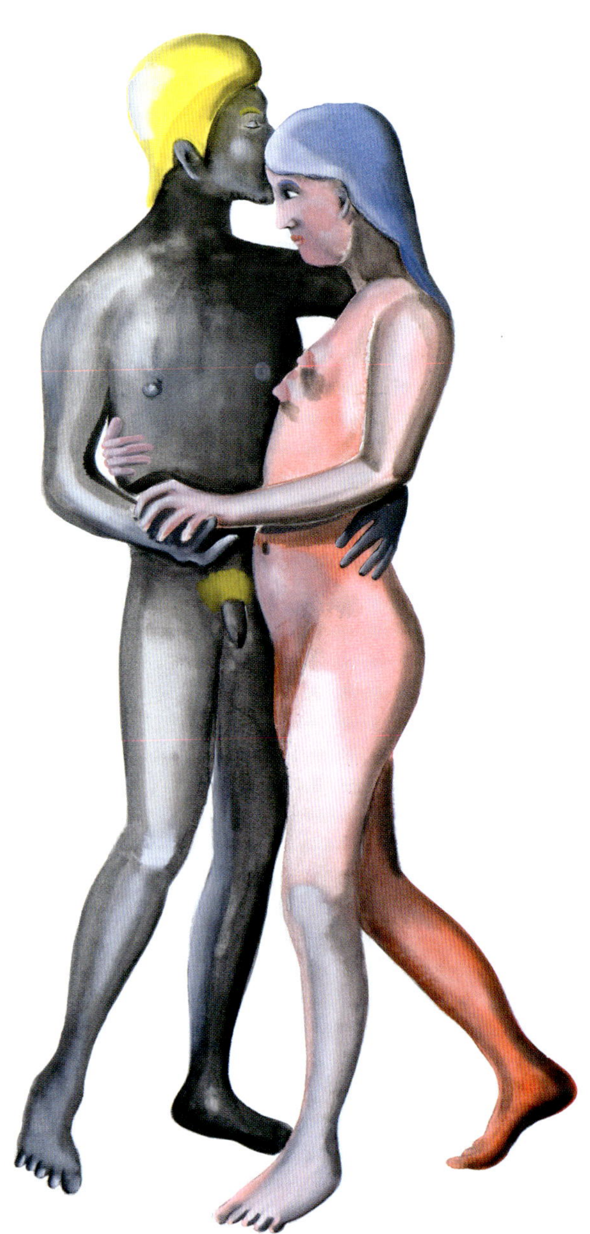

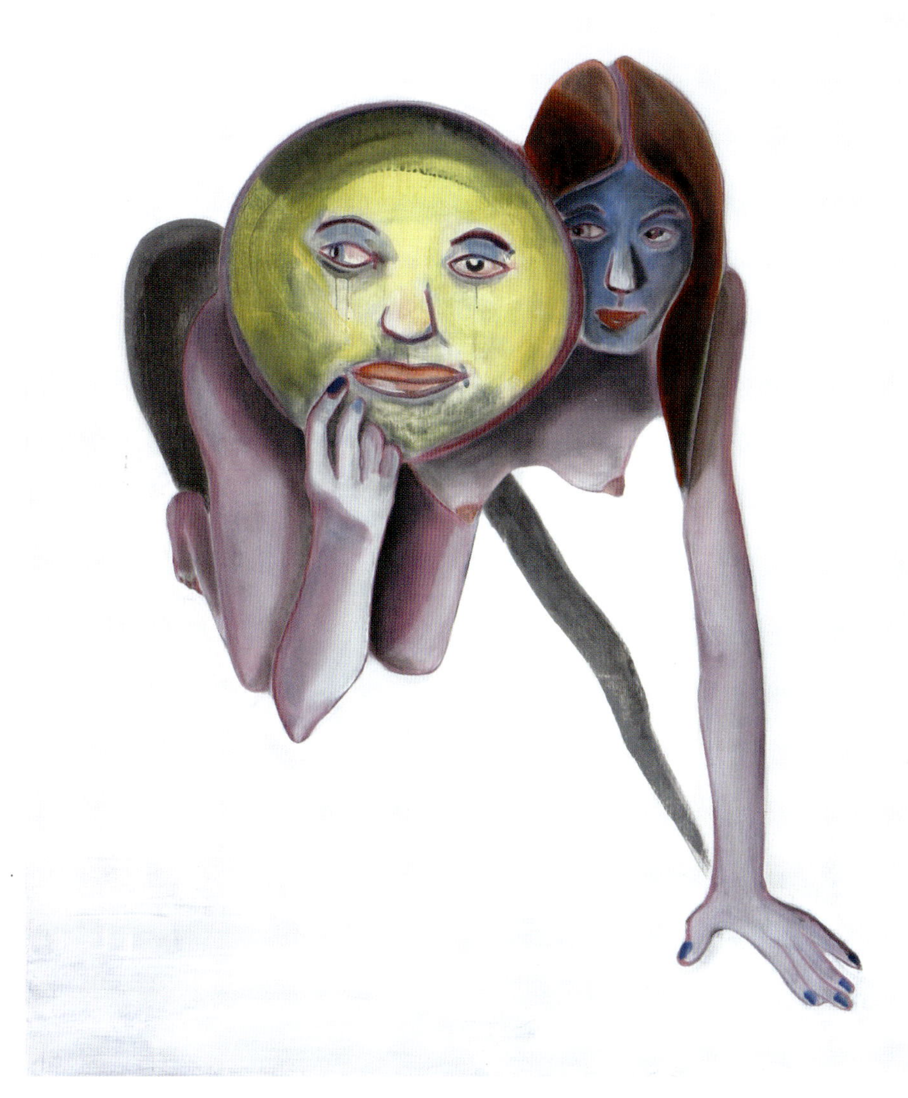

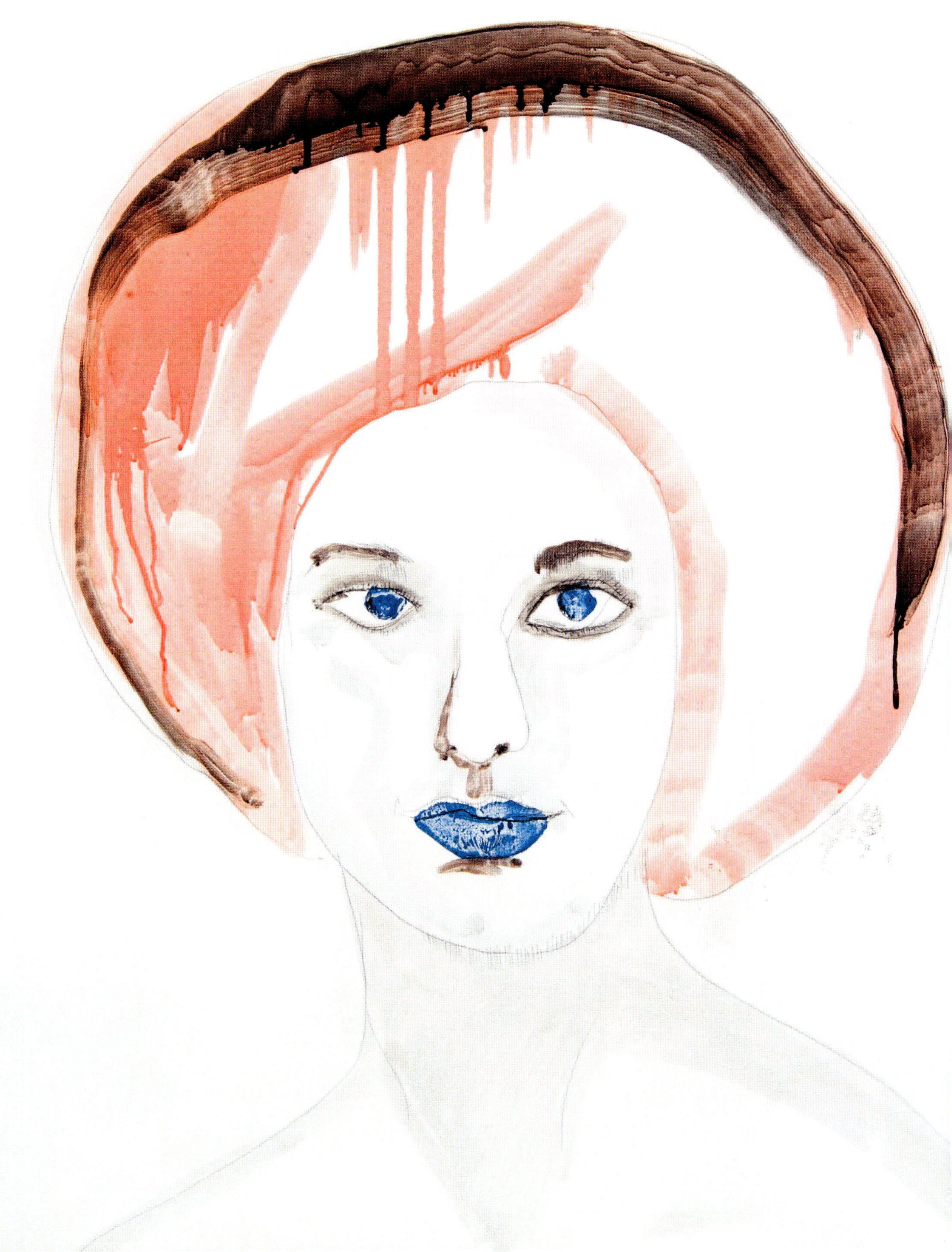

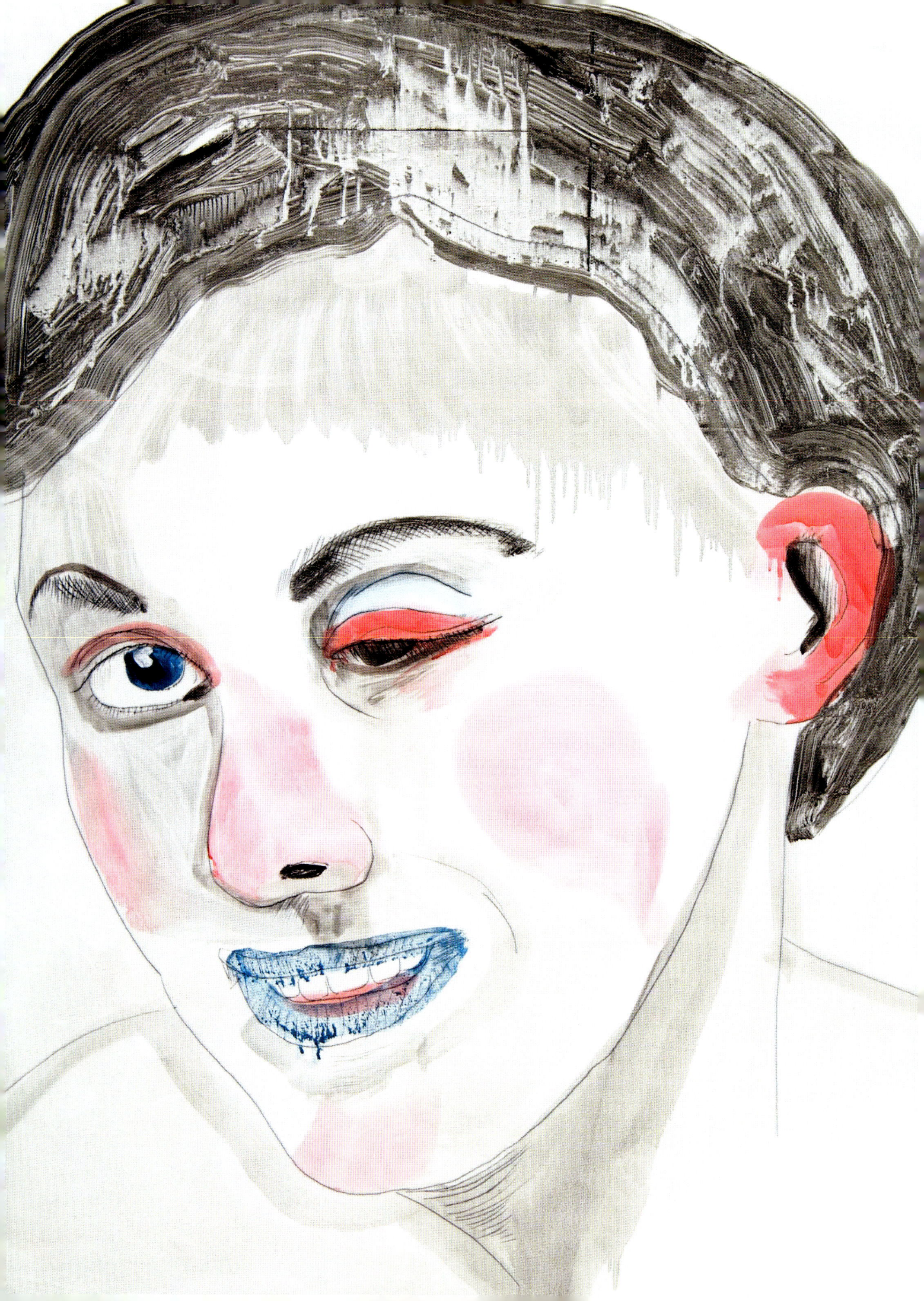

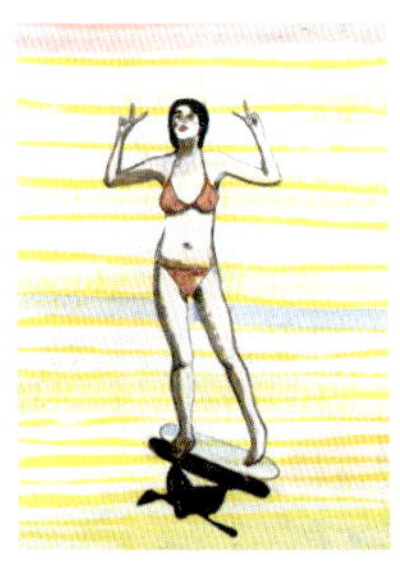

Day Ride, 2003
Oil on Canvas
42 x 36 inches

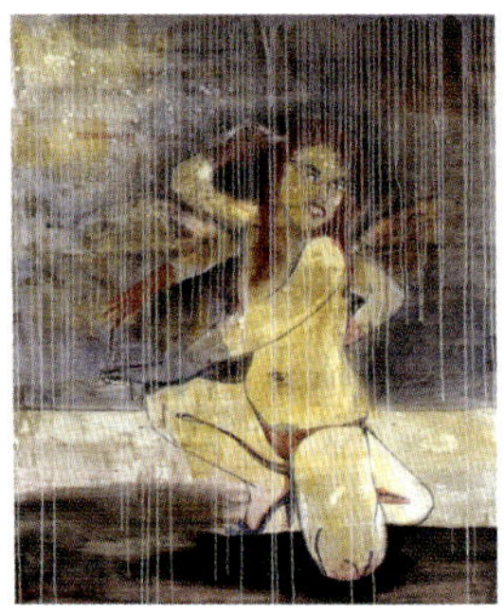

Annapurna, 1999/00
Oil and Enamel on Wood
60 x 48 inches

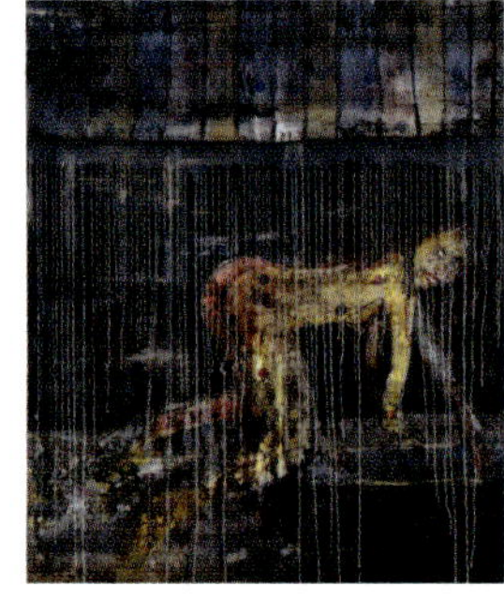

Dablam, 1999/00
Oil and Enamel on Canvas
61 x 49 inches

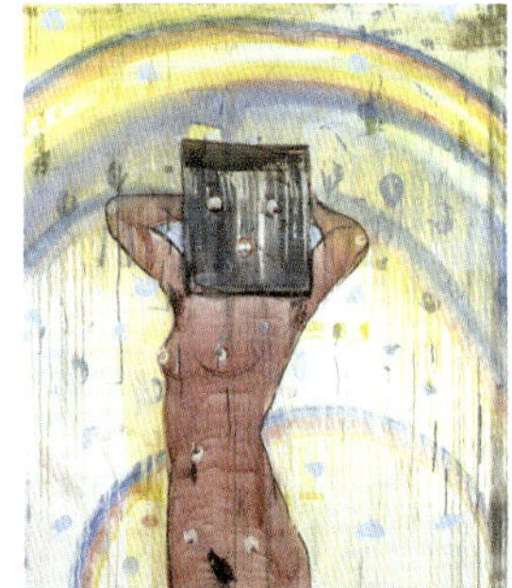

Flemish Cap, 2000
Oil and Enamel on Canvas
62 inches x 56 inches

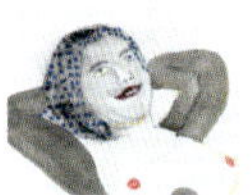

Untitled, 1999
Oil on Paper
27 1/2 x 20 inches

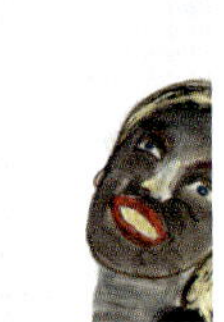

Untitled, 1999
Oil on Paper
27 1/2 x 20 inches

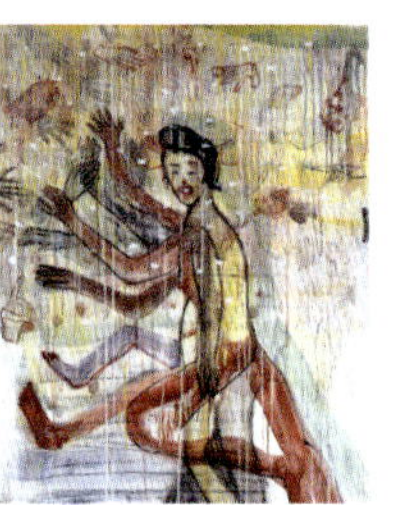

*All these moments lost in time
like tears in the rain, 1999/00*
Oil and Enamel on Canvas
61 1/2 x 49 inches

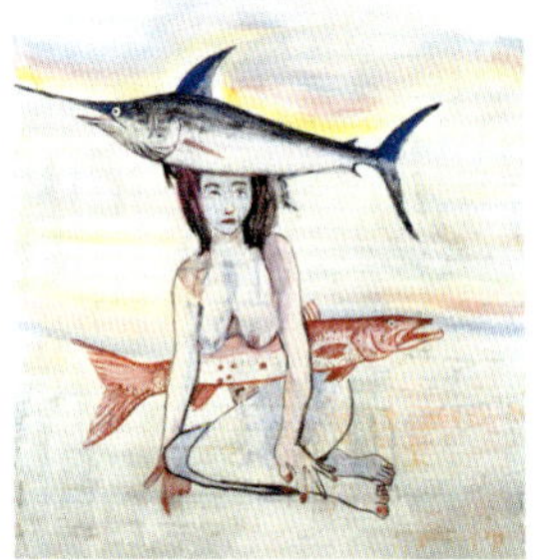

The Gift, 1999-2000
Oil and Enamel on Canvas
66 x 60 inches

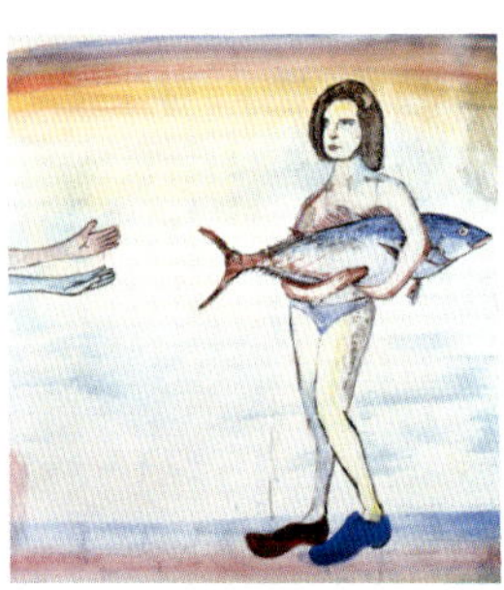

The Odessa Style, 2001
Oil on Canvas
66 x 60 inches

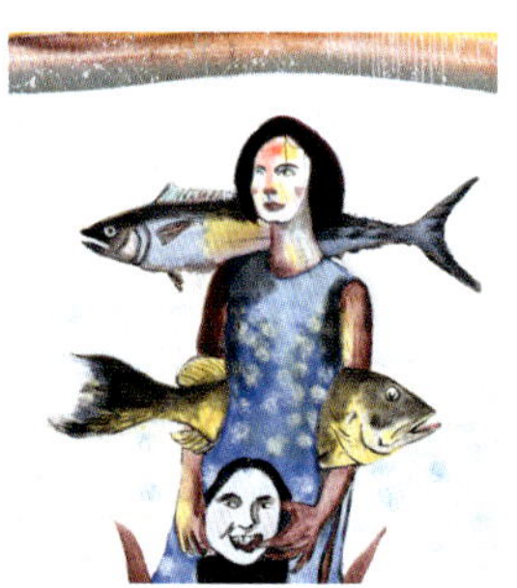

Magdelena Bay, 2001
Oil and Enamel on Canvas
62 x 56 inches

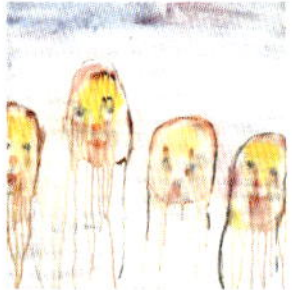

Finger Bank, 2001
Oil and Enamel on canvas
30 inches x 30 inches

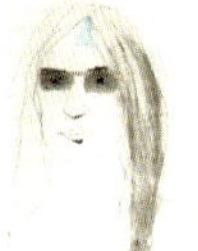

Untitled, 2005
Oil on Paper
27 x 20 inches

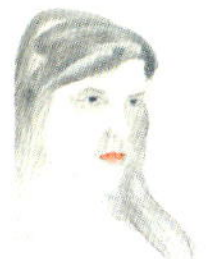

Untitled, 2005
Oil on Paper
27 x 20 inches

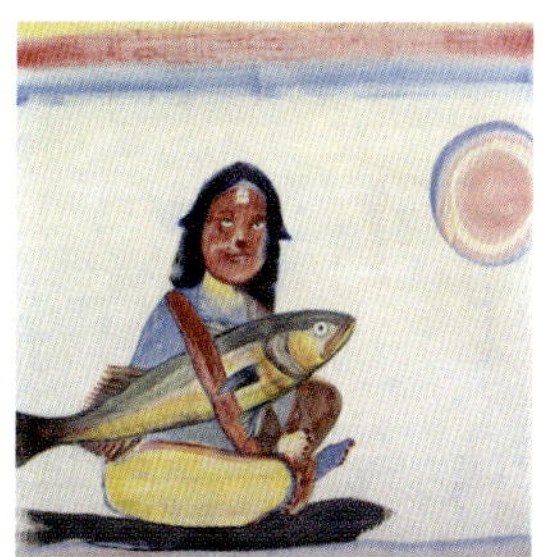

The Shotokan Bank, 2001
Oil enamel on Canvas
66 x 60 inches

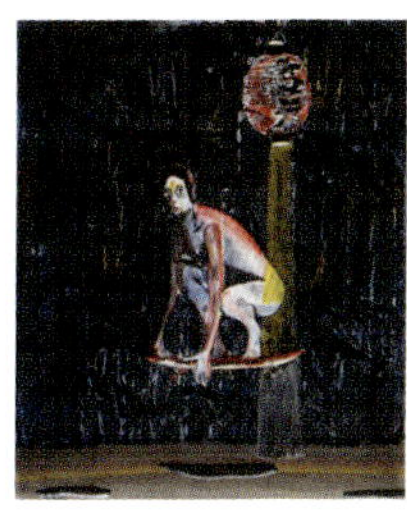

Jump, 2003
Oil on Canvas
36 x 30 inches

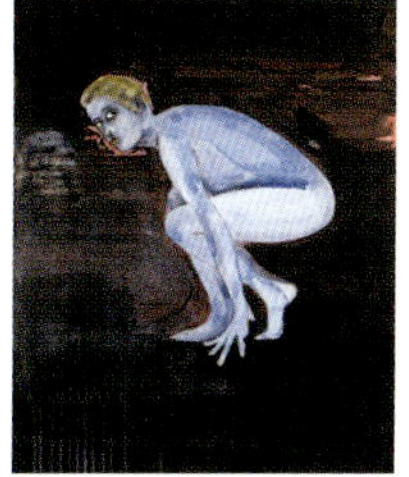

Race, 2006
Oil on Canvas
36 x 30 inches

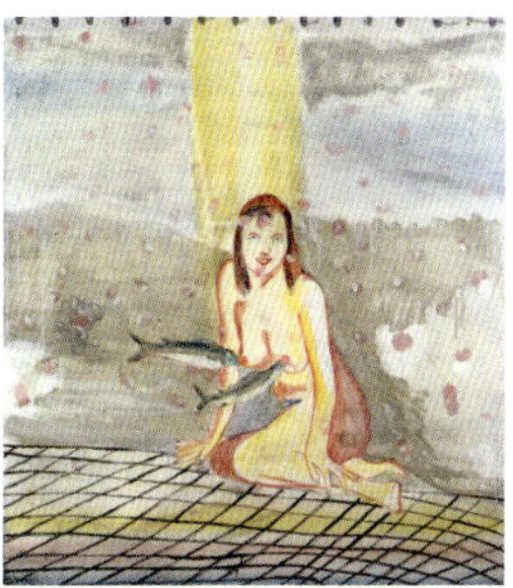

Springs, 2003
Oil on Canvas
62 x 56 inches

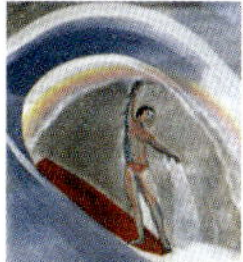

Overhead, 2003
Oil on Canvas
36 x 30 inches

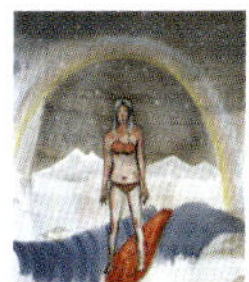

Surfside, 2003
Oil on Canvas
36 x 30 inches

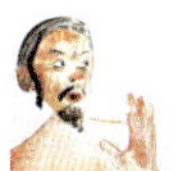

Untitled, 2005
Oil on Paper
27 x 20 inches

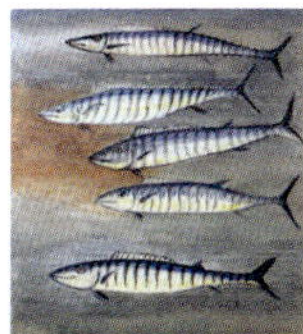

Pacific Vibrations, 2004
Oil on Canvas
66 x 60 inches

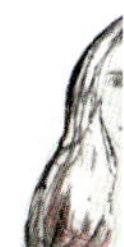

Untitled, 2005
Oil on Paper
27 x 20 inches

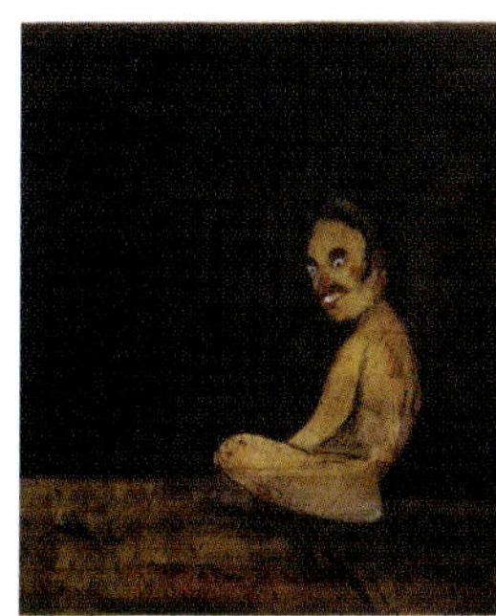

Nightwatch, 1998
Oil and Enamel on Canvas
60 x 66 in.

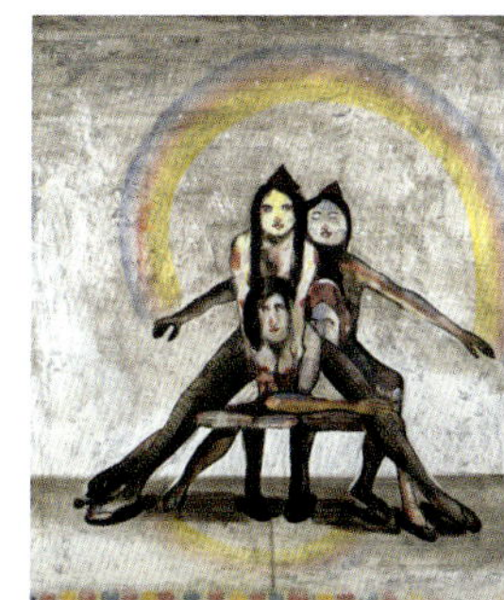

Pina Bausch, 2003
Enamel and Oil on Canvas
68 x 60 inches

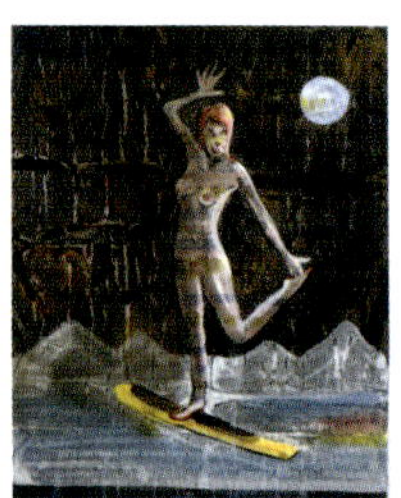

Boxed Fin, 2004
Oil on Canvas
30 x 24 inches

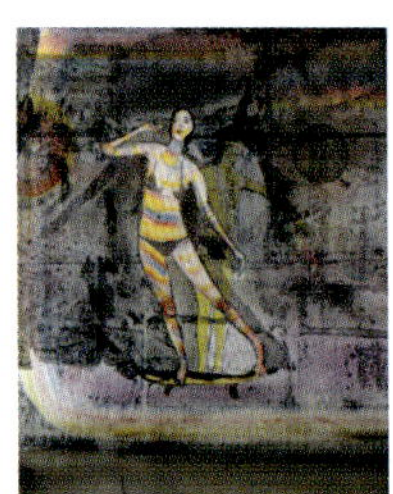

Nite Ride, 2003
Oil on Canvas
42 x 36 inches

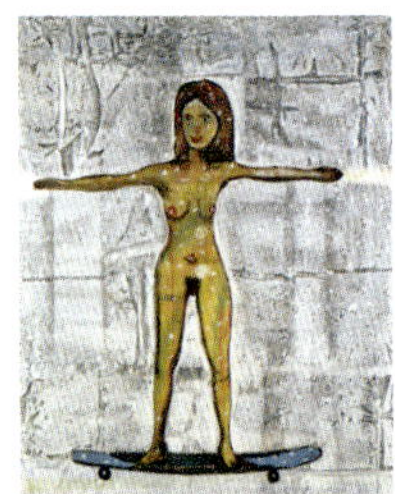

Paris, 2003
Oil on Canvas
59 x 45 inches

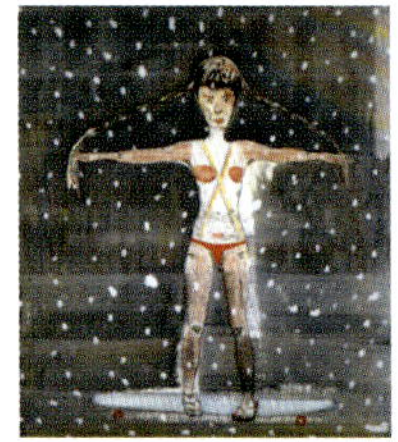

Night Tide, 2003
Oil on Canvas
62 x 56 inches

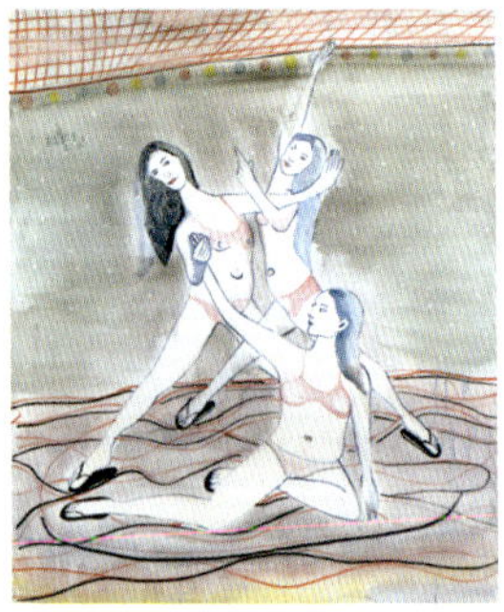

Dancers, 2003
Oil on Canvas
74 x 62 inches

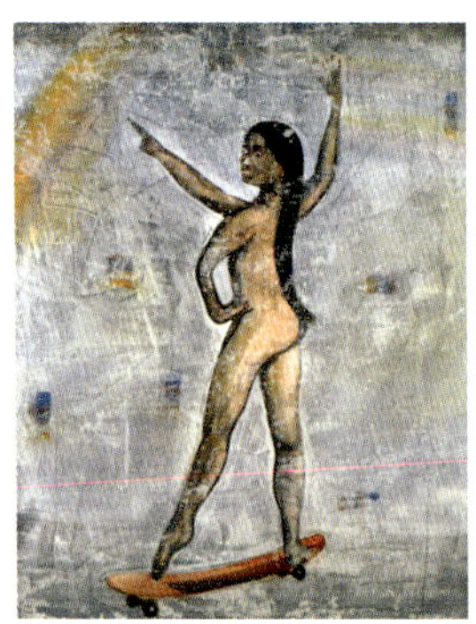

Snowboard, 2003
Oil on Canvas
59 x 45 inches

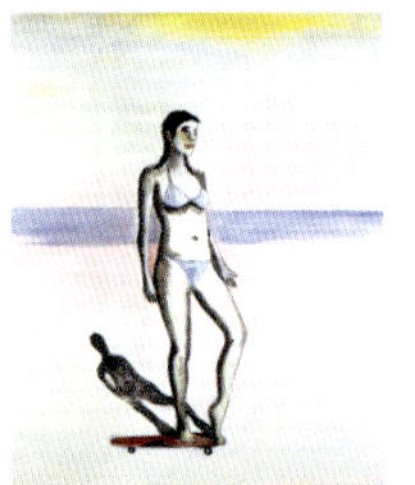

Untitled, 2003
Oil on Canvas
42 x 36 inches

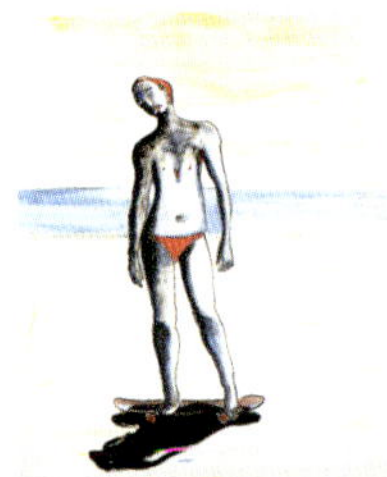

Untitled, 2003
Oil on Canvas
42 x 36 inches

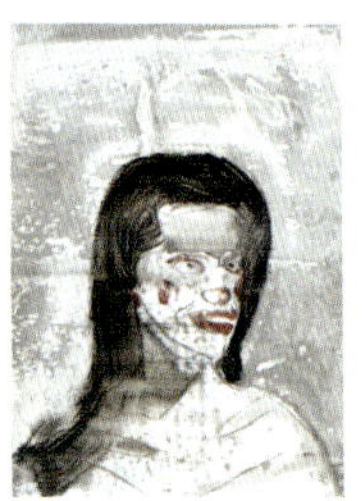

Untitled, 2003
Mixed Media on Paper
27 3/4 x 19 3/4 inches

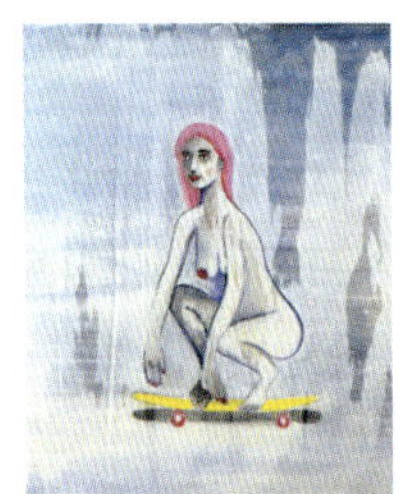

Skater Dater, 2004
Oil on Canvas
49 x 43 inches

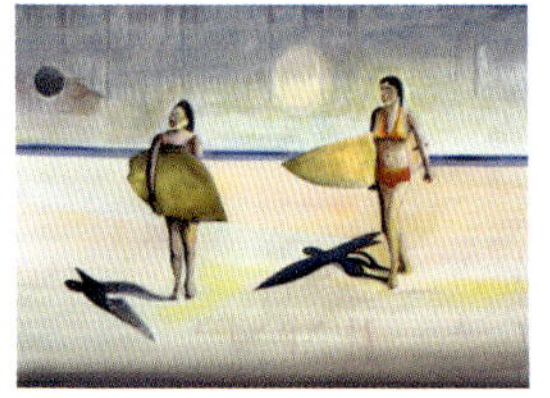

Sunset Beach Sunset, 2004
Oil on Canvas
54 x 78 inches

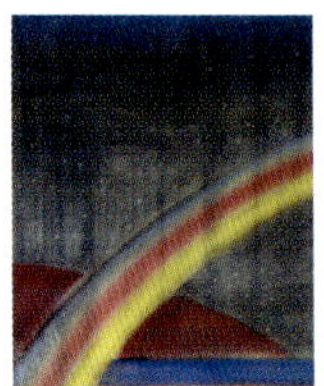

Friends Red Night (detail), 2004
Oil on Canvas
60 x 66 inches

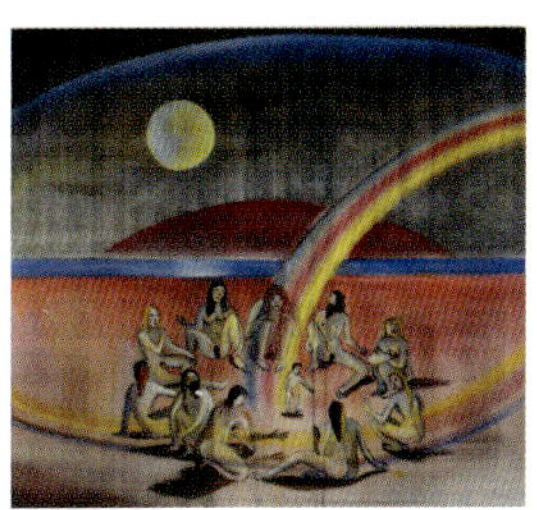

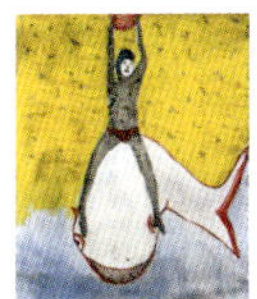

White Shark, 2004
Oil on Canvas
36 x 30 inches

Friends Red Night, 2004
Oil on Canvas
60 x 66 inches

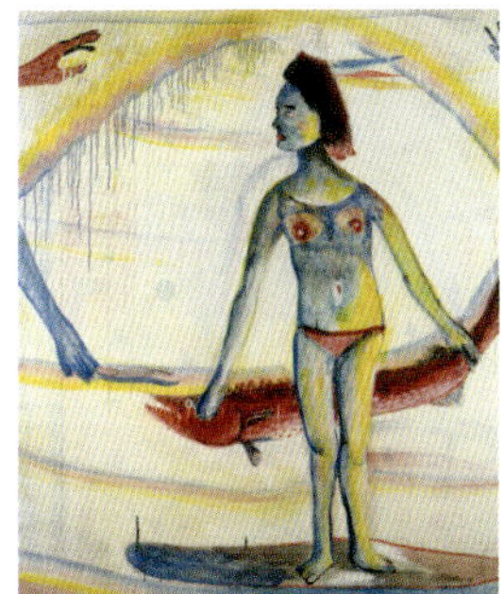

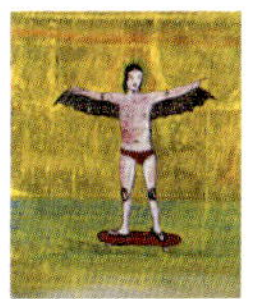

Sunrise Highway, 2004
Oil on Canvas
36 x 30 inches

Brighton Beach Rocks, 2001
Oil enamel on Canvas
62 x 56 inches

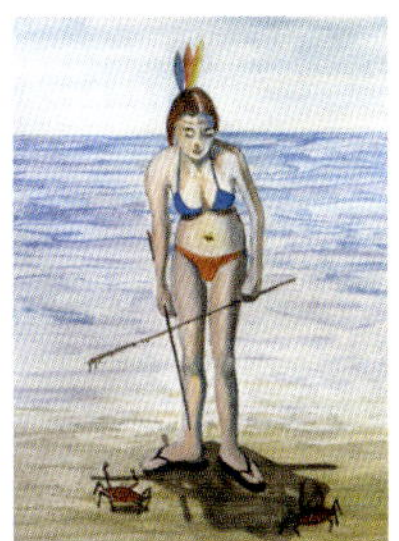

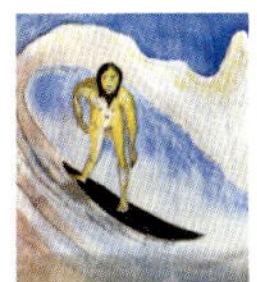

Blacks Beach, 2005
Oil on Canvas
36 x 30 inches

North East Coast, 2005
Oil on Canvas
49 x 43 inches

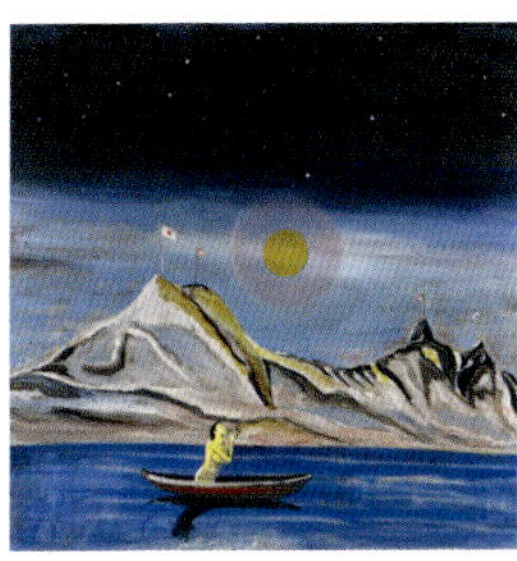

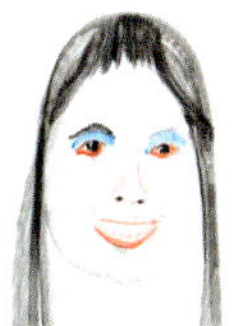

Untitled, 2007
Oil on Paper
34 x 27 inches

Kyoto Protocol, 2005
Oil on Canvas
48 x 52 inches

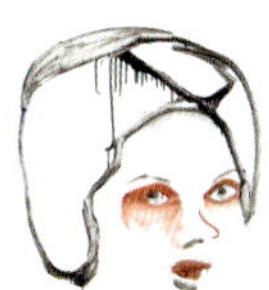

Untitled, 2007
Oil on Paper
30 x 28 inches

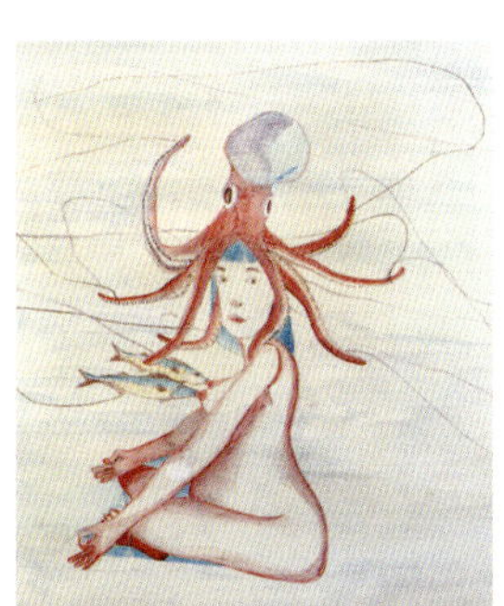

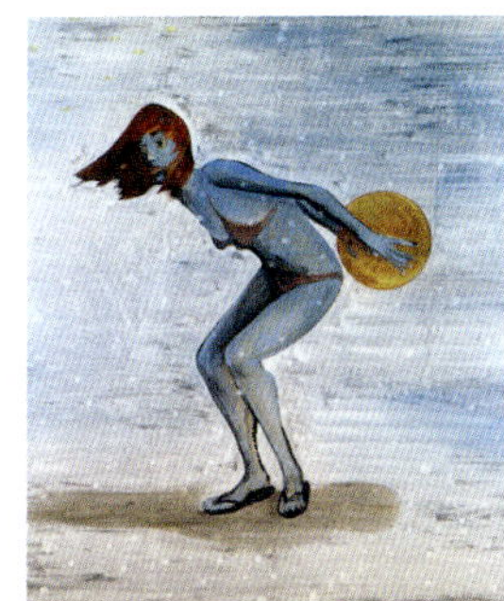

Mary Half Day (detail), 2005
Oil on Canvas
52 x 46 inches

Spring Sea, 2002
Oil and Enamel on Canvas
62 x 56 inches

Mary Half Day, 2005
Oil on Canvas
52 x 46 inches

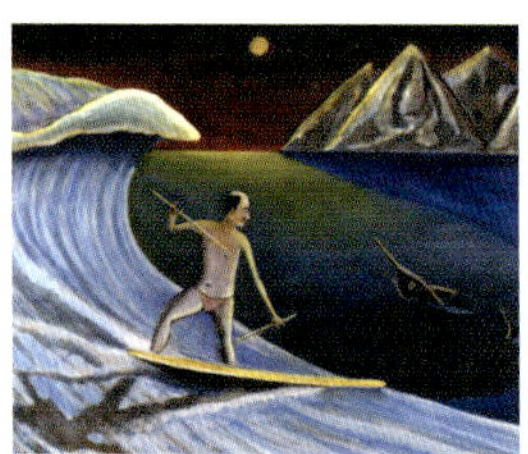

Nite Channel Crossing, 2005
Oil on Canvas
55 x 80 inches

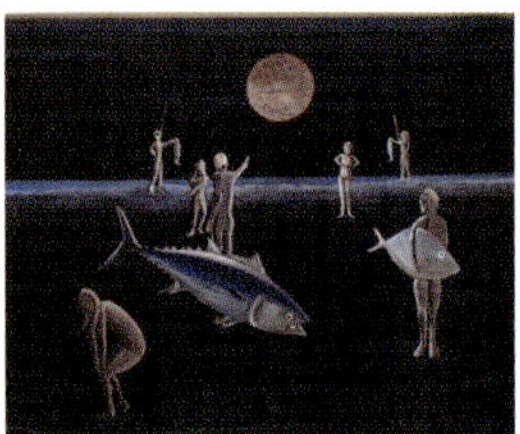

Wet Black Sand, 2005
Oil on Canvas
59 x 84 inches

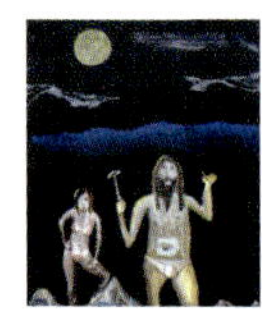

Alpine Carpenter II, 2005
Oil on Canvas
36 x 30 inches

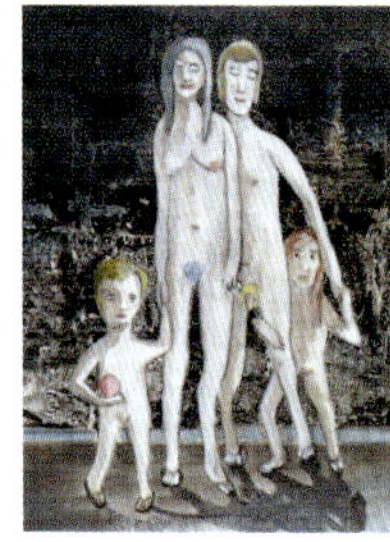

Young Family, 2005
Oil on Canvas
59 x 45 1/4 inches

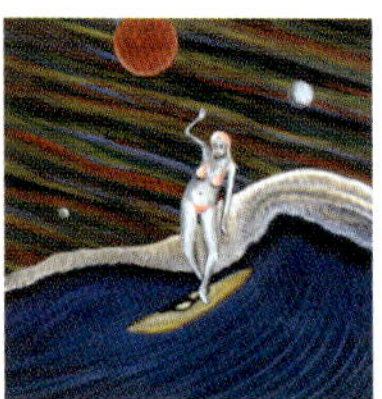

Towards the Nose, 2005
Oil on Canvas
62 x 68 inches

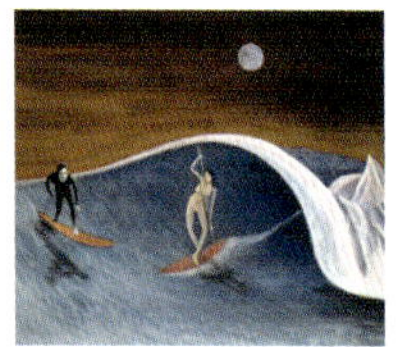

Last Day in October / Last Wave, 2005
Oil on Canvas
47 x 49 inches

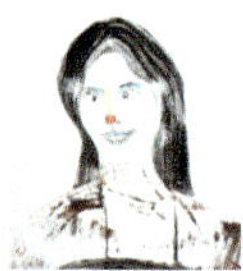

Untitled, 2001
Oil on Paper
27 x 19 inches

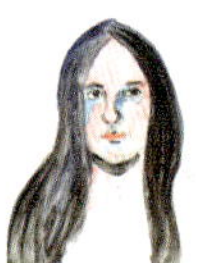

Untitled, 2005
Oil on Paper
27 x 20 inches

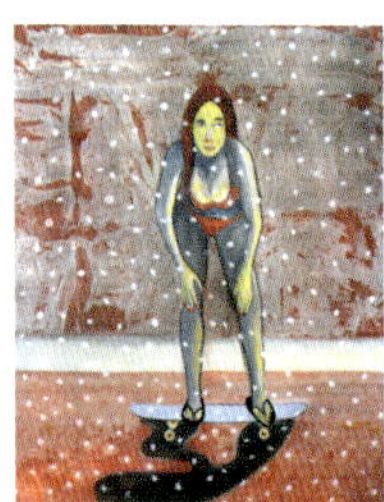

Little Cortez, 2004
Oil on Canvas
49 x 43 inches

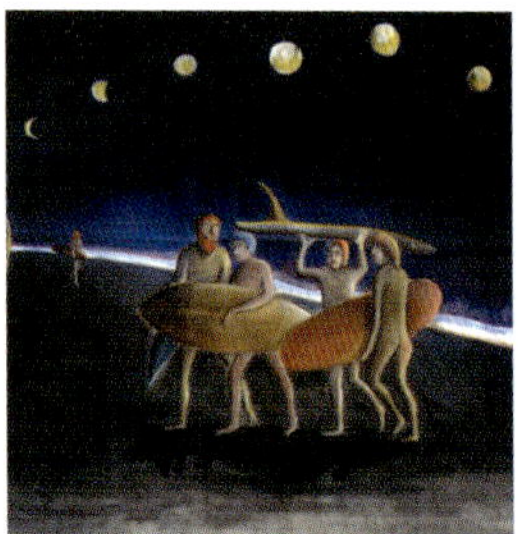

Seven Summer Stories, 2005
Oil on Canvas
59 x 66 inches

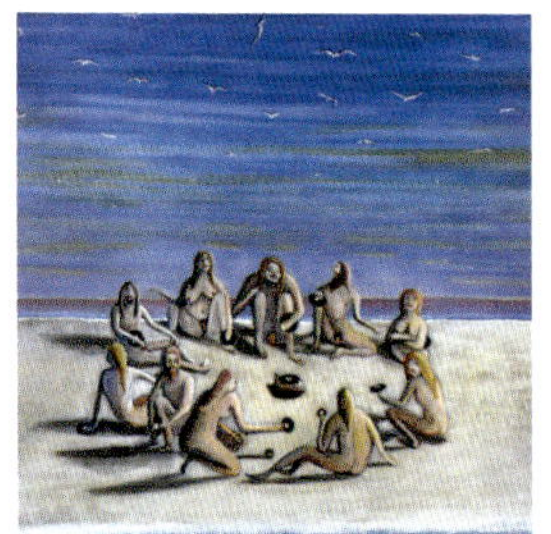

The Best of Friends, 2005
Oil on Canvas
62 x 68 inches

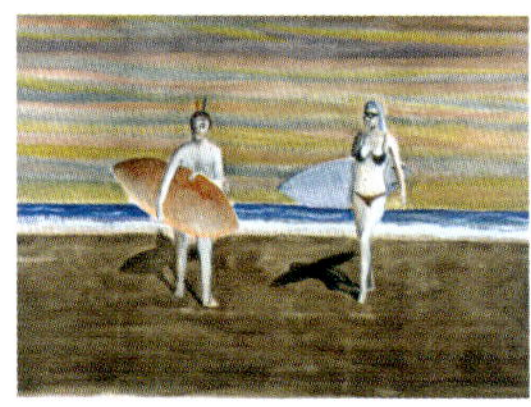

The New Boards, 2005
Oil on Canvas
54 x 78 inches

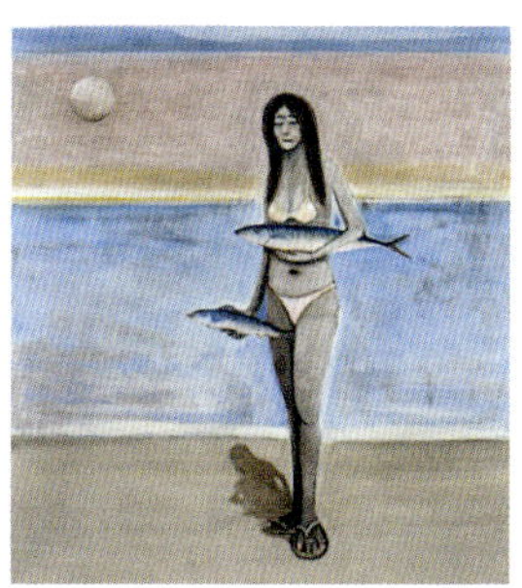

The Mackerel Bank, 2005
Oil on Canvas
62 x 56 inches

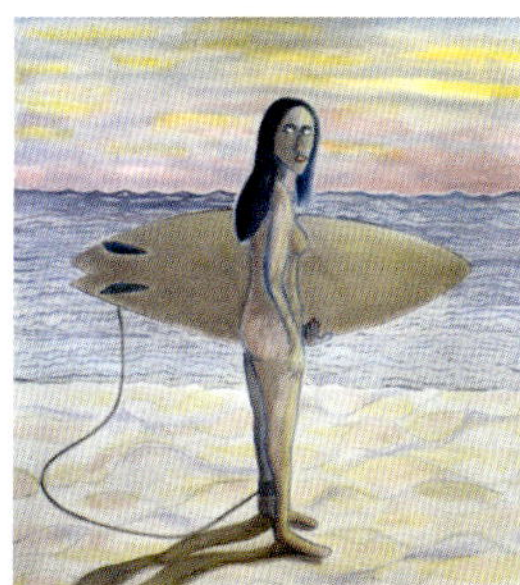

Look Back Sunset, 2005
Oil on Canvas
62 x 56 inches

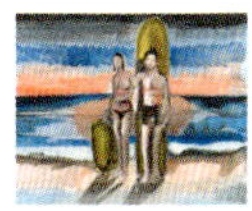

Laguna, 2007
Oil on Canvas
14 x 18 inches

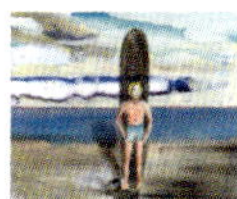

Solo Act, 2007
Oil on Canvas
14 x 18 inches

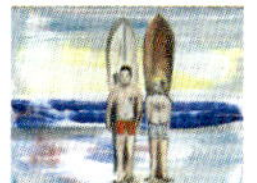

Japan, 2007
Oil on Canvas
14 x 18 inches

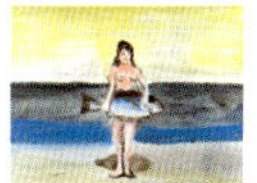

Salt Back, 2007
Oil on Canvas
14 x 18 inches

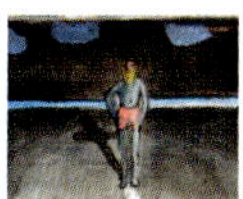

Night Walk, 2007
Oil on Canvas
14 x 18 inches

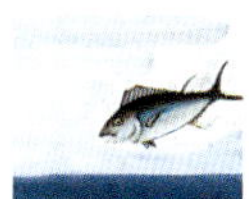

Blue, 2007
Oil on Canvas
12 x 16 inches

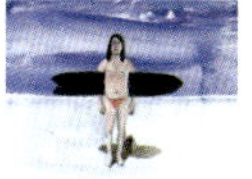

Nada Surf, 2006
Oil on Canvas
11 x 14 inches

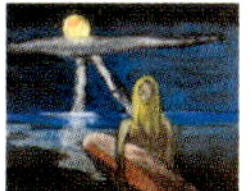

Full Moon, 2007
Oil on Canvas
14 x 18 inches

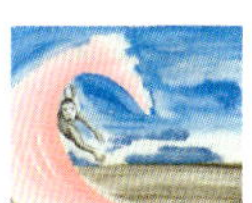

Wedge, 2007
Oil on Canvas
12 x 16 inches

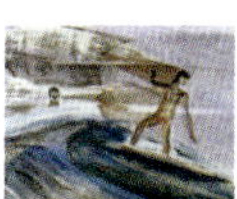

Flying, 2006
Oil on Canvas
18 x 24 inches

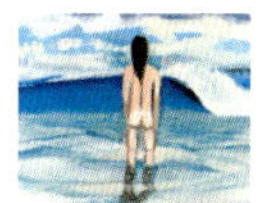

Off Shore, 2007
Oil on Canvas
14 x 18 inches

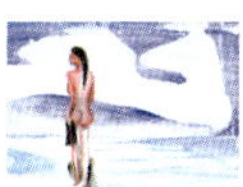

Surf del Cuerpo, 2006
Oil on Canvas
11 x 14 inches

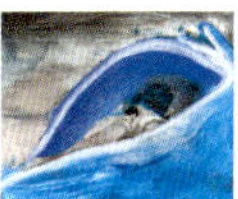

Tapped, 2007
Oil on Canvas
14 x 18 inches

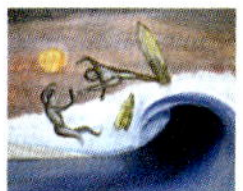

Wipeout, 2006
Oil on Canvas
18 x 24 inches

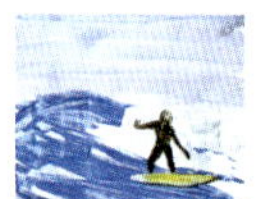

Blue Ride, 2006
Oil on Canvas
16 x 20 inches

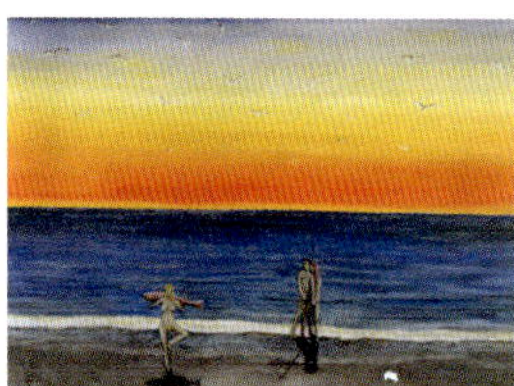

South Fork Sound, 2005
Oil on Canvas
56 x 78 inches

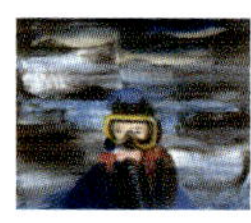

Zambulidor, 2006
Oil on Canvas
16 x 20 inches

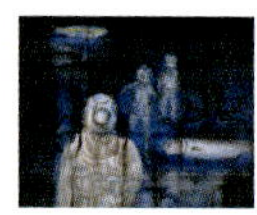

Sea Floor, 2006
Oil on Canvas
18 x 24 inches

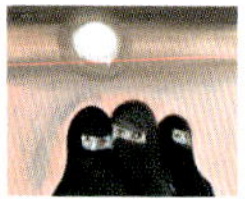

Fez, 2007
Oil on Canvas
14 x 18 inches

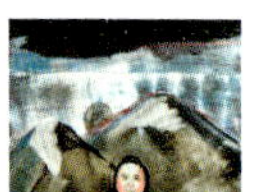

Winter Moon, 2007
Oil on Canvas
14 x 18 inches

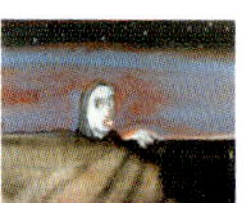

Wall Board, 2007
Oil on Canvas
14 x 18 inches

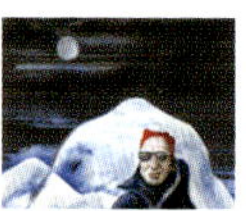

El Porta, 2006
Oil on Canvas
16 x 20 inches

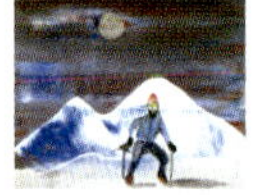

Night Moves, 2006
Oil on Canvas
16 x 20 inches

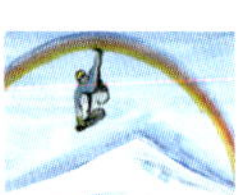

Altiplano, 2006
Oil on Canvas
14 x 18 inches

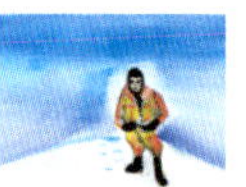

Peaked, 2007
Oil on Canvas
14 x 18 inches

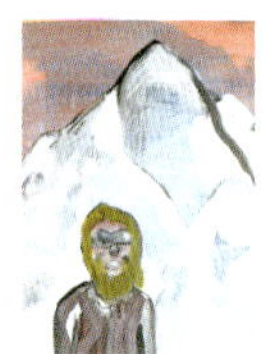

Guide, 2006
Oil on Canvas
14 x 11 inches

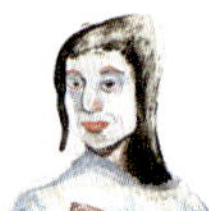

Untitled, 2003
Mixed Media on Paper
27 3/4 x 19 3/4 in

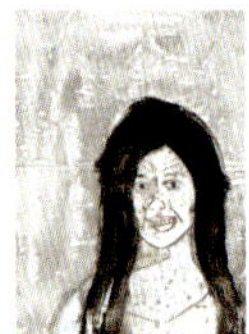

Untitled, 2003
Mixed Media on Paper
27 3/4 x 19 3/4 in

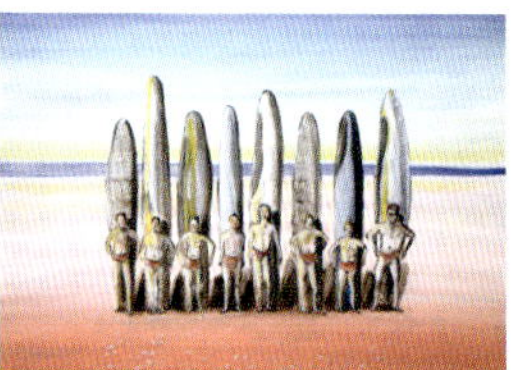

Lifeguards, 2006
Oil on Canvas
46 x 68 inches

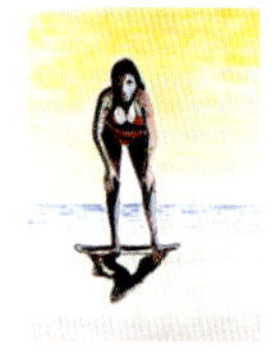

Untitled,2003
Oil on Canvas
42 x 36 inches

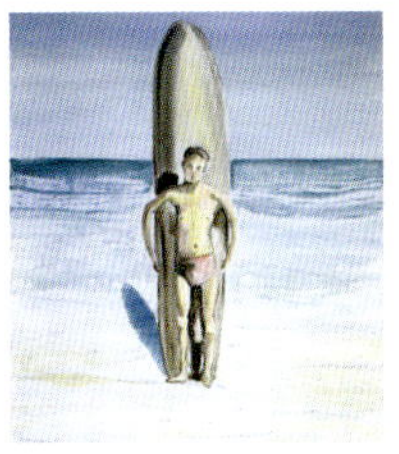

Youth, 2006
Oil on Canvas
49 x 43 inches

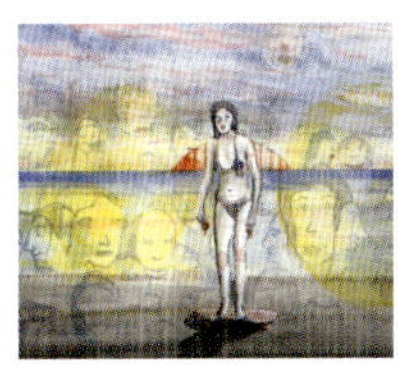

September Sun, 2005
Oil on Canvas
47 x 59 inches

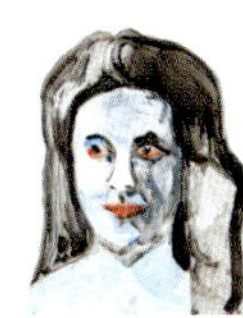

Untitled, 2007
Oil on Paper
30 x 28 inches

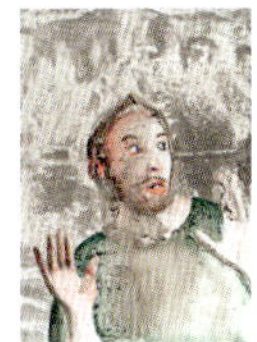

Untitled, 2005
Oil on Paper
27 x 20 inches

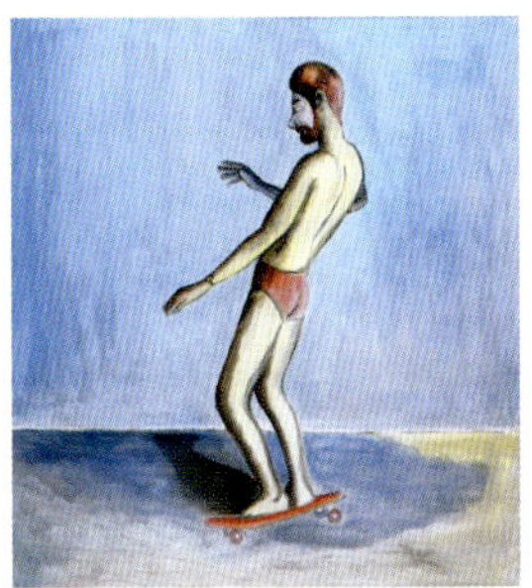

Lonely, 2006
Oil on Canvas
62 x 56 inches

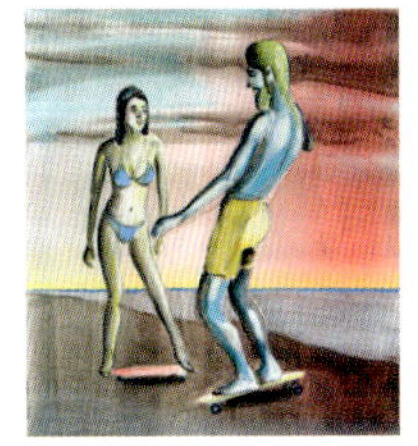

Twilight,2006
Oil on Canvas
42 x 36 inches

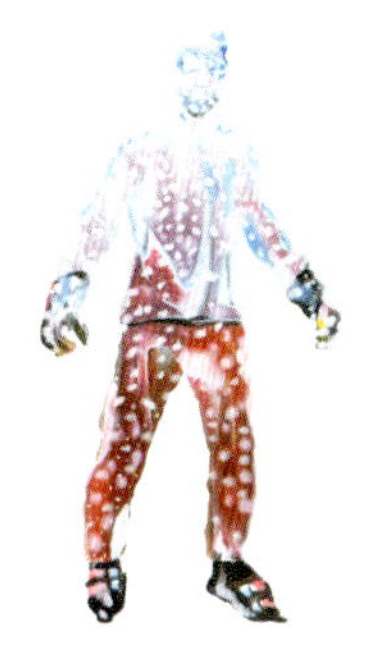

Wasatch White, 2006
Oil on Canvas
65 x 44 inches

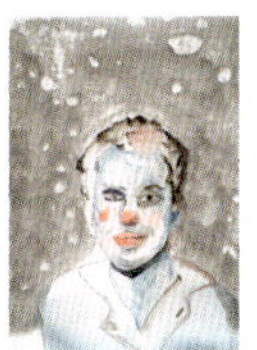

Untitled, 2005
Oil on Paper
27 x 20 inches

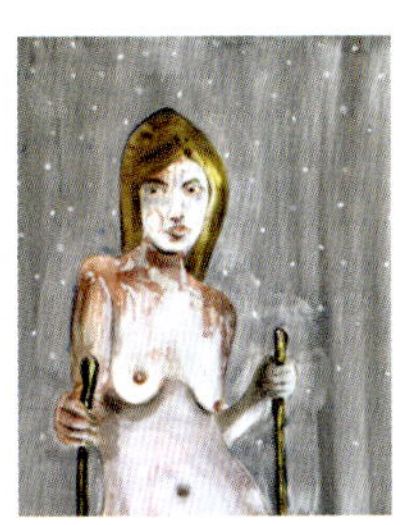

Ski Poles, 2006
Oil on Canvas
42 x 36 inches

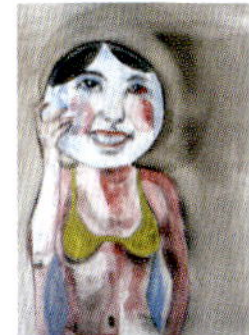

Eclipse, 2006
Oil on Canvas
36 x 30 inches

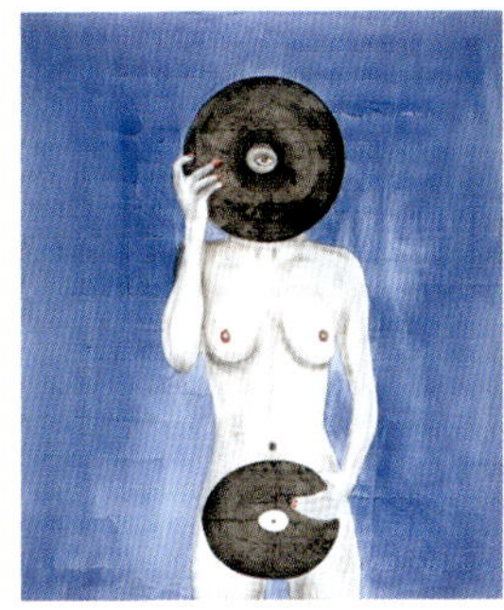

Untitled, 2006
Oil on Canvas
52 x 46 inches

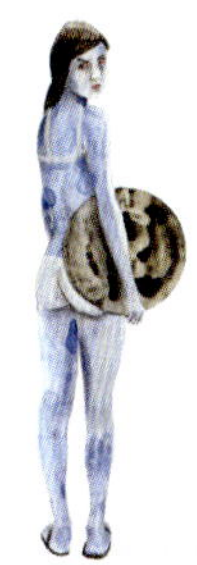

Black Ball, 2006
Oil on Canvas
58 x 40 inches

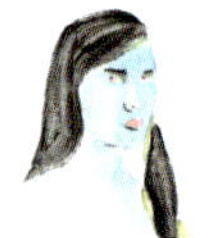

Untitled, 2005
Oil on Paper
27 x 20 inches

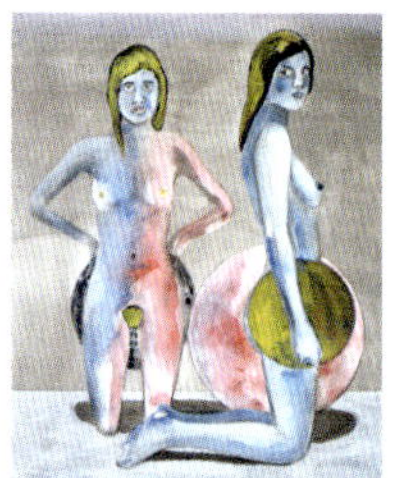

North/East, 2006
Oil on Canvas
42 x 36 inches

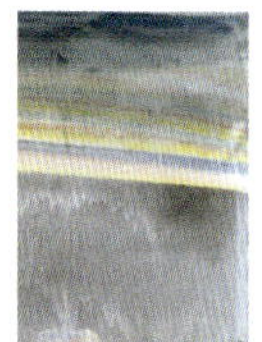

5 AM (detail), 2003
Oil on Canvas
60 x 72 inches

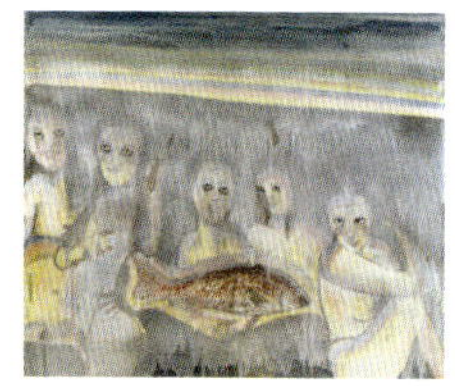

5 AM, 2003
Oil on Canvas
60 x 72 inches

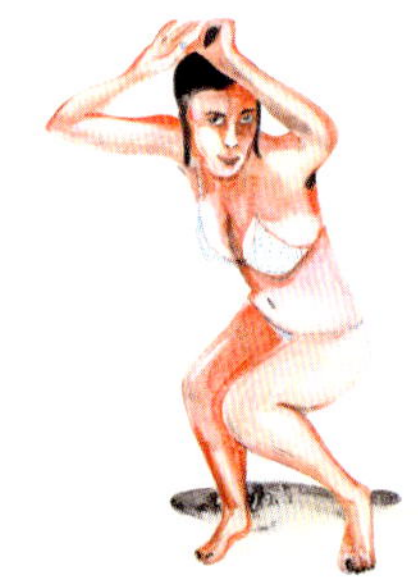

July, 2006
Oil on Canvas
49 x 43 inches

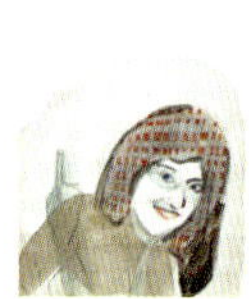

Untitled, 1999
Oil on Paper
27 1/2 x 20 inches

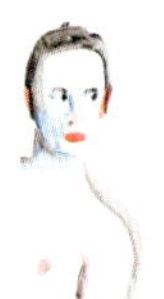

Untitled, 2007
Oil on Paper
30 x 28 inches

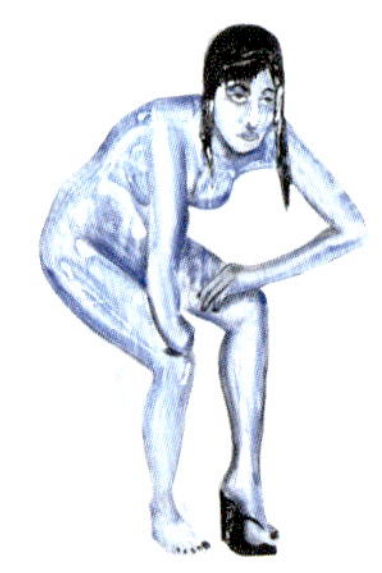

Pantera, 2006
Oil on Canvas
53 x 45 inches

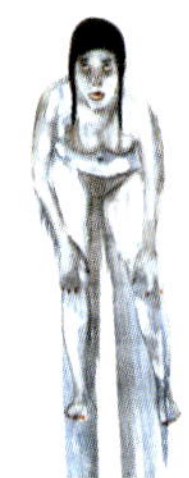

Waitress, 2006
Oil on Canvas
36 x 30 inches

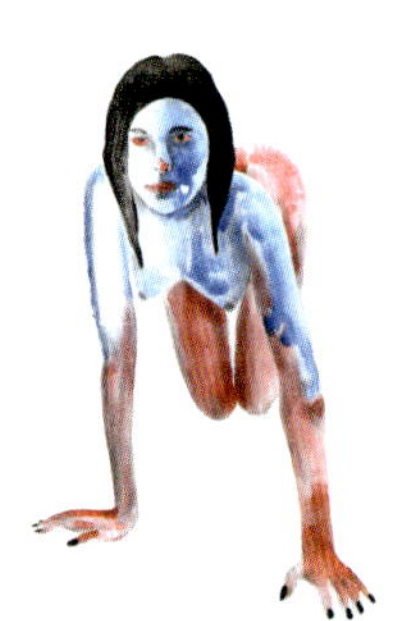

Through the Night, 2006
Oil on Canvas
52 x 46 inches

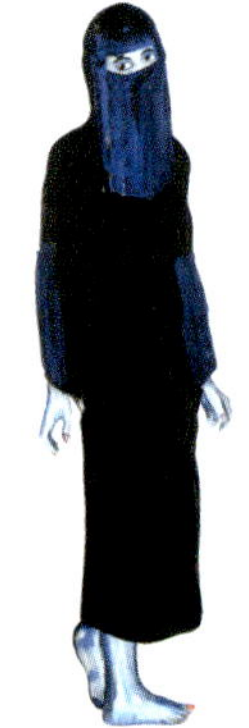

Black Drum, 2007
Oil on Canvas
67 x 45 inches

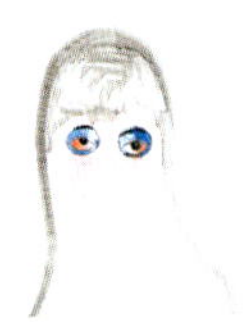

Untitled, 2007
Oil on Paper
34 x 28 inches

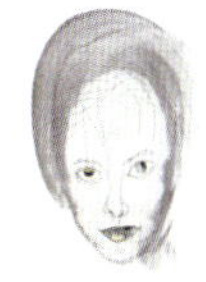

Untitled, 2005
Oil on Paper
27 x 20 inches

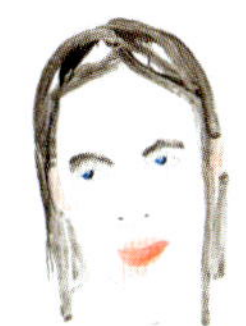

Untitled, 2007
Oil on Paper
34 x 28 inches

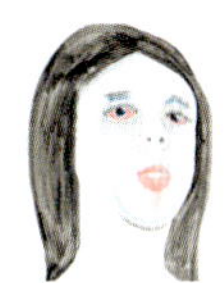

Untitled, 2007
Oil on Paper
34 x 28 inches

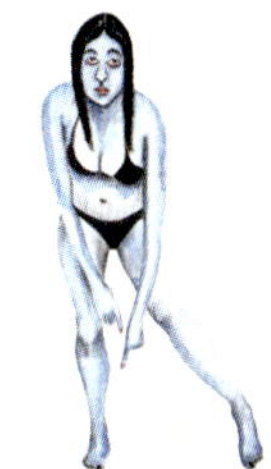

Blue Swag, 2007
Oil on Canvas
53 x 45 inches

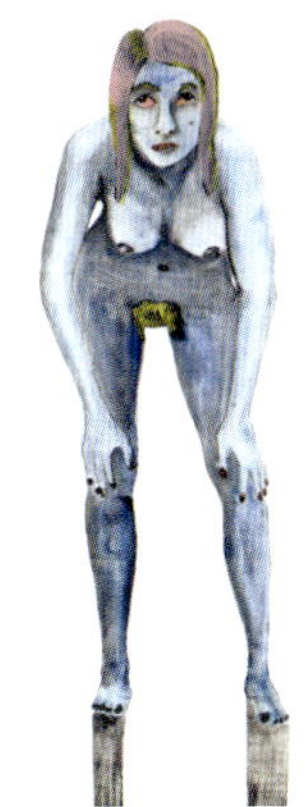

Crystal Cove, 2007
Oil on Canvas
65 x 44 inches

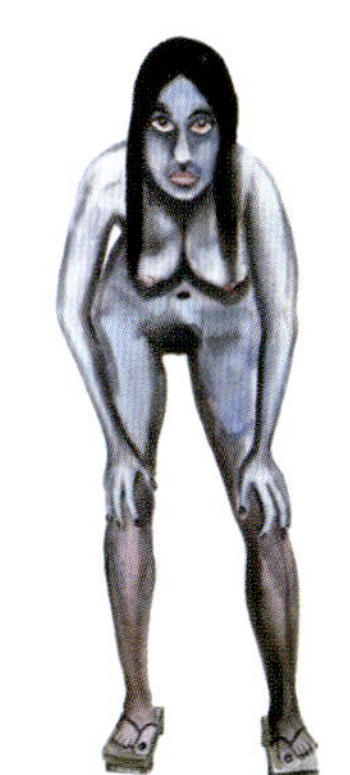

Wooden Shoes, 2007
Oil on Canvas
69 x 44 inches

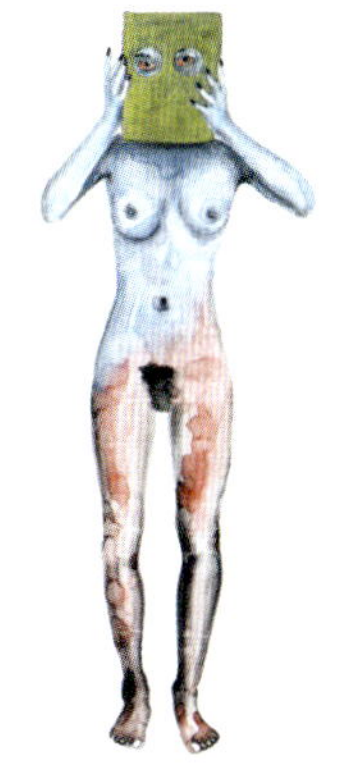

Box Set, 2007
Oil on Canvas
69 x 46 inches

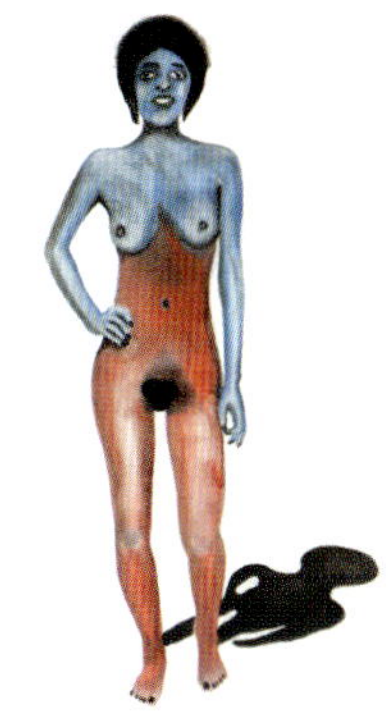

Golden West, 2007
Oil on Canvas
82 x 60 inches

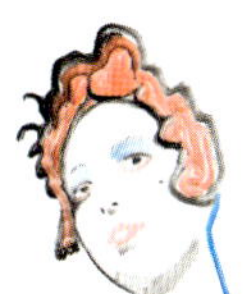

Untitled, 2007
Oil on Paper
30 x 28 inches

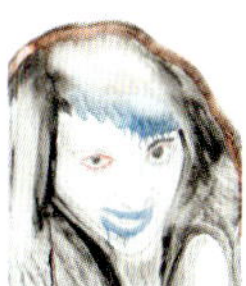

Untitled, 2007
Oil on Paper
34 x 28 inches

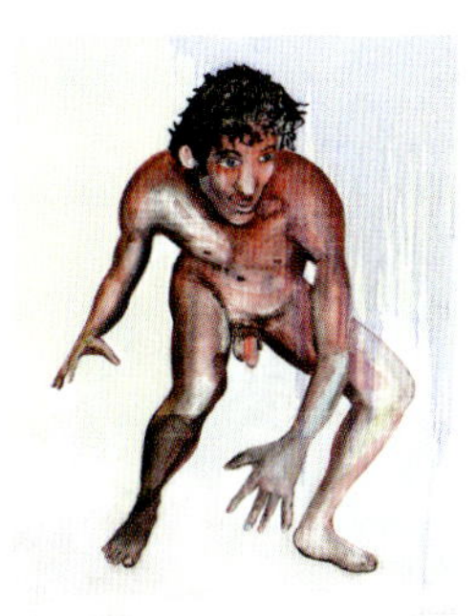

Swiss Army, 2007
Oil on Canvas
70 x 55 inches

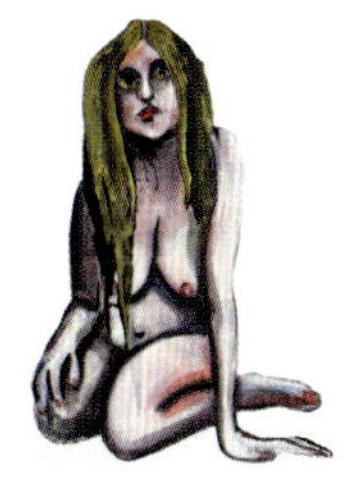

Wishful Thinking, 2007
Oil on Canvas
54 x 46 inches

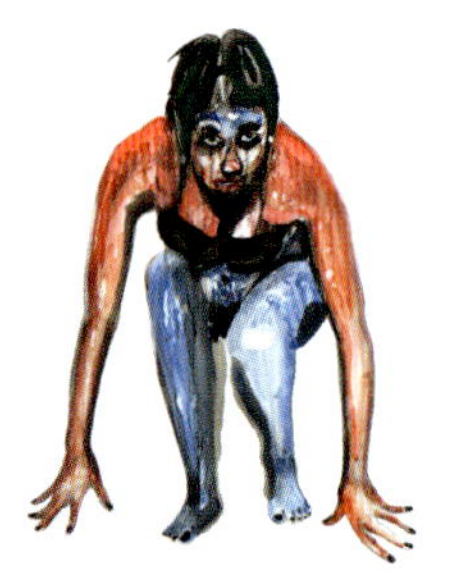

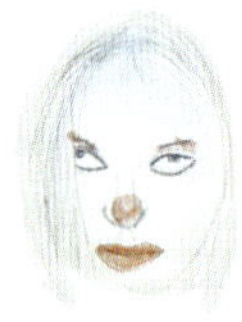

Untitled, 1999
Oil on Paper
26 x 20 inches

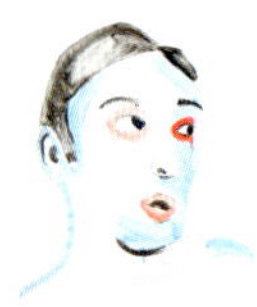

Untitled, 2007
Oil on Paper
34 x 28 inches

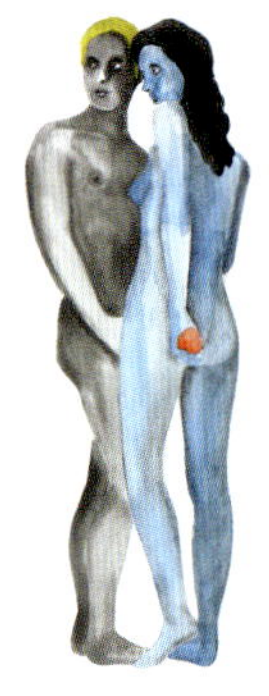

Outside Set, 2006
Oil on Canvas
52 x 46 inches

San Blas Commune, 2007
Oil on Canvas
83 x 59 inches

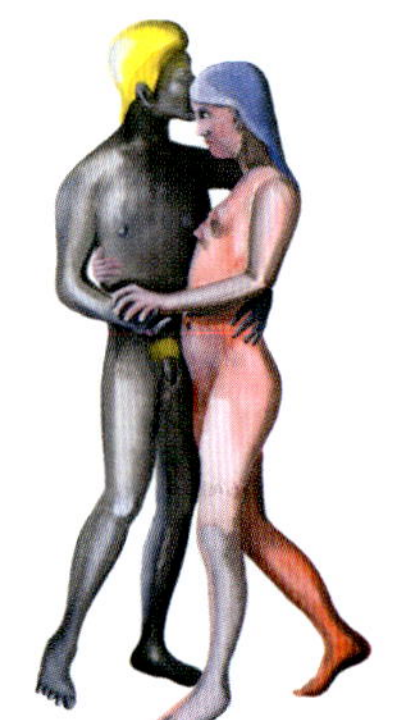

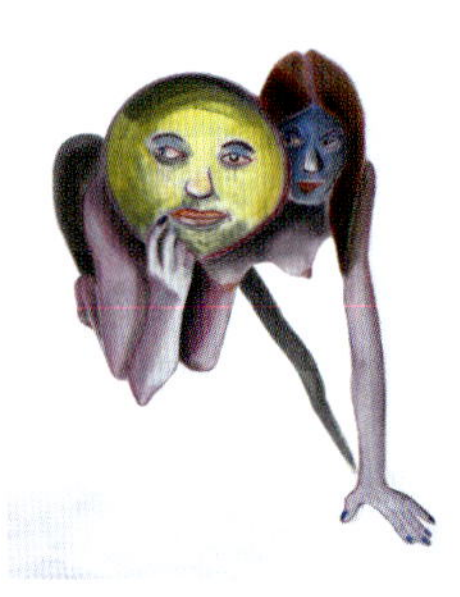

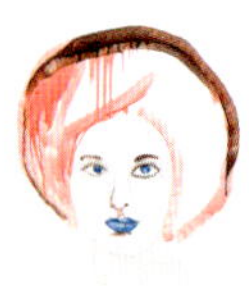

Untitled, 2007
Oil on Paper
34 x 28 inches

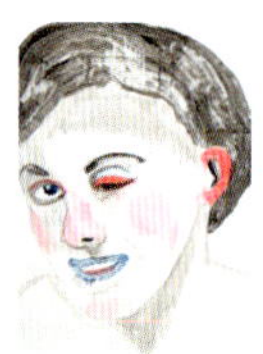

Untitled, 2007
Oil on Paper
34 x 28 inches

Del Mar Commune, 2007
Oil on Canvas
67 x 53 inches

Sunrise Pony, 2007
Oil on Canvas
71 x 59 inches

Dan McCarthy would like to thank:
For making this book possible,
Anton Kern and Marc Blondeau.

And special thanks to:
Sean Carmody,
Lionel Carvalho,
Michael Clifton,
Philippe Davet,
Bridget Finn,
Annet Gelink,
Christoph Gerozissis,
Corinne Gilbert,
Frank and Ralf Lehmann,
Karola Matschke,
Jeanette Mundt,
Michael Nevin,
Jack Pierson,
Jeffrey Porterfield,
Emily Schroeder,
Nick Stillman,
Elodie Trouche-Perrin,
and Suzanne Tarasieve.